Research Perspectives

Thought and Practice
in Music Education

A volume in
Advances in Music Education Research
Linda K. Thompson and Mark Robin Campbell, *Series Editors*

ADVANCES IN MUSIC EDUCATION RESEARCH

Editors

Linda K. Thompson
Lee University
Cleveland, TN

Mark Robin Campbell
The Crane School of Music
The State University of New York at Potsdam
Potsdam, NY

Editorial Board

William Bauer
Case Western Reserve University
Cleveland, OH

Susan Wharton Conkling
Eastman School of Music
University of Rochester
Rochester, NY

Colleen Conway
University of Michigan
Ann Arbor, MI

Regina Murphy
St. Patrick's College
Dublin City University
Dublin, Ireland

Kathy Scherler
University of Texas at Arlington
Wichita Falls, TX

Advances in Music Education Research is published yearly in April by the Music Education Special Interest Group of the American Educational Research Association. All editorial correspondence and manuscripts should be sent to Linda Thompson or Mark Robin Campbell.

Research Perspectives

Thought and Practice in Music Education

Linda K. Thompson
Lee University

Mark Robin Campbell
*The Crane School of Music
SUNY–Potsdam*

IAP

INFORMATION AGE PUBLISHING, INC.
Charlotte, NC • www.infoagepub.com

Library of Congress Cataloging-in-Publication Data

Research perspectives : thought and practice in music education / [edited by] Linda K. Thompson, Mark Robin Campbell.
    p. cm. – (Advances in music education research)
  Includes bibliographical references.
  ISBN 978-1-60752-089-4 (pbk.) – ISBN 978-1-60752-090-0 (hardcover)
1. Music–Instruction and study. I. Thompson, Linda K. II. Campbell, Mark Robin.
  MT1.R511 2009
  780.71–dc22
                                                                    2009006752

Copyright © 2009 Information Age Publishing Inc.

All rights reserved. No part of this publication may be reproduced, stored in a retrieval system, or transmitted, in any form or by any means, electronic, mechanical, photocopying, microfilming, recording or otherwise, without written permission from the publisher.

Printed in the United States of America

CONTENTS

Foreword vii
    Linda K. Thompson and Mark Robin Campbell

Preface xv
    Mary Ross Hookey

1 Elliot Eisner and Music Education: Eight Big Ideas about the
    Arts in Education 1
    Matthew D. Thibeault/Elliot Eisner

2 Developmentally Appropriate Practice: Historic Roots and
    Evolving Paradigms 7
    Martina L. Miranda

3 Type, Function, and Musical Features of Preschool Children's
    Spontaneous Songs 37
    Peter Whiteman

4 Preservice Teachers' Perceptions and Perspectives on Early
    Childhood Music Education: A Comparative Analysis
    of the United States and Korea 63
    Jinyoung Kim and Seung Yeon Lee

5 An Investigation of the 2 × 2 Achievement Goal Framework
    in the Context of Instrumental Music 81
    Peter Miksza

6 In-Service Music Teachers' Perceptions of Professional Development 101
William I. Bauer, Jere Forsythe, and Daryl Kinney

7 Developing Professional Knowledge about Music Teaching and Learning through Collaborative Conversations 125
Lisa M. Gruenhagen

8 Notes for a Moment in Music Education Research 153
Sandra L. Stauffer

About the Contributors 171

FOREWORD

Linda K. Thompson and Mark Robin Campbell

The title chosen for this volume of *Advances in Music Education* was selected to illustrate thinking about research and the practice of research. In the Preface, Mary Ross Hookey encourages us to think about the processes of research, reviewing, and publishing. In doing so, she provides clarity by examining both standards and guidelines, including the assumptions apparent in, and the implications of reviewing and reporting. Her questions provoke continued thought about the power of the processes, particularly as they relate to moving research in music education forward.

At the 2008 Music Education Special Interest Group business meeting of the American Educational Research Association (AERA) in New York City, Elliot Eisner was invited to give an address on a topic of his choosing. Because of Eisner's substantial work in arts education and research, we were confident that his address would be thought provoking and affirmative. His address, entitled "Eight Big Ideas in Arts Education," was all that and more, and provides a framework for both thought and practice, as well as a reflective point for research in the arts. Just as Bresler communicated in Volume 1 of *Advances in Music Education Research* about the intensity of engagement and the interaction of process and product as key elements within research endeavors, Eisner succinctly enumerates what educators can learn from the arts. By extension, we can apply these same ideas in the research context; this can be understood by substituting "research" for "education" in his address.

For Chapter 1, we asked Matthew Thibeault, one of Eisner's last doctoral students at Stanford University, to provide a snapshot of the context from which Eisner's perspectives have been generated. In doing so, Thibeault discusses Eisner's impact on the education and research communities, his contributions to thought and practice in arts and research, his personal involvement in the arts, and most importantly, the lasting legacy and impact of his passionate involvement in arts education and research. Eisner's address brings us back to a point of clarity and perspective on our individual roles as artists/educators/researchers.

Chapters 2 through 7 of *Research Perspectives: Thought and Practice in Music Education* represent the work of presenters at the 2008 AERA conference in New York City and reflect thought and practice in a variety of forms. As you examine these chapters, we encourage you to continue to consider Eisner's address as an interpretive lens—to consider how each article illustrates that form and content cannot be separated, that nuance does matter, that surprise is not an intruder in the art of inquiry but a source of reward, and that slowing perception allows us to see more clearly what is there. We invite you to look for Eisner's main themes as we see them in each of the chapters. We also challenge you to consider Hookey's thoughts and questions as delineated in the Preface.

Chapters 2 through 4 of this volume call our attention to various aspects of the rapidly expanding field of early childhood music education. Providing a background for much of the development in this area is Martina Miranda's psychohistoric examination of "Developmentally Appropriate Practice (DAP): Historic Roots and Evolving Paradigms." Her thorough examination of the foundations of child-development theories and the Kindergarten movement provides a solid backdrop for her summary of the development of the National Association for the Education of Young Children (NAEYC), leading to the emergence of DAP in the 1980s.

While presented in a somewhat linear manner, Miranda's writing clearly communicates the complexity inherent in the development of theories of learning. The 1997 revisions to the original DAP document of 1986 illustrate not only this complexity, but the purposeful intent of NAEYC to insure that DAP is not seen as a single, static theory, but rather interpreted as integrated and interconnected theories that are evolving and responsive to current research, practice, and sociocultural considerations. What then, does this mean for early childhood music education practices? Do the tenets of DAP hold implications for students in upper grades, as the author questions? How will emerging research confirm or contest the present conception of DAP? This chapter clearly creates a challenge for researchers to explore music educators' current notions of DAP and ways in which those ideas are enacted in classrooms. As Miranda indicates, this chapter, summarizing past and present events and influences in early childhood education, provides a foundation for considering future influences of DAP. Miranda's chapter additionally provides a comprehensive, important historical framework for researchers interested in furthering this growing area of study.

Peter Whiteman's engaging study of "Type, Function, and Musical Features of Preschool Children's Spontaneous Songs" is both a lesson for teachers and a compelling demonstration of how common assumptions about child development and musical understanding might be reexamined and rethought in light of new theoretical thinking supported by strong data and analysis. The idea that children's understanding of the world changes over the course of their maturation and development in a rather linear fashion has been a strong and productive force in developmental psychology. A significant body of research in children's musical development parallels this mode of thinking. Whiteman, however, challenges this thinking (drawing primarily on the work of Corsaro, 2005), suggesting that musical development should be viewed as *interpretative acts* based upon how individuals use cultural information. Whiteman claims that the data he reports on preschool children's spontaneous singing show a multiplicity of song types, functions, and music features, and not necessarily nascent examples of ultimately mature forms. His analysis, rather, supports a nonlinear interpretation of development. In short, Whiteman suggests that development may be thought of as generative, multidimensional, collective, and culturally situated. The means through which children acquire and transmit musical signs is seen as dynamic, interactive, socially constructed, self-referential, and to some extent, unable to be referenced or fit into a predetermined framework. Development and its attendant processes are more analogous to a spider web and the way spiders make them. This, according to Whiteman, should be a summons to call into question the organization of many early childhood learning programs, especially those based upon "grand theories" of child development, including traditional age-stage descriptions of when children are most likely to execute specific musical skills or display an understanding of specific musical concepts. In Whiteman's view, it is imperative that the early childhood classroom truly be a child-centered place. That is, a place where multiple pathways are available for children to exhibit their songs, particularly as a manifestation of how they negotiate the musical signs and information afforded them as maturing members of a culture.

Jinyoung Kim's and Seung Yeon Lee's study of "Preservice Teachers' Perceptions of and Perspectives on Early Childhood Music Education: A Comparative Analysis of the United States and Korea" provides readers with an opportunity to think more globally about what it means to be a "highly qualified" early childhood music teacher. The idea that teachers from both the United States and Korea value music in the education and experiential lives of young children should come as no surprise. Music as an integral part of the socialization and educational processes of cultures does seem to be a universal phenomenon. What counts as valuable within those social and educational processes is, however, culturally constructed. In other words, what actually does contribute to the differences found between skills and attitudes when the two groups of preservice teachers are compared? Like Gruenhagen's study of professional development, the differences may be more about a *whole web* of cultural values than anything else—different musical values; different curricular values within the educational systems; different individual, family, or social values. Furthermore, if the reports of Kim and Lee's study participants are reliable, then differences between Korean and U.S. teachers may also be matters of gradations, rather than kinds.

From a research practice perspective, Kim and Lee's study is an important reminder for thinking about differences between statistically significant and substantively significant in reporting results. What may be statistically significant may not be substantively significant. Equally, what may be substantively significant may never appear in a statistic. The chapter also offers an opportunity to think about the idea of generalizeability, both in terms of the specific context of this study and the analytical and interpretative tools used (e.g., sample size, representativeness). Furthermore, the chapter lets us think about how we position our work within broader interpretative frameworks; for example, international comparison in math and science (TIMMS) and reading (PIRL) (see for example, NCES, 2008). Lastly, Kim and Lee's study is a reminder about the importance of formulating good questions; for example, in the overall design of a research study and in the specific instruments used to gather, construct, and analyze data.

Understanding how and why students are motivated to pursue competence in music is an ongoing question in the profession. Peter Miksza's chapter, "Investigation of the 2×2 Achievement Goal Framework in the Context of Instrumental Music," explores this issue and provides readers an example of the research practice of adapting and testing the validity, reliability, and applicability of theories, from educational psychology to a music context. His approach to developing a psychometric tool reinforces the importance of acknowledging that validity and reliability in a given domain do not necessarily transfer to other domains. However, Miksza's findings do generally support the achievement goal research in other academic areas and in sports. Of particular interest is Miksza's determination that the 4-factor model is only a "fair" fit to the data, and thus not the only viable model for examining students' motivations for competence in music. Specifically, Miksza questions the applicability of the four orientations to instrumental music contexts, in that it is very possible some participants did not perceive the differences between the approach and avoid statements or the performance and mastery statements. Moving beyond the model, Miksza's analysis of descriptive data related to the questionnaire items indicated that primary motivations for the participants in this study included satisfying their expectations for personal accomplishment and maximizing band experiences. The author concludes with several suggestions for ongoing research into this important topic of motivation. Moving beyond this specific research model, one wonders what other motivational factors drive students toward competence in music education. Further thinking about the description raises questions of what, and even when, is competence.

The timely issue of professional development is the theme of Chapters 6 and 7 of this volume. In their chapter, "In-service Music Teachers' Perceptions of Professional Development," Bauer, Forsythe, and Kinney summarize music teachers' self-reports regarding the value of various approaches to professional development, the teachers' motivations for pursuing professional development opportunities, and preference for various delivery methods. While their findings likely confirm what we suspect about the teachers' perceptions, this chapter raises numerous questions for further investigation. There is the issue of identifying the population of music educators, particularly those who are not members of state music organizations. While the majority of respondents were members of the Ohio Music Educators Association, 6% were not. Why are they not members? Is there a disconnect between their perceived needs and what they feel the organization provides in terms of professional development? How can these members be identified and what can the profession provide to further their professional development? With regard to the delivery of professional development, the authors note the need for further research to "confirm or deny" what are perceived to be trends. What is the actual demand for online learning opportunities? What is the direction of the general field of professional development as it pertains to both content and delivery? How do new developments, technologies, and trends in the general field translate to the music education profession? What are the unique needs of music educators working in varied contexts and different levels of instruction? What is the impact of states' requirements for completed master's degrees on the perception of, and demand for, professional development opportunities? How do professional development needs change based on length of career? What approaches can be developed to provide sustained, meaningful professional development, acknowledging the need for extended time and reflection? As the authors point out, there is a tremendous need for further research in this important area, with a variety of research designs required to provide as comprehensive a picture as possible of this complex issue. While we have rather vague information about those who leave our profession, certainly a greater understanding of teachers' needs and of meaningful and specific professional development practices could make a difference in the support and retention of those uncertain about their futures in music education.

In "Developing Professional Knowledge about Music Teaching and Learning through Collaborative Conversations," Lisa Gruenhagen takes an in-depth look at the conversations of a group of early childhood music teachers and wonders to what extent these conversations function as a form of professional development. As many music teachers will tell you—whether currently teaching or long since retired—most models designed to address continuous professional growth and changes in practice are patently inadequate. Think of the typical in-service model, the "focus week" in the summer, the weekend immersion class. All fail to address the fundamental processes involved in professional growth and change: time, focus on teaching and context, problem analysis and reflection, and collaboration and critique, to name just a few.

The insights gleaned from Gruenhagen's study are fully in accord with current thinking regarding professional development: (a) Ongoing and teacher learning is important and is a key link in improving student learning; (b) Focusing on content knowledge and how students learn particular concepts/skills, coupled with collective and active participation in a "community of practice" leads to changes in instructional skills and practice; and (c) Aligning developmental work with curriculum issues and directly linking professional learning to teachers' actual work experiences is vital (see for example, Resnick, 2005). Perhaps of additional concern—one that acts as an ongoing tension throughout Gruenhagen's chapter, although not directly discussed—is the issue or perception of the value of professional development itself. In her study, we wonder why several participants dropped out. We also wonder why the teachers had to meet beyond the school day and at Gruenhagen's home. Why wasn't professional development a matter of institutional policy—an ongoing and embedded part of the teachers' work. What administrative acts actually took place that had an impact on several participants' participation? Why did the researcher herself have to create a space for the inclusion of ongoing teacher learning in the first place? These questions, among others, are as much dispositional as institutional, individual as collective. Change in values that undergird schools and their practices, as Fine and Raack (1994) note, "is the result of both individual *and* organizational development" (p. 2). Gruenhagen has certainly given us much to think about regarding both.

The concluding chapter of this volume features the invited perspectives of Sandra Stauffer. Her essay not only provides a discussion of the chapters in Volume 2, but also exemplifies the public review process described by Hookey in the Preface. In our invitation to review the articles, we asked Stauffer to reflect on their meanings for music education research. What she points out is that we in music education research are in a new moment. This moment, Stauffer asserts, is marked by diversity and complementarity, an "inquiry symbiosis" holding potential and possibility. Volume 1 of *Advances in Music Education Research*, with its diverse methodologies as a focus, is an example of the beginning of this moment. In Stauffer's discussion of the current volume, she advances the understanding of what diversity means in research. In addition, she highlights that the moment also takes into account the political context in which music education research is lived and practiced. Stauffer's analysis of practice, pedagogy, people, and place support her call for a shift from contestation in research to a position of complementarity—a recognition of the validity of diverse thought and practice in music education research.

As Mary Hookey describes in the preface, the advancement of music education research is dependent "in significant ways" on the peer-review process. So in conclusion, we wish to acknowledge and thank the editorial board of AMER for their careful work and attention to detail as reviewers. Certainly the production of this volume was dependent upon the participation of each board member in the review process, and for this we extend our sincere thanks.

REFERENCES

Resnick, L. B. (Ed.). (2005). Teaching teachers: Professional development to improve student achievement. *Research points: Essential information for education policy, 3,* 1–4.

Corsaro, W. A. (2005). *The sociology of childhood* (2nd ed.). Thousand Oaks, CA: Pine Forge Press.

Fine, C., & Raack, L. (1994). *Professional development: Changing times.* Policy Briefs, Report 4. Oak Brook, IL: North Central Regional Educational Laboratory. Retrieved December 5, 2008, from http://www.ncrel.org/sdrs/areas/issues/envrnmnt/go/94-4over.htm

National Center for Education Statistics. (2008). International Comparisons in Education. United States Department of Education and the Institute of Education Sciences. Retrieved December 5, 2008, from http://nces.ed.gov/surveys/international/

PREFACE

MUSIC EDUCATION RESEARCH REPORTING AND REVIEW IN THE AERA CONTEXT

Exploring the Potential for Music Education Research Advancement

Mary Ross Hookey

What are the implications of reporting our work within the context of the American Educational Research Association (AERA)? This edition of *Advances in Music Education Research* promises you something more than the last music research journal you read, with its collection of diverse articles. It has the potential to shift your reading focus to the question of how the AERA context, particularly its interdisciplinary nature and various research standards (e.g., 1999, 2000, 2006) might influence music education research reporting and review.

All the chapters in this book have emerged from a long process of review, reporting, and discussion associated with the annual meeting of the AERA. This Preface invites you to consider the issues and opportunities related

Research Perspectives: Thought and Practice in Music Education, pages xv–xx
Copyright © 2009 by Information Age Publishing
All rights of reproduction in any form reserved.

to the advancement of research that are available to music education researchers within the context of the AERA.

The AERA context is more than just the annual general meeting. Interdisciplinary research reports, critiques of methodologies, and review of research are only a few of the ways that AERA publications offer an interdisciplinary research perspective. While a number of music education researchers have made ongoing contributions to the dialogue, a group successfully met the criteria in 1996 for establishing the AERA's Music Education Special Interest Group (SIG). Their purpose is "to provide a professional forum for the dissemination of current research related to music teaching and learning." Beyond their own SIG, members may also be interested in learning about and contributing to the development of research methodologies from other SIGs. *Narrative and Research* and *Qualitative Research* are two examples where music educators now actively contribute. Some subject-matter SIGs have a history of drawing liberally on interdisciplinary research to broaden knowledge in their fields. Art, mathematics, reading, science, and social studies are leading examples.

In her 1996 Senior Researcher Award acceptance address, Cornelia Yarbrough made some recommendations that speak to the advancement of music education research practice through an interdisciplinary perspective:

> Improvement in scholarly process depends upon repeated research efforts resulting in products that are accepted by a wider scholarly community.... An interdisciplinary approach allows us to transfer appropriate knowledge and techniques from another area to our own. (1996, pp. 197–198)

Yarbrough's advice was not only for researchers.

> As we approach the 21st century, we, as musicians, teachers, and scholars, need to broaden ourselves by developing interdisciplinary knowledge and skills. Music historians need the techniques of anthropology and broad exposure to the humanities and liberal arts; applied music teachers need the skills of psychology and sociology; music educators need the rigor of scientific methodology coupled with strong orientations in the humanities and other liberal arts; and music therapists need the procedures of science, the knowledge of medicine, and the breadth of psychology, sociology, and the humanities. Most important, all of us need research techniques, so that we can get outside of our subjectivity and view our musicianship, teaching, and scholarship more objectively. (1996, pp. 197–198)

In 1996 no one might have anticipated the debates around the meaning of scientific research that would ensue in the following decade. The relevant point here is that the AERA context offers music education researchers the opportunity to become aware of and to consider how interdisciplinary research may affect how they shape their own research program. Each year at the AERA annual meeting, I meet people who are attending for the first time. They are usually impressed, and a bit overwhelmed, with the sheer volume and diversity of research reports, scholarly presentations, and debates on educational issues. AERA presentations undergo various forms of scrutiny for quality such as an electronic review process for acceptance and critique of presentations by discussants.

Improving the quality of published research is also dependent in significant ways upon the reviews of peers. Prior to publication in this edition of *Advances in Music Education Research* (AMER), the chapters in this volume were first prepared as proposals according to detailed AERA guidelines and submitted to double-blind peer review. Once the papers were accepted for presentation, many of them were formally discussed by their authors' peers during *Music Education SIG* sessions. Before formal acceptance for this book, they underwent additional peer review and editorial direction. While reviewing has recognized flaws, research shows that researchers and scholars believe that peer reviewing improves the quality of published work (Ware, 2008).

One approach is to expand our examination of the chapters in *Advances in Music Education Research* beyond music education content to the ways that research is theorized, questions are posed, methodology is explained, and methods are chosen. In a recent editorial, Burnard challenged us to look more closely at our research practice with this question: "How should we, as a research community, assess the methodological rigour and analytic defensibility of our work in music education research?" (2006, p. 143). The title of her editorial subtly suggests that we are only "telling half the story" if we do not make the "significance of methods and methodologies" explicit. Now, what questions can we, as readers, ask about these chapters from a methodological perspective?

Do these chapters represent links to interdisciplinary research and scholarship reported at the annual general meeting of AERA or found in AERA journals? This challenge to us as readers and researchers could generate a host of questions that we could consider as we read the chapters:

1. Is there an explicit link between the methodology underpinning the work and its influence on what we can know?
2. Does the author discuss the methodology that guides the studies in the literature review?
3. Does the author justify his/her/their research methodology in terms of the approaches discussed in the literature review?

Standards and guidelines published by AERA are designed to guide the work of researchers in education. Some publications, such as the *Standards for Educational and Psychological and Psychological Testing* (1999) and the revised *Ethical Standards* (2000) have had an important impact on practice. These testing and ethical standards may also support or amplify standards already established by other research disciplines, organizations, or Institutional Review Boards (IRBs). Those who present at the annual meeting or submit to AERA journals are expected to consider these standards. One of the Ethics Standards speaks directly to our responsibility to the field of educational research.

> To maintain the integrity of research, educational researchers should warrant their research conclusions adequately in a way consistent with the standards of their own theoretical and methodological perspectives. They should keep themselves well informed in both their own and competing paradigms where those are relevant to their research, and they should continually evaluate the criteria of adequacy by which research is judged. (AERA, 2000)

Other sets of standards published by AERA are educational documents. The latest set is *Standards for Reporting on Empirical Social Science Research in AERA Publications* (2006). The word "standards" appears in the title, but "guidelines" may be used as a substitute in the document. The authors emphasize that these standards are intended for reviewers and those submitting proposals and papers to AERA, but also suggest that these standards may be useful to researchers in other fields. The *Standards for Reporting on Empirical Social Science Research in AERA Publications* are focused on empirical research, with special sections for quantitative and for qualitative research. They are not intended for use with historical research reviews, conceptual essays, and other forms of scholarship. Once more, these standards draw our attention to matters of methodology.

> The purpose in specifying these standards is to provide guidance about the kinds of information essential to understanding both the nature of the research and the importance of the results.... The rationale for the conceptual, methodological, or theoretical orientation of the study should be described and explained with relevant citations to what others have written about it. (AERA, 2007)

While the stated audience includes "authors, editors, reviewers and readers of AERA journals" (AERA, 2007), the *Standards for Reporting on Empirical Social Science Research in AERA Publications* (2006) includes a list of situations where they should not be used. The panel who prepared these standards seems well aware of the misuse of standards to "define the conduct of empirical research, define or determine the format for writing" or to determine acceptability by using a standards checklist. The principles underlying the standards are transparency and sufficiency of the warrant. Standards are organized according to eight sections: (a) problem formulation; (b) design and logic of the study; (c) sources of evidence; (d) measurement and classification; (e) analysis and interpretation; (f) generalization; (g) ethics in reporting; and (h) title, abstract, and headings (AERA, 2006). Again, the information in each of these areas can be turned into a question to pose for reading, reviewing, and your own writing. As an example: Does the report contain a rationale for the conceptual, methodological, and theoretical choices made in addressing the problem? Does the quality of this rationale clarify why the research was undertaken? These questions may seem like second nature to experienced researchers, or the stuff of doctoral programs, but general concerns over the quality of published educational reports suggest that these and other questions may need to be raised in peer reviews. Reviewing is a scholarly practice that one can refine through experience. Some research into how music educators engage in the process could inform us as it illuminates how individual content and research expertise shapes the nature of a review. In one study of publication review practices (Godoy, 2006), experienced and novice reviewers reviewed articles that had already been assessed by expert reviewers. The results showed that experienced reviewers rated the articles similarly to the opinions expressed in the original assessment; however, the novice reviews were less likely to agree with the original reviewer opinions.

I have not made a connection between other contexts for review and publication review. The line between varied forms of review can be blurred when peer review of grants or promotions is discussed (e.g., Godoy, 2006; British Academy, 2007). Dialogue about the use of these AERA standards as publication standards has already begun. In providing a critique of the empirical research standards in terms of qualitative work, Freeman, deMarrais, Preissle, Roulston, and St. Pierre (2007) convey a sense of the urgency for dialogue and questioning of the need for standards through calling their article an "incitement." This requires exploring the possibilities and issues in the various AERA standards. The potential is there for additional music education researchers to take a central role in shaping quality in reviewing and reporting within the interdisciplinary context of education research.

REFERENCES

American Educational Research Association. (2000). *Ethical standards*. Retrieved September 24, 2008, from http://www.aera.net/AboutAERA/Default.aspx?menu_id=90&id=222&terms=ethical+standards

American Educational Research Association. (2006). *Standards for reporting on empirical social science research in AERA publications*. Retrieved September 24, 2008, from http://www.aera.net/opportunities/?id=1850&terms=Standards+for+reporting+on+empirical+social+science+research+in+AERA+publications.

British Academy. (2007). *Peer review: The challenges for the humanities and social sciences.* Retrieved September 24, 2008, from http://www.britac.ac.uk/reports/peer-review/index.cfm

Burnard, P. (2006). Telling half the story: Making explicit the significance of methods and methodologies in music education research. *Music Education Research, 8*(2), 143–152.

Freeman, M., deMarrais, K., Preissle, J., Roulston, K., & S. Pierre, E. (2007). Standards of evidence in qualitative research: An incitement to discourse. *Educational Researcher, 36*(1), 1–8.

Godoy, L. (2006). Differences between experts and novices in the review of engineering journal papers [Electronic version]. *Journal of Professional Issues in Engineering Education & Practice, 132*(1), 24–28.

Ware, M. (2008). *Peer review in scholarly journals: Perspective of the scholarly community—Results from an international study.* IOS Press Information services & use [0167-5265] 28(2). Retrieved September 4, 2008, from ALJC Swetswise http://www.swetswise.com

Yarbrough, C. (1996). The future of scholarly inquiry in music education: 1996 Senior Researcher Award acceptance address. *Journal of Research in Music Education, 44*(3), 190.

CHAPTER 1

ELLIOT EISNER AND MUSIC EDUCATION

Matthew D. Thibeault
University of Illinois at Urbana–Champaign

ABSTRACT

This chapter presents Elliott Eisner's address to the Music Education Special Interest Group of AERA, given in New York City at the 2008 AERA National Conference. We invited Matthew Thibeault to present introductory thoughts and comments on Eisner, his contributions to arts education and research, and his 2008 address to the Music Education SIG.

Those of us who attended Elliot Eisner's address and wide-ranging question and answer discussion at the 2008 AERA Conference were deeply moved (literally, to a standing ovation) and inspired. It is a pleasure to introduce his notes from this occasion.

With over 40 years teaching at Stanford, Elliot Eisner's contributions have had a broad impact in education, the arts, school reform, and curriculum theory. His writing is a continual source of deep satisfaction and inspiration.

Music education has a reputation as an insular discipline, but most music educators have read from Elliot's many books and articles. The impact of his ideas are felt within our field despite the fact that many of his examples come from the visual arts through his background as a painter and teacher of the visual arts.

Each art form has its own particular challenges. Elliot has been oriented toward the central problems arising within visual arts education—providing a sequential curriculum within a domain where changing media every week or two is common, and working to recognize the important cognitive contributions of art beyond self-expression. Those of us in music who spent decades playing a single instrument in Western art ensembles know the need for a sequential curriculum is not an issue. However, having rarely been asked our opinion in interpreting a phrase or what piece of repertoire the ensemble should tackle next, self-expression is more often absent then at the core of the music curriculum.

The two art forms most commonly found in American schools, music and the visual arts, each seem to have excelled in a certain conception of the arts while downplaying, omitting, and neglecting other potentially important areas. If only we could share notes to positively influence each other! Visual arts want our sequential curriculum, while we want our students to have the individual voice in their work that visual arts often provide. Visual art teachers want to foster collaboration, while we want to recognize individuality. Visual art teachers want to reconnect more forcefully with their history, and we want to make room for informal and popular music of the present.

Elliot's works bring us a message from the other side, brilliantly articulated and beautifully written.

In our time together, Elliot often undersold his musical experience and understanding, claiming no special expertise. But Elliot is passionate about music. He often breaks into song, usually a show tune or older popular song, to illustrate a point. For many years he and his wife, Ellie, had season tickets to the San Francisco Symphony. They would talk about a recent concert; how one of Michael Tilson Thomas' interpretations of Mahler had moved them or electrified the whole house. The drive from Palo Alto to San Francisco was worth it because hearing real musicians playing together in a great hall was one of their greatest pleasures. And they were interested in all the musicians—one viola player gave Elliot and Ellie such delight over the years that they wrote her a fan letter to let her know how much her artistry had meant to them over many years of concerts. In his living room, where he holds court with colleagues or reading group sessions, Elliot had a wonderful stereo and would frequently play examples from jazz or classical recordings in his collection. In true Eisnerian form, music made forms of experience possible that no other form could present or communicate, and he continues to draw upon music to teach, to learn, to experience and enjoy life with others. Elliot attended many of the concerts my primary school students put on while I was teaching up the hill from Stanford in Portola Valley.

Recently Elliot has turned his attention toward what education can learn from the arts, regularly presenting and speaking on this topic and devoting to it a chapter in his most recent book, *The Arts and the Creation of Mind*. In speaking to the music education SIG, Elliot drew directly upon this work. Now, when education seems to be more tightly constrained by the model of the sciences with each passing week, recognition of the contribution made by the humanities and the arts to the endeavor of education is critical.

Elliot's ideas have permanently altered the educational landscape in profound ways. He has fought hard for a rich conception of education throughout schooling. A product of the University of Chicago in the early 1960s, he worked with Joe Schwab, Philip Jackson, John Goodlad, as well as Ralph Tyler and Bruno Bettelheim. It was uncommon for a doctoral student to focus on the arts at the University of Chicago at that time, and Elliot brought away with him an uncommon viewpoint within art education.

Elliot's work presents most of us with an opportunity to return to the core reasons we are in teaching: a passion for working with people, helping them make the most of the opportunity of living. This manifests itself in unusual ways with different groups.

For example, I attended a talk Elliot gave to a group of superintendents in New Hampshire. He showed a video of an art teacher in Los Angeles, with students engaged in poetic contemplation of cream being added to coffee in clear glasses. These superintendents ate up what he had to share. They talked about the deep importance of the arts in thinking, and their hopes to instill imagination and creativity into their own curricula. After the talk, Elliot and I shared lunch, and I conveyed my amazement that these pragmatic administrators could be so poetic. He replied, "Although they have to deal with the day-to-day, in their heart of hearts they entered the field for a different reason."

Over the last several years Elliot has sent me drafts of speeches or printed copies of talks he gave. Many of these, particularly more recently, have consisted of a set of ideas he wanted to speak about in exactly the format presented here; broad ideas and one or two specific examples that he would then riff on, filling in and driving home serious points with humor, anecdotes, and rich examples from his own experiences tailored to the audience and context.

Such a list and skeletal outline does no justice to the event as experienced. What Elliot provides us now is modest compared with the presentation many of us attended. The metaphor of a jazz chart is an apt one, where melody and a set of chord changes present the bare beginnings to be exhaustively explored, improvised upon, challenged, expanded, and rethought. I have often brought these lists into my classroom in exactly this way, and my students respond with a rich discussion when working off a short list of such potent ideas. And so, if educational ideas be the food of music education reform, jam on.

EIGHT BIG IDEAS ABOUT THE ARTS IN EDUCATION

Address to the Music Education SIG of AERA
Elliot W. Eisner
March 25, 2008

1. Education can learn from the arts that form and content cannot be separated. How something is said or done shapes the content of experience.

   Since form shapes feeling, form is not a neutral entity but a force that can invigorate or impede. Consider the form of schools. For many schools, the closest formal analogy is the egg crate. Right angles dominate. One can only speculate how school experience would differ if schools had more soft surfaces, less right angles, and more curves.

2. Education can learn from the arts that everything interacts; there is no content without form, and there is no form without content.

   One of the major lessons people learn from listening to music, creating a painting, writing a story, is that components define each other. What a color, for example, looks like depends upon the setting in which it is encountered. I am reminded of a story of a man interested in buying a suit. He walked into a men's store and told the salesperson that he wanted to buy a suit. The salesperson asked what color he wanted. The man replied that he would like a green suit. Quizzically, the salesman asked, "A green suit?" to which the man replied, "Yes, a green suit." The salesman turned around and shouted to his colleague at the back of the store, "Max, turn on the yellow lights! The man wants a green suit." As I said, everything interacts. Consider the design of company logos. They are designed in ways that are intended to express the character of the business.

3. Education can learn from the arts that nuance matters. Heaven lives in the details.

   I was visiting a school one day, a secondary school, and encountered a young student working on the underside of a table. There he was, oil, turpentine, and steel wool in hand, smoothing out a part of the bottom of the table, a part that no one would ever see. You could say the student was concerned with nuance, but even more, he was concerned with perfection. It was his table and he wanted it to be as perfect as he could make it.

   There is another sense in which nuance matters. Nuance is the delicate, qualitative modulation of some form, whether it is an auditory form that you find in music or the visual form that you find in visual art. Crafting the nuance of it supports the whole that is being crafted and is what this is all about. Hence, students learning the color of language, its force and its delicacy, learn to pay attention to nuance, this time in a written form. Nuance also shows up in arguments designed to persuade readers of some conclusion at which the author has arrived.

4. Education can learn from the arts that surprise is not an intruder in the process of inquiry, it is a source of reward.

   The arts often push the rim of possibility. Students are encouraged to work at the edge of incompetence. To try things they don't know how to do. To develop work which is called "imaginative." Such features are applicable to all kinds of work in school, and the arts provide an example when they are well taught of what this looks like in their work.

5. Education can learn from the arts that slowing down perception is the most promising way to see or hear what is actually there.

   The culture puts a premium on being speedy, quick, fast, efficient. Such personal features are seldom related to the kinds of satisfactions that come out of savoring a qualitative or symbolic field. Learning how to pay attention to such particulars is one of the important lessons the arts teach and is a potential feature not only in the arts, but in virtually every disciplinary activity that we undertake with the young.

6. Education can learn from the arts that the limits of language are not the limits of cognition. We know more than we can tell.

   How does one get a feel for the rightness of a solution or the insight of an idea? Solutions and ideas are not limited to the arts. Can we design tasks whose solutions are judged right by feel rather than by rule? Can the ideas that explain history provide the sense of completion that we use to appraise the quality of a work? Can we get away, at least for a time, from problems that are solved by algorithm and which are proved with certainty?

7. Education can learn from the arts that somatic experience is one of the most important indicators that someone has gotten it right.

   In gestalt psychology, the law of pragnanz is the law of good fit. In contemporary philosophy, rightness of fit is an important criterion in judging the adequacy of a solution. Can we design activities in which students can make judgments about the rightness of fit that they have arrived at in looking at their solution in relation to the work before them? Can we promote activities which rely upon body knowledge, or, as I have called it, somatic knowledge, in order to determine how adequate a solution is?

8. Education can learn from the arts that open-ended tasks permit the exercise of imagination and that it is imagination, not necessity, that is the mother of invention.

   So much of the way we test students teaches them the tacit lesson that there is a single correct answer to every question that is posed and a single correct solution to any problem that is addressed. Can we design tasks that provide open ended opportunities for students to arrive at solutions that are not closed, not fixed, not permanent, not certain, but are open ended and which permit, indeed, encourage, the generation of alternative possibilities. If people learn what they have an opportunity to do, then to have tasks which are open ended gives students the opportunities to become imaginative and problem solving in their orientation to the world. Not a bad aspiration; it's an even better potential reality.

CHAPTER 2

DEVELOPMENTALLY APPROPRIATE PRACTICE

Historic Roots and Evolving Paradigms

Martina L. Miranda
University of Colorado–Boulder

ABSTRACT

In 1987 the NAEYC released its first publication on Developmentally Appropriate Practice (DAP). While music educators have been aware of DAP for over 20 years, the purpose of this chapter is to offer a historical perspective on DAP through a psychohistorical approach—one in which historical events are interpreted as they were shaped by social events and developmental theories. This chapter examines the historic roots of DAP as represented in four overlapping, yet distinct psychological and social eras: (a) foundations of child development theory (1600–1950), (b) the Kindergarten movement (1800–1896), (c) the organizational beginnings of the NAEYC (1896–1950), and (d) the period of change (1950–1980) that led to the emergence of DAP in the 1980s. With that backdrop, the chapter concludes with the emergence of DAP (1987–1997), the contemporary influences of DAP (including its first major revision in 1997), and implications from the proposed second revision due for publication in 2009.

INTRODUCTION

Beginning in the 1980s, music educators began a dialog with leading members of the National Association for the Education of Young Children (NAEYC) about emerging ideas on "appropriate practices" for those working with young children. In 1987 the NAEYC released its first publication on Developmentally Appropriate Practice (DAP). While music educators have been aware of DAP for over 20 years, the purpose of this chapter is to offer a historical perspective on DAP, through a psychohistorical approach—one in which historical events are interpreted as they were shaped by social events and developmental theories. Historical reports can be approached in multiple ways, such as chronological accounts, oral histories, comparative histories, and quantitative histories (Phelps et al., 2005). Psychohistorical approaches aim to place a phenomenon (e.g., event, individual's life) in a larger context with the goal of providing an explanation of the surrounding influences on that phenomenon. Rainbow and Froehlich (1987) observe that, "historical developments have often been instigated by specific individuals who either worked with socio-political groups or alone" (p. 115). For this study, DAP is situated in information from historical documents and interviews with contemporary NAEYC leaders. Ultimately, this historical reflection affords the foundation to consider future influences of DAP, based on an understanding of past and present events.

As a multifaceted compilation, DAP does not represent one theoretical view of early childhood education; hence it is not a singular theory. Rather, DAP is an integration of theories (Miranda, 2004) in response to the interrelated nature of children's physical, social, and cognitive development including:

1. Characteristics of physical development that affect a child's ability to engage in the learning environment (Berk, 1997).
2. Influence of social relationships on children's development (Hartup & Moore, 1990; Howes, 1998; Stipek et al., 1992).
3. The biological foundation for language acquisition (Chomsky, 1968), as well as the influence of the child's environmental experiences on communicative competence (Hart & Risley, 1995).
4. Vygotsky's sociocultural theory (1978), Piaget's preoperational theory (1952), and information-processing theories on short- and long-term memory ability and use of cognitive strategies (Siegler, 1983; Seifert, 1993), as well as appropriate intellectual and perceptual challenges (Katz & Chard, 1989).
5. Play theory (Smilansky & Shefatya, 1990) as a means to promote cognitive, socioemotional, and academic development.

DAP can be linked in many respects to constructivism; however, that link has been debated in the literature (Blasi & Enge, 1998). In addition, arriving at a definition of DAP is complicated by the varied perceptions and presentations of what DAP means in the literature (Miranda, 2000). The following three principles offered by Kostelnik, Soderman, and Whiren (1993) provide an operational definition of DAP:

1. Developmentally appropriate means taking into account what is known about how young children develop and learn, and matching that to the content and strategies they encounter in early childhood programs.
2. Developmentally appropriate means approaching children as individuals, not as a cohort group.
3. Developmentally appropriate means treating children with respect—understanding children's changing capacities and having faith in children's continuing capacity to change (pp. 32–33).

One premise of DAP is that the domains of development are interconnected across all areas of learning. Music educators have considered the implications of DAP for music education. In 1982 the Music Educators National Conference (now known as MENC: The National Association for Music Education) sponsored an early childhood conference titled, "The Young Child and Music: Contemporary Principles in Child Development and Music Education." Andress conveyed that, in addition to several leading early childhood music educators, leading members of the NAEYC attended the conference—an event that served as an avenue for key connections between music educators and the NAEYC (B. Andress, personal communication, July 2000). These events marked the beginning of music educators' attention to emergent ideas about appropriate practice formulated by the NAEYC. In 1986 the MENC sponsored the first Music and Young Children day at its national biennial conference.

Several publications by the MENC incorporated DAP guidelines into their recommended practices (e.g., Andress & Walker, 1992; MENC, 1993; Sims, 1995). Additionally, the NAEYC arranged for the publication of chapters on music in early childhood by leading music educators (e.g., Andress, 1995; Kenney, 1997) prior to the second revision. The voluntary national standards in music as published in *The School Music Program: A New Vision* (MENC, 1994) reflect DAP principles in the Pre-Kindergarten standards (pp. 9–12). Authors of these standards describe the teacher's role in framing children's musical explorations in playful contexts within a stimulating environment. The authors recommend that music teachers recognize the holistic nature of young children's development and plan experiences with concrete materials in which the children explore and express choice.

As a result of developmentally appropriate musical experiences, children should show curiosity about music and initiate musical play, both individually and collaboratively.

Through an examination of the historical roots of DAP, and in particular the ways in which thinking about young children has evolved over time, early childhood educators of all disciplines may realize the potential for reciprocal dialogue and further research endeavors. The succeeding section presents the historic roots of DAP as represented in four overlapping, yet distinct psychological and social eras: (a) foundations of child development theory (1600–1950), (b) the Kindergarten movement (1800–1896), (c) the organizational beginnings of the NAEYC (1896–1950), and (d) the period of change (1950–1980) that led to the emergence of DAP in the 1980s. With that backdrop, the chapter concludes with the emergence of DAP (1987–1997), and the contemporary influences of DAP, including its first major revision in 1997 and the proposed second revision due for publication in 2009.

1600–1950: FOUNDATIONS OF CHILD DEVELOPMENT THEORY

Perhaps no single movement has affected early childhood education more than the emergence and articulation of developmental theories. Each educational theory, pedagogical application, or curricular choice reflects a core belief on who children are, what children are capable of, and in what ways children learn best. Further, developmental theories are not static, isolated constructs. Rather, from the beginning of child development history, each theory has informed the next either through expansion, contrast, or creating a new perspective through some combination of theories.

I recognize that the work of keystone individuals (e.g., Rousseau, Locke) and subsequent theorists (e.g., Darwin, Skinner, Hall) served as the roots of several other significant educational movements (e.g., Progressive Education) and pedagogical practices beyond the focus of this chapter. For example, I have examined connections between the period of 1600–1880 and the work of individuals involved in the child-study movement (Miranda, 2006), with clear overlap in the historical accounts.

For the purpose of this section, an examination of the historical roots of DAP from the beginnings of child development theory to the introduction of DAP in the 1980s is not meant to provide a detailed discussion of each theorist or imply a direct line from the whole of each theorist's constructs to DAP. Instead, my intent is to identify how core developmental ideas of each successive theorist informed the early leaders of the NAEYC, shaped the mission of their organization, and established groundwork for the key ideas of DAP. To that end, I have provided a guide of key individuals and movements that have influenced DAP (see Figure 2.1). The intent of this figure is to illustrate the flow of ideas leading to DAP, not present a comprehensive view of developmental theory. For example, I have identified Locke's work as a precursor to behaviorism, but have not followed that idea by including other key individuals and movements that build on the behaviorist view.

17th/18th Century

Rousseau "nature" (precursor to Pestalozzi)

"Nature vs. Nurture Debate"

Locke "nurture" (precursor to behaviorism)

19th Century

Pestalozzi (sense experiences)

Froebel: Kindergarten (precursor to purist vs. eclectic pedagogy)

Darwin "baby journals" (precursor to learning from the child)

Hall/Gesell "Child Study" (precursor to Progressive Education/ Dewey)

Baldwin "maturationist" (precursor to stage theories)

20th Century

American kindergarten; IKU of 1896

S. Blow "purist view; teacher-directed" IKU to ACEI

P. S. Hill "eclectic view; child-initiated" NANE to NAEYC

Other Dev. Theories (physical, social, emotional, cognitive, language, play)

Piaget/Vygotsky (1987 DAP)

Constructivism (1997 DAP)

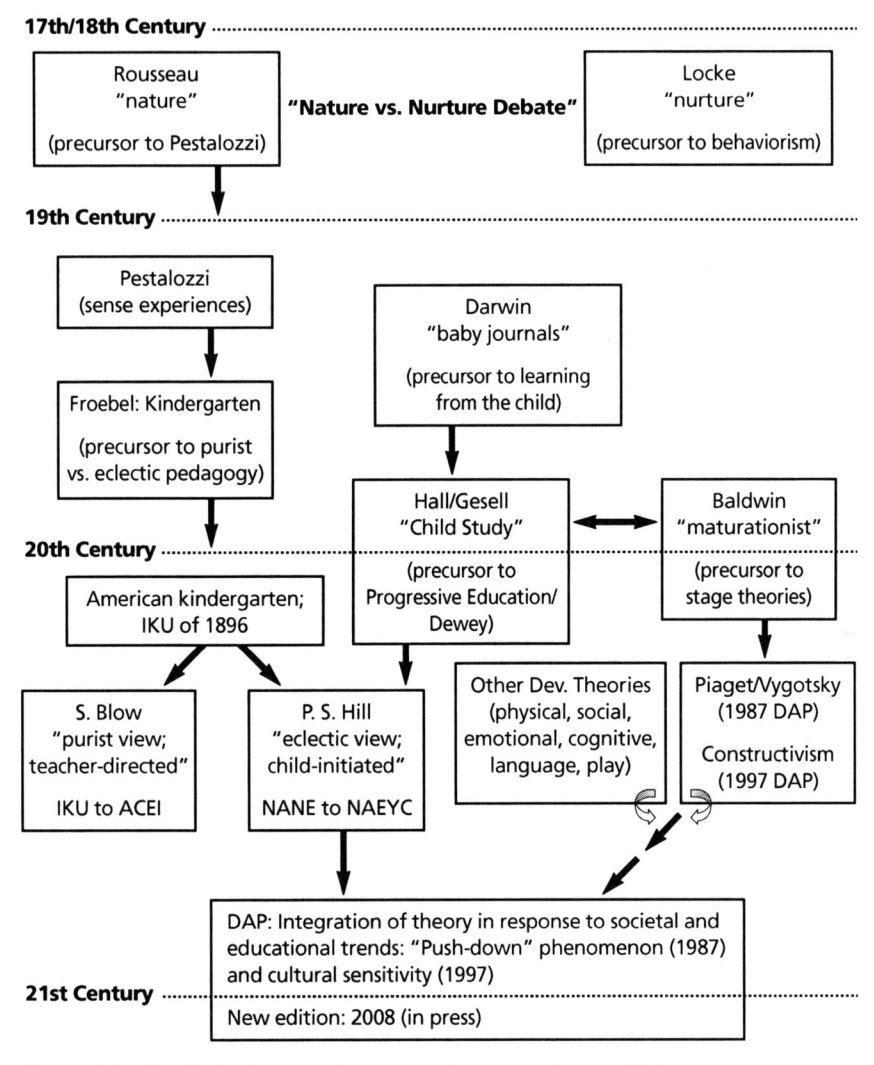

DAP: Integration of theory in response to societal and educational trends: "Push-down" phenomenon (1987) and cultural sensitivity (1997)

21st Century

New edition: 2008 (in press)

Figure 2.1 Key individuals and movements connecting to DAP.

The roots of the perspectives that would set the groundwork for DAP can be traced back to the 17th century (Gordon & Browne, 1993). As the 17th century began, children were viewed not as different from adults, but as inherently evil and in need of strict control. In contrast, John Locke (1632–1704) viewed children as neutral, and emphasized the idea of "nurture," a position that does not trust natural development, but sees the child as needing to be shaped (see Table 2.1). In his conclusion to *Some Thoughts Concerning Education* (1693/1964), Locke represented children as passive and moldable:

> But having had here only some general views in reference to the main end and aims in education, and those designed for a gentlemen's son whom, being then very little, I considered only as white paper or wax to be moulded and fashioned as one pleases.... (p. 235)

More than two centuries later, B.F. Skinner (1904–1990) represented this behaviorist school of thought by positing that external forces, such as a system of rewards, shape the child's behavior. Locke's view of children as "miniature adults" who are not distinct individuals would later prove to be the antithesis of a core tenet of DAP—a developmental perspective predicated on the importance of seeing and responding to children as individuals who are not simply "versions" of adults, but participants in a distinctive growth processes qualitatively different from adults.

In contrast to Locke, Jacques Rousseau (1712–1778), a French philosopher, placed significance not on the external but rather on internal factors that determined growth. One of his most famous works, *Emile* (1762/1962),

TABLE 2.1 Key Perspectives on Children

Key Individual	Philosophic Views on Development	Influence on Later Perspectives
Locke	"Nurture" Child as object to be shaped	Precursor to Skinner and Behaviorism (antithesis of DAP)
Rousseau	"Nature" Child follows innate processes influenced by environment	Precursor to Pestalozzi and Froebel (beginnings of child-centered educational practices)
Darwin	Scientific Approach Child as object to be studied	Precursor to Hall & Gesell; child-study movement; reciprocal learning
Baldwin	"Maturationist" Reciprocal relationship between nature and nurture	Precursor to developmental stage theorists, with particular connections to constructivism

is an account of a fictitious boy raised according to Rousseau's theories on child rearing. Although the account of *Emile* was anecdotal, it presented a philosophical position on parenting and educational practices. Rousseau viewed children as naturally good, with an innate curiosity and capacity to reach their maximum potential optimized by environmental factors (Brewer, 1998; Seefeldt & Barbour, 1998), a perspective often referred to as "nature," out of a belief in predetermined, natural developmental processes. With respect to DAP, Rousseau's recognition of inherent differences between children and adults, with a trust in children to be active participants and initiators, provided the foundation for the "child-centered" instruction that permeates the DAP position statement and guidelines (see Table 2.1).

In the 19th century, Charles Darwin's (1809–1882) work emerged. Through Darwin's introduction of a systematic method of studying children through recording "baby journals" of his son, descriptive research emerged as a viable avenue for scientific study (e.g., Preyer, 1882/1888). Darwin's approach reversed prior thought, suggesting that observation of children could contribute to knowledge (see Table 2.1), and thus served as a precursor to the child-study movement (Dixon & Lerner, 1992; Miranda, 2006; Shapiro, 1983). In retrospect, Darwin's scientific respect for observational knowledge can be seen as a precursor to the operational definition of DAP as teacher decision-making based on observational knowledge and investigation of each child. Conrad (1998) suggests that Darwin's observational approach was not unidirectional, but relational, involving "mutual construction of meaning" (p. 63), a further connection to constructivist practices encouraged in DAP. Darwin's examination of the adaptations of children (Berk, 1997; Oates, 1994) influenced two significant figures in developmental psychology: G. Stanley Hall (1844–1924) and his student Arnold Gesell (1880–1961).

Hall earned his doctorate at Harvard University, established a learning laboratory at Johns Hopkins University, and became the first president of Clark University in 1881 (Mark, 2007). Hall's educational background, coupled with his prominent positions in the academic community, assisted in the widespread influence of his research. In particular, Hall shaped the educational landscape through the influence of his ideas on students like Gesell and Dewey, and contemporaries like Baldwin.

Hall's landmark study, *The Contents of Children's Minds Upon Entering Schools* (Hall, 1907/1975), compiled children's knowledge of people, places, and events in their natural environment, based on interview data from over 200 Boston schoolchildren (Humphreys, 1985). Known for his efforts to employ scientific methods in understanding children, Hall became the impetus for the child-study movement of 1880–1910 (Gordon & Browne, 1993; Mark, 2007). Keene (1987) stated:

> While the antecedents of Hall's psychology go back to Pestalozzi and Rousseau... his theories, as well as those of others, brought about a change in the thinking of the public and of the educational establishment in relation to the school curriculum. (p. 222)

In particular, Hall's efforts to construct a normative profile of children based on observational data introduced a key idea that would find expression in the work of developmental-stage theorists (Rideout, 1982), and in the integration of stage theory with DAP (see Figure 2.1).

Gesell established a research center at Yale University, where he investigated the potential of genetic programming to account for the predictability of development (Gesell, 1939/1975). While Gesell identified a common sequential pattern for development, he strongly believed in the individual character of children, an idea that would resonate in DAP publications. Gesell wrote about the developmental influence of maturation and acculturation while upholding the unique response of each child to the environment. In *Child Development* (1949), Gesell and Ilg state:

> In the hey-day of Behaviorism [sic] there was a popular impression that all babies are very much alike at birth, and that the differences which become apparent as they mature are due to conditioned reflexes.... There is no evidence, however, that infants are not individuals to the same degree that adults are individuals.... In a boundlessly complex world he [the infant] says, in effect, "Lo, I too am here!" (pp. 40–41)

Hall and Gesell gathered information about children from infancy to adolescence and provided the foundation for the subsequent work of developmental theorists. An explanation of how children develop and the reasons connected with developmental events became the next challenge for child development theorists.

James Mark Baldwin (1861–1934), a contemporary of Hall and Gesell, contributed a developmental-stage theory to the knowledge base that existed during the first part of the 20th century (Cairns, 1992). While this contribution was significant, it was Baldwin's position on the nature-versus-nurture debate that influenced the study of child development for the next century. Baldwin maintained that nature and nurture held a reciprocal relationship and acted as joint influences in the child's development (see Table 2.1). The use of a dialectic process, integrating the views of Locke and Rousseau, created a middle ground or "maturationist" position that would later influence the development of constructivist theory (DeVries & Kohlberg, 1987). Further, beyond the influence of constructivist thought on DAP, it may be that Baldwin's efforts to merge two conflicting views set a precedent that is echoed in the efforts of DAP writers to merge multiple developmental theories into a holistic model (see Figure 2.1).

1800–1896: THE KINDERGARTEN MOVEMENT

The era of 1856–1896 marked a distinct time in American educational history as the "Kindergartners," or early kindergarten leaders established the first kindergarten programs in North America, based on the European ideas of Pestalozzi and Froebel. By 1896, due to the growth in the kindergarten movement, the first professional kindergarten organization was established—one that would lead to the origin of the NAEYC. What pedagogical perspectives did these early kindergarten leaders hold? What was the source for these views? The beginnings of kindergarten philosophy began in Europe with the ideas of Johann Pestalozzi (1746–1827).

Pestalozzi favored "natural" education, which emphasized the intrinsic curiosity of children and their innate desire to learn (Rusk, 1951). Further, in contrast to Rousseau's emphasis on education for the privileged male children, Pestalozzi believed education was for all children, regardless of gender or social status (Weber, 1984), a belief that would resonate in DAP principles. In his 1801 text, *How Gertrude Teaches Her Children*, Pestalozzi advocated learning experiences in which children form increasingly complex "sense-impressions" of objects through active investigation (Pestalozzi, 1801/1973).

> Pestalozzi abandoned the tradition of interminable lectures followed by student recitation that characterized typical instruction for all age groups, in favor of more active, hands-on activities and what he termed *Anschauung*: "object lessons" or direct, concrete observation. The long reign of pedagogical terror, enforced by flogging, was to give way to voluntary obedience elicited by respect for the dignity of each beloved pupil. (Brosterman, 1997, p. 19)

Pestalozzian educational principles included, among other things, introducing sounds before signs, emphasis on active instead of passive learning, sequential instruction focused on one concept at a time, and practice prior to introduction of formal terminology and theory (Birge, 1988). The influence of these principles can be observed in many contemporary educational methods. With the introduction of Pestalozzian ideas, the educational field experienced a shift in focus from discussions of "who" the child is to pedagogical applications of "how" to best present instruction to all children, an idea that would resonate in American public education.

The origins of the modern kindergarten are found in the writings and work of one of Pestalozzi's most famous pupils, Friedrich Froebel (1771–1852). Froebel, widely regarded as the founder of kindergarten, had a profound influence on the future of education in Europe and North America. He established his first school with primary-aged children (seven years of age and older) in Germany in 1816. Froebel remained at the Institute until 1830 and, after teaching in Switzerland, he returned to Germany. In 1837 he opened a school for younger children called "Kleinkinderbeschaftigungsanstalt"—a German term meaning "institution where small children are occupied" (Wolfe, 2000). The actual name of "kindergarten" was adopted in 1840 (Shapiro, 1983). "The Garden for Children is the Kindergarten" was the official title Froebel gave to the blueprint he sketched of the school, and the classroom layout set in a literal garden represented his tenet of "unity," or a place of both social and spiritual growth (Brosterman, 1997).

Two significant components of Froebel's method were the "gifts" and "occupations" of the children. The gifts were geometric play objects. The occupations consisted of the children's playful engagement with the gifts and the learning achieved through these and other activities (Graves, 1971). As stated by Froebel (1861/1909):

> The plays and occupations of children should by no means be treated as offering merely the means for passing the time, hence only as an outside activity, but rather that by means of such plays and employments the child's innermost nature must be satisfied. (p. 108)

The importance of play objects extends beyond the pervasiveness of these materials in contemporary early childhood education. Froebel's idea that use of these materials connected with the child's "innermost nature" echoes the philosophic position of Rousseau's natural development and Pestalozzi's hands-on activities (see Figure 2.1). Congruent with pedagogical practices of DAP, Froebel believed that play experiences common to a child-centered environment provide teachers an opportunity to "cultivate" the child's natural interests.

In the United States, changes in the educational landscape set the stage for Froebelian methods to become a part of kindergarten education. The model of the rural one-room schoolhouse, in which children aged 3 to 18 were grouped by ability (Wortham, 1992) grew obsolete in the industrialized settings of many American cities. Margarethe Schurz (1832–1876), a pupil of Froebel, established the first American kindergarten in 1856. Schurz began her kindergarten in Watertown, Wisconsin as a private school for German-speaking children.

Four years later, Elizabeth Peabody (1804–1894) opened a private kindergarten in Boston using Froebel's *Education of Man* as a guide (Snyder, 1972). Interest in Froebel's child-centered approach continued to grow; however, Peabody was not pleased with the results:

> But even seven years of experience with my so-called kindergarten, though it has had a pecuniary success and a very considerable popularity, stimulating to other attempts, convinced me that we were not practicing Froebel's fine art.... (p. 45)

In 1867 Peabody traveled to Europe to visit several Froebelian kindergartens and teacher training programs. After more than a year of study, she returned to America, revised her previous publications and materials, and devoted time to improving both materials and teacher training (Ross, 1976).

The first public-school kindergarten was established in St. Louis in 1873, with Susan Blow (1843–1916) as the leader. Blow had previously visited Froebelian kindergartens in Europe and was familiar with Peabody's work in America. By 1876 the St. Louis program had become a national center for kindergarten administration and teaching training (Shapiro, 1983). Blow left the St. Louis area in 1896 to join the faculty at Teachers College, Columbia University.

By the second half of the 1880s Henry Bernard, the first U. S. Commissioner of Education (Lawler & Bauch, 1988), established kindergarten as the voluntary entry grade for public school, and the kindergarten movement continued to grow. Training courses for kindergarten teachers were added to public and private institutions (Beatty, 1995). School superintendents began to establish double sessions (morning/afternoon) in part because of fiscal concerns and parental demand (Beatty, 1995). The popularity of kindergarten education spread quickly, and by the turn of the century there were more than 200,000 kindergartens in the United States, with 58% of them in public schools (Labuta & Smith, 1997).

1896–1950: ORGANIZATIONAL BEGINNINGS OF THE NAEYC

The beginnings of early childhood education in the United States can be traced back to the late 1800s as professional organizations formed in response to the growth of preschool and kindergarten programs. In 1896 the International Kindergarten Union (IKU) formed in response to the need for professional support for training programs and new teachers. However, a debate soon grew among the members. Although founded on Froebelian philosophy and pedagogy, a portion of the membership contemplated the implications of child-study research (Snyder, 1972), led by Patty Smith Hill (1868–1946). Hill employed the Froebelian methods, but also the ideas of others (see Table 2.2), including Maria Montessori, whose work was the most controversial (International Kindergarten Union, 1913). Whereas Froebel advocated a strict order of presentation in his gifts and occupations, Montessori believed that the child should be free to interact with classroom materials. The contrast between these two pedagogical perspectives was at the core of the division between the kindergarten leaders (Shapiro, 1983). The debates between Blow, who represented a purist application of Froebel's methods, and Hill, who represented an eclectic view,

TABLE 2.2   1896–1926: Debates and Division

Factions	Purist Division	Eclectic Division
Theoretical view	Froebel	Froebel as informed by Child Study research & Dewey, Hall, Montessori
Leader	Susan Blow	Patty Smith Hill
Materials	Strict order of presentation of gifts and occupations	Freedom to interact with materials
Teaching approach	Teacher-directed	Play based, child-centered
Resulting organization	IKU becomes the ACEI	NANE becomes the NAEYC

resulted in dramatic shifts. Kindergartens and laboratory schools based on child-study principles increased in number (Miranda, 2006), the view of the child became central to professional conversations, and the leading early childhood organization moved toward a dramatic split.

In 1905 Hill joined the faculty of Teachers College, Columbia University, where the debate over kindergarten pedagogy intensified. The IKU voted in 1903 to appoint the Committee of Nineteen to examine the matter. According to Bredekamp (1990):

> The now famous outcome of that group's work was the issuance of three reports: One by Susan Blow that advocated a relatively structured, teacher-directed instructional approach; one by Patty Smith Hill that supported a more play-based, child-initiated, progressive educational emphasis; and an attempted compromise report by Lucy Wheelock [committee chair] that apparently satisfied no one. (p. 177)

The reports were published in 1913 (International Kindergarten Union, 1913; Ross, 1976). The result was a split in the organization, with Blow's traditional view officially adopted by the IKU (S. Bredekamp, personal communication, November 1999). In 1926 the National Association for Nursery Education (NANE), begun by Hill to assist the growing nursery school movement, adopted Hill's eclectic, or developmental, approach (Hewes, 1976), while the IKU retained a strict Froebelian pedagogy (see Figure 2.1).

During the 1930s the IKU expanded its membership to include the elementary grades and changed its name to the Association for Childhood Education (ACE), eventually becoming the Association for Childhood Education International (ACEI). Meanwhile, the NANE shifted its focus to a new issue when, in 1933, the U.S. Office of Education announced the beginning of a national preschool system (Beatty, 1995). The organization continued to grow over the next three decades; in 1964 the name was changed to the National Association for the Education of Young Children (NAEYC) (Hewes, 1976). As the NAEYC expanded, new educational ideas (e.g., Progressive Education) had an influence on their thinking, but the core view of the child as an agent in learning (as exemplified in a child-centered pedagogy) remained constant.

While professional organizations focused on issues related to growth, psychologists and educators explored developmental implications for curriculum. Weber (1984) identifies the 1940s and 1950s as a time when a growing body of literature emerging from the child-study movement served as a catalyst to examine the relationship of developmental growth to curriculum planning. Specifically, the period of 1950–1980 was marked by significant attention to discussion of child development theories, accompanied by societal changes that set the stage for the NAEYC to draft and approve the first position statement on DAP in 1986 (see Figure 2.1).

1950–1980: THEORETICAL AND SOCIETAL CHANGES

Jean Jacques Piaget (1896–1980), one of the pioneers of child psychology in the 20th century (Gardner, 2000), began his study of children in 1920 while working at the Binet Laboratory in Paris. Through analysis of children's incorrect responses to standardized intelligence tests, coupled with many hours of clinical interviews, Piaget began to develop a new approach to defining intelligence in children. In 1969 Piaget commented during an interview:

> I became interested immediately in the way the child reasoned and the difficulties he encountered, the mistakes he made, his reasons for making them, and the methods he came up with in order to get the right answers. From the outset I did what I've been doing ever since: I made qualitative analyses instead of preparing statistics about right and wrong answers. (Bringuier, 1980, p. 9)

By placing emphasis on the child's way of thinking as opposed to the number of correct test responses, Piaget concluded that children's adaptation to their social and physical environment reflects their stage of cognition (Piaget, 1932). The stages of cognitive development he defined have influenced all areas of education. Sigel (1969) elaborates: "Piaget's conceptualization of the psychology of intelligence is developmental in format, substantive in content, and operational in behavior. These characteristics make the theory eminently germane, if not essential, for education" (p. 466).

Piaget analyzed the behavior of children from a genetic epistemological perspective. He believed that the child constructs cognitive structures that develop in a sequential manner, regardless of age or environment. Through a process of adaptation, characterized by assimilation and accommodation, cognitive structures are modified and reconstructed at subsequent points in the child's development (Ginsburg & Opper, 1979). The process of adaptation allows children to construct cognitive stability as they mature (Sigel, 1969).

American researchers became familiar with Piaget's findings in the 1930s, but did not give them significant attention until the 1960s, largely because of the strength of the behaviorist school in America through the first half of the century (Berk, 1997), as well as criticisms of Piaget's development of a theory based on a case study of his own children. Regardless, two factors combined at the Woods Hole Conference in 1959 to bring attention to Piaget's thinking: Jerome Bruner's report, *The Process of Education*, and the participation of Piaget's collaborator, Barbel Inhelder (Duckworth, 1987). The original purpose of the Woods Hole Conference was to examine science education, but the meeting became the inspiration for many curriculum studies (Mark, 2007).

The debates of the Woods Hole Conference brought focus to the area of cognitive science and served as a catalyst for educational research beginning in the 1960s, leading to widespread attention focused on Piaget's research in the United States. Gardner (1987) observes:

> But Piaget did more than simply help to keep alive the cognitive flame during the behaviorist hegemony. More than nearly any of his predecessors, he launched an entire field of psychology—that concerned with human cognitive development—and provided the research agenda that keeps it occupied until this day. Even disproofs of his specific claims are a tribute to his general influence. (p. 118)

Mixed perspectives on Piaget's theory have implications for later revisions of DAP. From a historical perspective, Piagetian perspectives on stage-related development informed the DAP writers as they studied child development, earned their degrees, and began their teaching careers.

The Russian theorist Lev Vygotsky (1896–1934) became known in the United States during the late 1970s, when several of Vygotsky's writings were published in English. Vygotsky's theory is often referred to as sociocultural, because he considered the historical and cultural contexts of children and families as germane to his views on development (Berk & Winsler, 1995).

Vygotsky viewed the child as an active learner situated in the context of the social relationships within the child's personal environment. In *Mind in Society* (1978) he stated:

> We propose that an essential feature of learning is that it creates the zone of proximal development; that is, learning awakens a variety of internal developmental processes that are able to operate only when the child is interacting with people in his environment and in cooperation with his peers. Once these

developmental processes are internalized, they become part of the child's independent developmental achievement. (p. 90)

The zone of proximal development, then, encompasses the child's mental age based on what can be accomplished with the assistance of an adult or "more knowledgeable" other (Pass, 2004). In Vygotsky's perspective, the larger the zone of proximal development, the more likely the child will succeed in school (Vygotsky, 1934/1986).

Vygotsky believed that children work out their ideas in the social context of their environment prior to internalizing concepts through a form of dialogue he called "private speech," in which children think aloud as a means of guiding their actions (Vygotsky, 1934/1986). Piaget theorized that mental constructs are initially worked out by children through internal processes, which then transfer to become a part of their social interactions (Vygotsky, 1934/1986). In contrast, Vygotsky theorized that children use private speech to work out concepts in a social context (external) before internalizing the new concept.

As implications of these developmental theories became a part of the educational literature, social change beginning in the late 1960s caused the preschool movement to experience unprecedented growth, as an increasing number of mothers entered the workforce. Statistics reported in *The State of America's Children Yearbook* (Children's Defense Fund, 2001) show that the percentage of mothers with children under the age of 6 who were employed grew from 30.3 to 65.3 between 1973 and 2000. The percentage of children under the age of 6 enrolled in childcare centers also increased from 13 in 1977 to 25.1 in 1995. In 2000 an estimated 13 million children under the age of 6 spent part of their day in childcare, regardless of the mother's employment status.

Concurrently, the number and variety of educational programs designed for young children paralleled the increasing enrollments in preschool facilities. Still younger children were enrolled in programs in response to the needs of employed families (Bredekamp, 1987). The federal government founded Project Head Start in 1965 to address the needs of economically disadvantaged preschool children (Kostelnik, Soderman, & Whiren, 1993). The goals of the project centered on promoting child development through parent education and proactive health initiatives. Several similar versions of this project were established through private funding in subsequent years (Peck, McCraig, & Sapp, 1988; Seefeldt & Galper, 1998).

At the same time, early childhood education experienced a shift toward formal academic instruction. The length of the program day for preschools was extended and both half-day and full-day options for kindergarten increased. The trend toward formal instruction was the antithesis of developmental practices based on children's play, and many early childhood educators expressed concern (e.g., Kagan & Zigler, 1987; Spodek, 1999):

> Kindergarten used to mean brightly colored painting, music, clay, block building, bursting curiosity, and intensive exploration. Now the kindergarten's exuberance is being muted, its color drained, and spirit flattened, leaving us with stacks of paperwork and teacher manuals. (Martin, 1985, p. 318)

Katz described the formal trend as the "push-down" phenomenon, in which the academic expectations and curriculum once used in first grade are pushed down into the kindergarten and preschool (Katz, 1988).

Elkind described frustration and stress exhibited in young children in *The Hurried Child: Growing Up Too Fast, Too Soon* (1981). Elkind identified parents of the 1970s as overwhelmed individuals who rushed their children to grow up in order to relieve their own stress. He specifically described pressures placed on young children for early intellectual achievement, the changing nature of children's recreational experiences, and the influence of the media toward an "miniature adult" lifestyle. In 1987 Elkind published a second work, *Miseducation: Preschoolers At Risk*, in which he expanded on his earlier views to include parents of the 1980s who sought to develop "superstar" children.

1987–1997: DAP EMERGES INTO THE EDUCATIONAL LANDSCAPE

From its inception in 1926 the NAEYC connected pedagogical practice with a child-centered view. As their 50th anniversary neared, educational policy moved in a direction opposite to their philosophic beliefs. In 1986 NAEYC responded with the release of a position statement that defines best practice as an integration of theories addressing the holistic development of children, or what has come to be known in the literature as DAP. Hirtz (1992) comments: "There are two basic assumptions underlying DAP. First, young children have somewhat different physical, social, emotional, and learning needs than older children and adults.... Second, there are individual differences that should impact teaching practices" (p. 310).

In 1984 the NAEYC leadership appointed a Commission on Appropriate Education for Four- and Five-Year-Old Children (Hymes, 1991) to develop an official response to concerns expressed by Katz, Elkind, and many early childhood educators. The commission's work resulted in the adoption of an official position statement in 1986 entitled, "Developmentally Appropriate Practice in Early Childhood Programs Serving Children from Birth through Age 8." The following year this statement was published within a larger document titled, "Developmentally Appropriate Practice in Early Childhood Programs" (Bredekamp, 1987). The larger document contains the official position statement of the NAEYC (Part 1), an examination of the teacher decision-making process (Part 2), and additional guidelines for implementation and age-specific applications (Parts 3 through 5). The document and subsequent publications on appropriate practice became known as developmentally appropriate practice guidelines and the practices based on them as "developmentally appropriate practice" or DAP.

Developmentally appropriate practice was defined as a set of guidelines to encourage "a way of teaching that's informed by child development knowledge, knowledge of the children as individuals, and the children in their social and family contexts" (S. Bredekamp, personal communication, November 1999). The DAP document published by the NAEYC served two purposes. The primary function was to provide a position statement to assist childcare agencies seeking accreditation with the NAEYC. A secondary function was to establish guidelines for childcare workers and to serve as a response to the growing movement toward formalized practices in early childhood programs nationwide.

With more than 700,000 copies sold, the DAP authors understood that the position statement would serve as a springboard for commentary and debate (Bredekamp, 2001). Further, there was a common expectation that theoretical perspectives on young children would change, and hence the authors included plans for a revision in 1997. While early childhood educators began to debate DAP as a construct, theoretical changes in the early childhood landscape occurred.

Researchers encountered difficulties verifying Piaget's theories. Piaget's concept of stage progression as invariant was not substantiated by cross-cultural research (e.g., Fahrmeier, 1978; Light & Perret-Clermont, 1989). Additional problems emerged as the results of replication studies varied according to materials used (e.g., Feldman, 1980; Flavell, 1971). Researchers found evidence of domain-specific knowledge, meaning that the child's cognitive stage varied depending on the type of activity encountered (Miller, 1993). In response to these difficulties, other perspectives on child development emerged as Piaget's ideas were examined (Case, 1985, 1992; Vygotsky, 1934/1986).

Piaget believed that the child constructs cognitive structures that develop in a sequential manner, regardless of age or environment. Vygotsky viewed the child as an active learner within the context of the social relationships that compose the child's personal environment. The difference of opinion on the role of external and internal cognitive processes points to the major difference between Piaget and Vygotsky. Piaget viewed the internal processes of assimilation and accommodation as a prelude leading to practice of the new skill in social interactions. Vygotsky viewed the inception of learning as occurring in social interactions and the child's subsequent internalization of each concept as the goal.

Constructivism emerged in the 1980s based on the work of Piaget and Vygotsky. While Piaget and Vygotsky differ in many respects, they share the position that knowledge is neither shaped nor optimized, but constructed through the child's interactions with the environment. The constructivist position is reminiscent of Baldwin's views on the reciprocal relationship of nature and nurture. The constructivist view also echoes the influence of Rousseau and Darwin, as Vygotsky (1934/1986) stated when commenting on Piaget's work:

> It [Piaget's idea] had already been expressed in the words of J.J. Rousseau, which Piaget himself quoted, that a child is not a miniature adult and his mind not the mind of an adult on a small scale. Behind this truth...stands another simple idea—the idea of evolution, which suffuses all of Piaget's studies with a brilliant light. (p. 13)

Vygotsky, while often identified with the constructivist school of thinking, actually saw himself as holding yet another position that rejected the other views (Vygotsky, 1978). Regardless, it is clear that Vygotsky contributed to the formation of the constructivist school of thought.

Constructivism is based on the premise that acquisition of knowledge is adaptive and emergent from the child. One goal of a constructivist classroom is to create an environment that fosters children's autonomy (DeVries & Kohlberg, 1987). Constructivist teachers see their role in the classroom as facilitators and supporters of the child's learning, creating environments in which teachers provide appropriate materials and opportunities for children's interaction and engagement. A constructivist pedagogy is not simply an active learning approach, but a much richer experience in which the teacher encourages reflective abstraction and higher thinking processes. Blasi and Enge (1998) state:

> They [teachers] must consider how to build into their practice the concepts of reflection, reorganization, problem-solving, discussion of problem-solving techniques, and connections across experiences. (p. 299)

Constructivist principles encourage children to raise questions, conduct open-ended investigations, reflect with co-learners, and dialogue within the community (Fosnot, 1996). Those who hold this theory view it as a paradigm that stands on new ground, and thus is different from the behaviorist and maturationist views that preceded it (Brewer, 1998; Fosnot, 1996).

CONTEMPORARY VIEWS OF DAP: 1997 TO THE PRESENT

As an integration of theories, DAP incorporates perspectives on physical, social, language, and cognitive development beyond the work of Piaget and Vygotsky. During the decade between the first and second edition of DAP, the emergence of constructivism attracted great attention in the literature. That is not to say that implications for DAP from other developmental areas (see Figure 2.1) were not also considered in DAP revisions. In fact, one interesting facet of DAP is that it was designed to be an evolving and not static model, one responsive to contemporary thinking and practice (see Table 2.3).

The period from 1987 to 1997 served as an introduction and subsequent discussion of DAP. The NAEYC viewed the discussion as healthy for the profession and sought to gather contributions from early childhood caregivers,

TABLE 2.3 Developmentally Appropriate Practice: Comparison of Revisions

Edition	Core Ideas/Contributions	Resultant Points of Debate
1987	Initial position statement on DAP	Lack of cultural sensitivity
	Construct representing multiple theories of development	Apparent "either/or" mentality: appropriate vs. inappropriate; teacher directed vs. child-centered approaches
	New lines of research	
	EC defined as Birth–Age 8	
	Strong base of Piagetian theory	
1997 2nd ed.	Inclusion of developmentally & "culturally" appropriate practices	Critical theory perspectives; stresses consensus, no discussion of widely differing perspectives
	Inclusion of constructivist principles	
	Clarification of nuanced view: continuum of practice—not either/or	Limited connections in grade-level classrooms
	Broader inclusion of Vygotsky's theory	
2009 3rd ed.	Revised definition of DAP	TBA
	Emphasis on teacher decision making	
	Efforts to connect Pre-K and elementary practices	
	Focus on reducing learning gaps	

teachers, and researchers during the late 1980s and early 1990s. Criticisms of the 1987 edition can be summarized as follows:

1. either/or oversimplification [appropriate or inappropriate dichotomy] of practice;
2. overemphasis on child development and underemphasis on curriculum content;
3. passivity of the teacher's role, the failure to recognize the value of teacher direction;
4. lack of awareness of the significant role of culture in development and learning (White, middle-class bias);
5. lack of application for children with disabilities and special needs;
6. overemphasis on the individual child and underemphasis on relationships and social construction of knowledge;
7. naïveté about the significant role of families (Bredekamp, 2001, p. 108).

Beginning in 1994, a review panel began the process of revisions to the original position statement and accompanying guidelines. Following a 2-year review process, the NAEYC Governing Board adopted a revised position statement in 1996, followed by the 1997 publication of the revised position statement and accompanying guidelines. The review panel considered current research and theory on child development (including constructivist theory), addressed emerging issues in the areas of curriculum and assessment, and looked to provide support for caregivers now concerned with diversity and cultural awareness (see Table 2.3). With respect to the changing climate of early childhood education in 2002, Dickinson observed:

> Gone are the alarmist concerns about academic pressures, replaced by discussion of increases in diversity of populations served, with reference to the importance of Head Start and welfare reform efforts.... Thus, instead of being a bulwark against overly academic pressures, DAP now is at least partly viewed as a means to ensure that disadvantaged populations receive high quality programs. (pp. 27–28)

The climate of early childhood education had changed, in part because of the influence of Vygotsky's sociocultural theory and constructivism. Thus it is not surprising that the 1997 revision reflected an emphasis on *culturally* and *individually* appropriate practices.

Further, the revision process allowed the authors to respond to the "increased conversation" about early childhood educational practices, correct widespread misinterpretations about DAP, and provide clear explanations about DAP as a framework for practice. Rather than framing DAP as an "appropriate/inappropriate" construct, the revised document encouraged a "both/and" continuum perspective in which there could be "many ways for practices to be developmentally appropriate," with the caveat that certain practices are harmful to children or inappropriate, as they result in undesirable results (Bredekamp & Copple, 1997).

Developmentally Appropriate Practice in Early Childhood Programs (Bredekamp & Copple, 1997) consists of several subsections critical to a comprehensive understanding of DAP: a rationale for DAP, a position statement, 12 broad principles of child development (see Table 2.4), implications for

TABLE 2.4 DAP Child Development Principles

1. Domains of children's development—physical, social, emotional, and cognitive—are closely related. Development in one domain influences and is influenced by development in other domains.
2. Development occurs in a relatively orderly sequence, with later abilities, skills, and knowledge building on those already acquired.
3. Development proceeds at varying rates from child to child as well as unevenly within different areas of each child's functioning.
4. Early experiences have both cumulative and delayed effects in individual children's development. Optimal periods exist for certain types of development and learning.
5. Development proceeds in predictable directions toward greater complexity, organization, and internalization.
6. Development and learning occur in and are influenced by multiple social and cultural contexts.
7. Children are active learners, drawing on direct physical and social experience as well as culturally transmitted knowledge to construct their own understandings of the world around them.
8. Development and learning result from interaction of biological maturation and the environment, which includes both the physical and social worlds children live in.
9. Play is an important vehicle for children's social, emotional, and cognitive development, as well as a reflection of their development.
10. Development advances when children have opportunities to practice newly acquired skills as well as when they experience a challenge just beyond their mastery level.
11. Children demonstrate different modes of knowing and learning and different ways of representing what they know.
12. Children develop and learn best in the context of a community where they are safe and valued, their physical needs are met, and they feel psychologically secure.

Note: From *Developmentally Appropriate Practice in Early Childhood Programs* (Rev. ed.) (pp. 10–15), by S. Bredekamp and C. Copple, Eds., 1997, Washington, DC: National Association for the Education of Young Children. Copyright 1997 by the National Association for the Education of Young Children. Adapted with permission.

policymakers, and 5 dimensions of early childhood practice that can serve as a guide for teachers' decision making:

> Creating a caring community of learners, teaching to enhance development and learning, constructing appropriate curriculum, assessing children's development and learning, and establishing reciprocal relationships with families. (Bredekamp & Copple, 1997, p. 16)

Although both the position statement on developmentally appropriate practice (Part 1), and subsequent sections (Parts 2 through 5) were published as one document, only the revised position statement (Part 1) reflects the official position of the NAEYC as adopted by the NAEYC Governing Board in July of 1996 (Bredekamp & Copple, 1997).

A comprehensive summary of DAP and its integration with curricula was published in 1997 in the form of a compilation by several early childhood specialists (Hart, Burts, & Charlesworth, 1997). In addition to generalized developmental information, the following specialized areas are the subjects of individual chapters: mathematics, science, music, physical education, social studies, visual arts, and literature. Authors of similar anthology chapters outlining the visual arts and early childhood education specifically addressed DAP issues (Seefeldt, 1999; Thompson, 1995). As previously discussed, music educators worked with the NAEYC to facilitate musical connections between DAP and early childhood music practice (e.g., Andress, 1995; Kenney, 1997). In 2003 the *Early Childhood Connections: Journal of Music- and Movement-Based Learning* published a special focus issue (Vol.9, Number 2) with several articles on DAP. In particular, I have investigated the implications of DAP for teaching and learning practices in kindergarten music classrooms (Miranda, 2000, 2002, 2004). However, few additional studies have investigated the implications of DAP for music teaching and learning settings in childcare and preschool settings, early childhood classes, or other early elementary grades.

In keeping with previous practice, the NAYEC is in final edits for the third edition (Copple-Bredekamp, 2009) of DAP (see Table 2.3). The authors acknowledge three current challenges—"reducing learning gaps to enable all children to succeed, bringing prekindergarten and elementary education together, and recognizing teacher decision-making as vital to educational effectiveness" (pp. 2–3). While revisions to the second edition considered cultural awareness, early drafts of the third edition acknowledge issues of poverty, second-language difficulties, and the impact of the 2001 No Child Left Behind (NCLB) legislation. Bowman (2001) observes, "Balancing research with values-based practice will continue to challenge us, particularly as we try to set standards that are responsive to children living in very different social worlds" (p. 175).

CONCLUSION

This chapter examined the historic roots of DAP as structured in these eras: (a) foundations of child development theory (1600–1950), (b) the Kindergarten movement (1800–1896), (c) the organizational beginnings of the NAEYC (1896–1950), and (d) the period of change (1950–1980) that led to the emergence of DAP in the 1980s. Several key principles from child development theory that are integrated in DAP include (a) recognizing fundamental differences between children and adults, (b) trusting children to be active participants in child-centered instruction, (c) teacher decision-making based on observational knowledge of individuals, and (d) implementing guidelines for practice based on an integrated model of developmental theory.

Concurrent to philosophical and theoretical changes, key individuals introduced educational practices for kindergarten education based on the work of Pestalozzi and Froebel. Early childhood education in the kindergartens flourished and led to the formation of the IKU. Although the quality of leadership and strength in numbers contributed to the formation of the IKU, it also revealed a sharp divide over applications of Froebelian practices and ultimately to an organizational split. At the core of the philosophic divide, leaders could not come to terms with a pedagogy driven by the *how*—as typified by a purist approach to Froebel's methods, or a pedagogy driven by the *child*—as illustrated by an adaptive approach. Clearly, the roots of DAP are evident in the child-centered approach that the NAEYC adapted, and the direction that mission took the NAEYC over time, culminating in the publication of DAP.

From my perspective, we are now at the beginning of a new cycle in early childhood education and can employ new lenses for conceptualizing developmentally appropriate practices. I have shown that our historical roots have led us from the philosophical debate over "nature" and "nurture" to a proposed integration of these views. The application of theory to pedagogy sparked the next debate of "child-centered" vs. "teacher-directed" pedagogy, followed closely by debates over Piaget vs. Vygotsky, and subsequently constructivism.

And now the question of what might come next is less clear. Early childhood research supports holistic development (physical, social, emotional, cognitive) through supportive relationships; yet many K–2 classrooms appear to emphasize subject content and skills, with less autonomy given to teachers to make individual decisions about what is best for their students. Moreover, while DAP is designed as a set of developmental principles for children from birth to age 8, is there not room to consider a parallel version of DAP for children in the third through fifth grades? Clearly that task is beyond the scope of the NAEYC, yet the opportunity exists to consider a partnership with a similar organization to address needs of children at the next part of their development.

If indeed there is a new revision of DAP in 2018, will it be shaped by societal changes, new understandings of children, or changes in teaching and learning shaped by reconfigurations of schools we have not yet envisioned? When one ponders what it might mean to "reconceptualize" early childhood education, one might imagine formulating a new understanding of what has been believed or experienced, with the hope of changing current practice. If one looks only to the past, the danger exists to look for ways to pursue changes only within the known paradigm. An alternate perspective sees "reconceptualizing" as a way to picture or imagine something new. Within the backdrop of historical precedent, and with the knowledge and understanding of children that these precedents provide, I believe we are poised to imagine an early childhood education in a new paradigm, one in which debates over "appropriate" and "inappropriate" have become historical topics, replaced by celebrations of children's inventiveness, voice, and creativity.

REFERENCES

Andress, B. (1992). Developmentally appropriate practice in early childhood programs serving children from birth through age eight. In B. Andress & L. Walker (Eds.), *Readings in early childhood education* (pp. 15–25). Reston, VA: Music Educators National Conference.

Andress, B. (1995). Transforming curriculum in music. In S. Bredekamp & T. R. Rosegrant (Eds.), *Reaching potentials: Transforming early childhood curriculum and assessment* (Vol. 2, pp. 99–108). Washington, DC: National Association for the Education of Young Children.

Beatty, B. (1995). *Preschool education in America: The culture of young children from the colonial era to the present.* New Haven, CT: Yale University Press.

Berk, L. E. (1997). *Child development* (4th ed.). Boston: Allyn and Bacon.

Berk, L. E., & Winsler, A. (1995). *Scaffolding children's learning: Vygotsky and early childhood education.* Washington, DC: National Association for the Education of Young Children.

Birge, E. B. (1988). *History of public school music in the United States.* Reston, VA: Music Educators National Conference. (Original work published 1928)

Blasi, M. J., & Enge, N. (1998). Under construction: Developmentally appropriate practice. What is constructivist about the revised developmentally appropriate practice. *Journal of Early Childhood Education, 19,* 293–300.

Bowman, B. (2001). Facing the future. In C. Copple (Ed.), *NAEYC at 75: Reflections on the past; challenges for the future.* Washington, DC: National Association for the Education of Young Children.

Bredekamp, S. (Ed.). (1987). *Developmentally appropriate practice in early childhood programs serving children from birth through age 8*. Washington, DC: National Association for the Education of Young Children.

Bredekamp, S. (1990). Defining standards for practice: The continuing debate. In C. Seefeldt & A. Galper (Eds.), *Continuing issues in early childhood education* (2nd ed., pp. 176–189). Upper Saddle River, NJ: Prentice-Hall.

Bredekamp, S. (2001). Improving professional practice: A letter to Patty Smith Hill. In C. Copple (Ed.), *NAEYC at 75: Reflections on the past, challenges for the future* (pp. 89–115). Washington, DC: National Association for the Education of Young Children.

Brewer, J. A. (1998). *Introduction to early childhood education: Preschool through primary grades* (3rd ed.). Boston: Allyn and Bacon.

Bringuier, J. (1980). *Conversations with Jean Piaget*. Chicago: University of Chicago Press.

Brosterman, N. (1997). *Inventing kindergarten*. New York: Harry N. Abrams.

Cairns, R. B. (1992). The making of developmental science: The contributions and intellectual heritage of James Mark Baldwin. *Developmental Psychology, 28*, 17–24.

Case, R. (1985). *Intellectual development: A systematic reinterpretation*. New York: Academic Press.

Case, R. (1992). *The mind's staircase: Exploring the conceptual underpinnings of children's thought and knowledge*. Hillsdale, NJ: Erlbaum.

Children's Defense Fund. (2001). *The state of America's children yearbook*. Washington, DC: Children's Defense Fund.

Chomsky, N. (1968). *Language and Mind*. New York: Macmillan.

Conrad, R. (1998). Darwin's baby and baby's Darwin: Mutual recognition in observational research. *Human Development, 41*, 47–64.

Copple, C., & Bredekamp, S. (Eds.). (2009). *Developmentally appropriate practice in early childhood programs* (3rd ed.). Washington, DC: National Association for the Education of Young Children.

DeVries, R., & Kohlberg, L. (1987). *Constructivist early education: Overview and comparison with other programs*. Washington, DC: National Association for the Education of Young Children.

Dickinson, D. K. (2002). Shifting images of developmentally appropriate practice as seen through different lenses. *Educational Researcher, 31*(1), 26–32.

Dixon, R. A., & Lerner, R. M. (1992). A history of systems in developmental psychology. In M. H. Bornstein & M. E. Lamb (Eds.), *Developmental psychology: An advanced textbook* (3rd ed., pp. 3–58). Hillsdale, NJ: Erlbaum.

Duckworth, E. (1987). *The having of wonderful ideas & other essays on life*. New York: Teachers College Press.

Fahrmeier, E. D. (1978). The development of concrete operations among the Hausa. *Journal of Cross-Cultural Psychology, 9*, 23–44.

Feldman, D. H. (1980). *Beyond universals in cognitive development*. Norwood, NJ: Ablex.

Flavell, J. H. (1971). Stage-related properties of cognitive development. *Cognitive Psychology, 2*, 421–453.

Fosnot, C. T. (1996). *Constructivism: Theory, perspectives, and practice.* New York: Teachers College Press.
Froebel, F. (1909). *Pedagogies of the kindergarten* (J. Jarvis, Trans.). New York: D. Appleton & Company. (Original work published 1861)
Gardner, H. (1987). *The mind's new science.* New York: Basic Books.
Gardner, H. (2000). *The disciplined mind.* New York: Penguin Books.
Gesell, A. (1975). *Biographies of child development: The mental growth careers of eighty-four infants and children.* New York: Arno Press. (Original work published 1939)
Gesell, A., & Ilg, F. (1949). *Child development: An introduction to the study of human growth.* New York: Harper & Row.
Ginsburg, H., & Opper, S. (1979). *Piaget's theory of intellectual development* (2nd ed.). Englewood Cliffs, NJ: Prentice-Hall.
Gordon, A.M., & Browne, K. W. (1993). *Beginnings & beyond: Foundations in early childhood education* (3rd ed.). Albany, NY: Delmar Publishers.
Graves, F. P. (1971). *Great educators of three centuries: Their work and its influence on modern education.* New York: AMS Press.
Hall, G. S. (1975). The contents of children's minds. In G. S. Hall (Ed.), *Aspects of child life and education* (pp. 1–52). Boston: Ginn & Company. (Original work published 1907)
Hart, C. H., Burts, D. C., & Charlesworth, R. (Eds.). (1997). *Integrated curriculum and developmentally appropriate practice.* Albany, NY: State University of New York Press.
Hart, B., & Risley, T. (1995). *Meaningful differences in the everyday experiences of young American children.* Baltimore: Paul H. Brooks.
Hartup, W.W., & Moore, S. G. (1990). Early peer relations: Developmental significance and prognostic implications. *Early Childhood Research Quarterly, 5*(1), 1–17.
Hewes, D. W. (1976). *NAEYC's first half century.* Washington, DC: National Association for the Education of Young Children.
Hirtz, R. (1992). Advocacy for developmentally appropriate practice. In L. S. Williams & D. P. Fromberg (Eds.), *Encyclopedia of early childhood education* (pp. 310–311). New York: Garland.
Howes, C. (1988). Relations between early child care and schooling. *Developmental Psychology, 24*(1), 53–57.
Humphreys, J. T. (1985). The child-study movement and public school music education. *Journal of Research in Music Education, 33*(2), 79–86.
Hymes, J. L., Jr. (1991). *Early childhood education: Twenty years in review. A look at 1971–1990.* Washington, DC: National Association for the Education of Young Children.
International Kindergarten Union. (1913). *The kindergarten: Reports of the committee of nineteen on the theory and practice of the kindergarten.* Cambridge, MA: Riverside Press.
Kagan, S. L., & Zigler, E. F. (1987). *Early schooling: The national debate.* New Haven, CT: Yale University Press.
Katz, L. (1988). *Early childhood education: What research tells us.* Bloomington, IN: Phi Beta Kappa Educational Foundation.

Katz. L., & Chard, S. (1989). *Engaging children's minds: The project approach.* Norwood, NJ: Ablex.

Keene, J. (1987). *A history of music education in the United States.* Hanover, NH: University Press of New England.

Kenney, S. (1997). Music in the developmentally appropriate integrated curriculum. In C. H. Hart, D. C. Burts, & R. Charlsworth (Eds.), *Integrated curriculum and developmentally appropriate practice* (pp. 103–144). Albany, NY: State University of New York Press.

Kostelnik, M. J., Soderman, A. K., & Whiren, A. P. (1993). *Developmentally appropriate programs in early childhood education.* New York: Macmillan.

Labuta, J. A., & Smith, D. A. (1997). *Music education: Historical contexts and perspectives.* Upper Saddle River, NJ: Prentice-Hall.

Lawler, S. D., & Bauch, J. P. (1988). The kindergarten in historical perspective. In J. P. Bauch (Ed.), *Early childhood education in the schools* (pp. 25–28). Washington, DC: National Education Association.

Light, P., & Perrett-Clermont, A. (1989). Social context effects in learning and testing. In A. H. R. Gellatly, D. Rogers, & J. Sloboda (Eds.), *Cognition and social worlds* (pp. 99–112). Oxford, UK: Claredon Press.

Locke, J. (1964). *Some thoughts concerning education.* (F. W. Garforth, Ed.). New York: Barron's Educational Series. (Original work published 1693)

Mark, M. L. (2007). *A history of American music education* (3rd ed.). Reston, VA: Music Educators National Conference.

Martin, A. (1985). Back to kindergarten basics. *Harvard Educational Review, 55,* 318–320.

MENC (Producer). (1993). Sing! Move! Listen! Music and young children. [Video]. Reston, VA: Music Educators National Conference.

MENC. (1994). *The school music program: A new vision.* Reston, VA: Music Educators National Conference.

Miller, P. H. (1993). *Theories of developmental psychology* (3rd ed.). New York: W. H. Freeman & Company.

Miranda, M. M. (2000). Developmentally appropriate practice in a Yamaha Music School. *Journal of Research in Music Education, 48*(4), 294–309.

Miranda, M. M. (2002). The seasons of kindergarten: Developmentally appropriate practices in the kindergarten music classroom (Doctoral dissertation, Arizona State University, 2002). Digital Dissertations AAT 3069834.

Miranda, M. M. (2004). The implications of developmentally appropriate practice for the kindergarten general music classroom. *Journal of Research in Music Education, 52*(1), 79–86.

Miranda, M. M. (2006). The child study movement: Historical roots and lasting influences. *The Mountain Lake Reader, 4,* 40–44.

Oates, J. (Ed.). (1994). *The foundations of child development.* Oxford, UK: Blackwell.

Pass, S. (2004). *Parallel paths to constructivism: Jean Piaget and Lev Vygotsky.* Greenwich, CT: Information Age.

Peck, J. T., McCraig, G., & Sapp, M. E. (1988). *Kindergarten policies: What is best for children?* Washington, DC: National Association for the Education of Young Children.

Pestalozzi, J. H. (1973). *How Gertrude teaches her children* (L. E. Holland & F. C. Turner, Trans.; E. Cooke, Ed.). New York: Gordon Press. (Original work published 1801)

Phelps, R. P., Sadoff, R. H., Warburton, E. C., & Ferrara, L. (2005). *A guide to research in music education.* Lanham, MD: Scarecrow Press.

Piaget, J. (1932). *Language and thought of the child* (2nd ed.). London: Routledge and Kegan Paul.

Piaget, J. (1952). *The origins of intelligence in children.* New York: Norton.

Preyer, W. (1888). *The mind of the child.* New York: Appleton. (Original work published 1882)

Rainbow, E. L., & Froehlich, H. C. (1987). *Research in music education.* New York: Schirmer.

Rideout, R. (1982). On early applications of psychology in music education. *Journal of Research in Music Education, 30*(3), 141–150.

Ross, E. D. (1976). *The kindergarten crusade: The establishment of preschool education in the United States.* Athens: Ohio University Press.

Rousseau, J. J. (1962). *The Emile of Jean Jacques Rousseau* (W. Boyd, Ed. & Trans.). New York: Bureau of Publications, Teachers College, Columbia University. (Original work published 1762)

Rusk, R. R. (1951). *A history of infant education.* London: University of London Press.

Seefeldt, C., & Barbour, N. (1998). *Early childhood education: An introduction.* Upper Saddle River, NJ: Prentice-Hall.

Seefeldt, C. (1999). Art for young children. In C. Seefeldt (Ed.), *The early childhood curriculum: Current findings in theory and practice* (pp. 201–217). New York: Teachers College Press.

Seefeldt, C., & Galper, A. (1998). *Continuing issues in early childhood education* (2nd ed.). Upper Saddle River, NJ: Prentice-Hall.

Seifert, K. (1993). Cognitive development and early childhood education. In B. Spodek (Ed.), *Handbook of research on the education of young children* (pp. 9–23). New York: Macmillan.

Shapiro, M. S. (1983). *Child's garden: The kindergarten movement from Froebel to Dewey.* University Park, PA: The Pennsylvania State University Press.

Siegler, R. (1983). Information processing approaches to child development. In P. Mussen (Ed.), *Handbook of child psychology* (Vol. 1, pp. 129–211). New York: Wiley.

Sigel, I. E. (1969). The Piagetian system and the world of education. In D. Elkind & J. Elkind (Eds.), *Studies in cognitive development* (pp. 465–489). New York: Oxford University Press.

Sims, W. L. (1995). *Strategies for teaching prekindergarten music.* Reston, VA: Music Educators National Conference.

Spodek, B. (1999). The kindergarten: A retrospective and contemporary view. In K. M. Paciorek & J. H. Munro (Eds.), *Sources: Notable selections in early childhood education* (pp. 101–111). New York: Dushkin/McGraw-Hill. (Reprinted from *Current Topics in Early Childhood Education, Vol. 4,* 173–191, by L. Katz, Ed., 1982, Norwood, NJ: Ablex.)

Smilansky, S., & Shefatya, L. (1990). *Facilitating play: A medium for promoting cognitive, socioemotional, and academic development in young children.* Gaithersburg, MD: Psychosocial & Educational Publications.

Snyder, A. (1972). *Dauntless women in childhood education, 1856–1931.* Washington, DC: Association for Childhood Education International.

Stipek, D., Daniels, D., Galluzzo, D., & Milburn, S. (1992). Characterizing early childhood education programs for poor and middle-class children. *Early Childhood Research Quarterly, 7*(1), 1–19.

Thompson, C. M. (1995). Transforming curriculum in the visual arts. In S. Bredekamp & T. R. Rosegrant (Eds.), *Reaching potentials: Transforming early childhood curriculum and assessment* (Vol. 2, pp. 81–96). Washington, DC: National Association for the Education of Young Children.

Vygotsky, L. (1978). *Mind in society: The development of higher psychological processes.* (M. Cole, M. John-Steiner, S. Scribner, & E. Souberman (Eds.). Cambridge: Harvard University Press. (Compilation of works from 1930 to 1934)

Vygotsky, L. (1986). *Thought and language.* (A. Kozulin, Trans. & Ed.). Cambridge: MIT Press. (Original work published 1934)

Weber, E. (1984). *Ideas influencing early childhood: A theoretical analysis.* New York: Teachers College Press.

Wolfe, J. (Ed.). (2000). *Learning from the past: Historical voices in early childhood education.* Alberta, CN: Piney Branch Press.

Wortham, S. C. (1992). *Childhood 1892–1992.* Maryland: Association for Childhood Education International.

CHAPTER 3

TYPE, FUNCTION, AND MUSICAL FEATURES OF PRESCHOOL CHILDREN'S SPONTANEOUS SONGS

Peter Whiteman
Macquarie University

ABSTRACT

This chapter reports aspects of a 3-year study of the singing of eight preschoolers. Monthly video recordings were made of the children's spontaneous singing during play. After transcription, these 443 songs and play episodes were coded for demographic, musical, and social aspects; the resultant dataset transferred to a qualitative software package (NUD•IST) for analysis and interpretation. Results exhibit some congruence with prior studies, especially those for which the social context of music making was considered important. The children used songs for specific purposes, but individual patterns of musical development were distinctly different. Findings expand previous developmentally based investigations by showing that conceptions based on a unidirectional model of musical development, closely linked to age, need to be refined to consider the diversity of social contexts and generative processes.

PURPOSE AND AIM

Early childhood is a time of tireless bustle in many domains that results in a burgeoning advancement in ways of knowing about the world. During this industrious activity, children sing countless spontaneous songs. It is through sensitive investigation of these that we can begin to understand what children know about music and the place that it is afforded in their social milieux. This chapter explores a corpus of 443 spontaneous songs produced by a group of eight preschool-aged children during play over 3 years. Specifically, it reports on the types of songs the children sang, their use while engaged in play, and the musical features of the songs. These data are drawn from a larger study of spontaneous singing. Other findings have been reported elsewhere.

PRESCHOOL CHILDREN AND SPONTANEOUS SINGING

The spontaneous songs of young children have been the subject of investigation for almost a century. It seems that early studies concentrated more on describing the children's music making. More recent research has been concerned with providing comprehensive explanations of how and why this musicking occurred, and locating the singers' behaviors and songs in wider educational provinces.

Describing Children's Spontaneous Songs and Musical Development

Werner (1917) proposed a series of 3-monthly stages through which 2- to 5-year-old children's musical development was purported to progress, based on children's improvisations. The main musical components he examined were melodic direction, repetition, a *gestalten* formal description, cadential content and placement, and range. Moorhead and Pond (1977) provided numerous detailed, naturalistic descriptions of young children's musicking in the Pillsbury Foundation School in the 1930s. This school opened in 1937 for children aged between 1½ and 8½ years, with the aim of developing musical understanding in young children, and, through the encouragement of free musical expression, to uncover principles that govern a child's relationship to music (Moorhead & Pond, 1977). In order to facilitate this, the program included "continuous opportunity for unregulated music-making, for hearing many kinds of music, and for receiving expert musical guidance and assistance" (Moorhead & Pond, 1977, p. 3). This was a significant landmark in music education since allowing children the time and space to experiment with musical expression was a somewhat radical variation on more teacher-oriented philosophies. The project is notable not only for its approach to curriculum but for the fact that it was documented in a naturalistic manner, which was quite distinct from the more experimental, quantitative nature of research at that time.

From the vast number of songs that they collected, Moorhead and Pond (1977) identified two distinct categories, drawing a distinction between "chants" and "songs." Chants were perceived as being based on speech; rhythmic and often based on rhythms of a quarter note followed by two eighth notes, then two quarter notes; repetitive; often associated with movement; and very social, more often produced by groups than individuals. Songs, on the other hand, were more complex and individual; rhythmically free, flexible, and irregular; often melismatic on important syllables; and not usually related to an observable tonal center.

In a section of a study of young twins and singletons, Alford (1966) reported on the quantity of the children's spontaneous songs and their rhythmic complexity. He reported that growth and experience affect children's responses to music, with older children singing more than younger children. He also found that the complexity of rhythmic patterns increased with the age of the child.

Like Moorhead and Pond (1977), Moog (1976a; 1976b) outlined clear differences in the spontaneous singing of preschoolers. Whereas Moorhead and Pond's categories of chant and song can both be found at various ages and in various forms, Moog presented a developmentally based taxonomy composed of five qualitatively different categories, which encompass "invented" songs as well as those that are imitations of songs that are normally sung to children by other members of their cultures. Stages were generally 12 months in duration, with the rhythmic and melodic features gradually acquiring characteristics of standard songs of the culture.

Interestingly, Moog (1976a; 1976b) reported on an additional form of spontaneous singing characterized by function rather than musical aspects. These sung monologues, "narrative songs," appeared to tell a story. The song text was not always logical or recognizable, was interspersed with "nonsensical interpolations," and usually sung without attempting to relate the story to anyone.

Explaining Children's Spontaneous Songs and Musical Development

More recent research has sought to explain the underlying cognitive processes involved in young children's spontaneous singing. Researchers generally concur that the context in which music is made and naturalistic data collection are important considerations.

McKernon (1979); Davidson, McKernon, and Gardner (1981); and Dowling (1984) traced rhythmic and melodic changes in children's singing. McKernon (1979) suggested that melodically, first spontaneous songs are characterized by an undulating melody, discrete pitches sometimes mixed with glissandi and spoken tones, and no sense of tonal center. Overall, Dowling (1984) concurred, with the exception of tonal organization, maintaining that these improvisations were based on a constantly drifting tonal center determined by intervals of highly variable size. Veldhuis (1984; 1992) confirmed the general observations of prior studies of spontaneous singing. She also provided insight into very short musical utterances in an attempt to tie purely musical information with the wider field of learning. Although without a major interest in the social context of singing, she provided a rudimentary acknowledgment of social conditions by distinguishing between the physical, social-emotional, and cognitive features of the two contexts (spontaneous and elicited) in which she collected children's songs.

Conformity of rhythmic characteristics was not evident in the songs collected by McKernon (1979) and Dowling (1984). According to McKernon, first spontaneous songs exhibit free and flexible rhythms (somewhat akin to those of speech) and display immense variation in rhythmic organization, ranging from random to metrical (although the latter is uncommon). Dowling, on the other hand, maintained that these songs are organized by a steady beat, albeit within phrases.

As children's spontaneous songs develop, environmental influences become more evident, with aspects of standard songs more frequently incorporated into spontaneous vocalizations (Bjørkvold, 1990; Davidson et al., 1981; Davidson & Scripp, 1989; Dowling, 1982, 1984; McKernon, 1979; Moog, 1976a, 1976b; Moorhead & Pond, 1977). By approximately 7 or 8 years of age, children produce spontaneous vocalizations and sing familiar (standard) songs, which demonstrates an assimilation of enculturated musical components such as "adult-like tonal stability, flexibility and nuance" (Davidson & Scripp, 1989). Initially, spontaneous and standard songs are closely linked, each affecting the other; a newly found musical element or skill in one area is very quickly imported into the other. However, at some point during their preschool years, children begin to produce versions of standard songs that are not always mirrored in their spontaneous output, with the organization of standard songs eventually forging ahead of their spontaneous counterparts.

Gardner and Wolf (1983) situated musical development in relationship to other domains of symbolic thought. While acknowledging "... that there is no ready translation of problems—let alone solutions—across symbolic domains" (p. 25), they maintain that children generally move from topological mapping (focusing on broad outlines such as melodic contours) to digital mapping (focusing on details such as tonal and rhythmic frameworks).

Bjørkvold (1990) collected examples of spontaneous singing from children in the United States, the former Soviet Union, and Norway. He perceived songs as basic components of children's play, and through analysis of situations where singing was part of play, formulated a three-level model (sound play, musical speech act, song accompaniment) of singing during play. Examination of the musical properties of the children's singing led Bjørkvold to categorize their song types in a fashion similar to that of McKernon (1979), Davidson, McKernon, and Gardner (1981) Dowling (1984), Davidson (1985), Davidson and Scripp (1988), Bamberger (1991) and Davidson (1994).

Adachi (1994) examined young children's spontaneous singing from the perspective of Vygotsky's zone of proximal development. During observations of social-musical interactions with children and adults, she identified three salient roles played by close adults: transmitter of musical signs; practice partner; and co-player, where adult and child participate equally in the music-making process.

While revealing various musical aspects congruent with prior studies, Burton's (2002) study also elicited some information from the children themselves. It would appear that this is the first investigation of young children's spontaneous singing, in which the singers have been considered valuable informers on their own songs.

METHOD

The contemporary view of children as valued and valuable co-constructors of their cultures (Broström, 2006; Dahlberg & Moss, 2005; James & Prout, 1997; Kjørholt, 2002) positions musical development and cultural construction as complex, socially located, collective actions. To investigate the musical development of a group of young children through this sociocultural lens, their spontaneous songs were collected via naturalistic observation over 3 years and analyzed from an ethnographic perspective using NUD•IST software. With context deemed crucial, analysis was undertaken in light of Miles and Huberman's (1994) six "analytic moves" through a course of "abductive influence" (Kelle, 1997), where theoretical presumptions were adjusted where needed as the structure of the data unfolded.

Setting

Data were collected over a 3-year period in a childcare center in a large city. The Center is licensed to cater to children from the age of 2 years until they begin school, and prides itself on its philosophy of equal footing for "care" and "education." Play is highly valued by staff and families, as are opportunities for children to play with others of varying ages. A total of 44 children (18 girls and 26 boys) attended the Center, with various attendance patterns of two, three, four, or five days per week.

The Center employs four full-time staff. The Director is a trained teacher. One staff member holds a 2-year paraprofessional qualification in childcare, while another was working toward this qualification. The final member of staff has extensive experience working with young children and families, but is untrained and works under the supervision of the Director. Additionally, an itinerant teacher of Japanese visited the Center once a week, and other support staff (e.g., speech pathologist) visited when necessary.

Participants

The four youngest girls and the four youngest boys attending the Center at the outset of the study were chosen to participate. The youngest children were chosen because of the likelihood of them remaining involved for the longest time before beginning school. At the commencement of the study, the children's ages ranged from 2 years, 6 months to 3 years, 6 months. All eight participated for the first 2 years of the study. With three leaving to attend school at the beginning of the third year, five children participated for the entire 3 years.

Henry

Henry was one of the older children at the commencement of the study and left to attend school after 2 years. He seemed to enjoy singing and used song frequently during play. An outgoing and confident child, Henry was usually very explicit about his feelings concerning this project, eagerly awaiting the researcher's arrival and typically announcing when he wanted the observations for the morning to stop. While Henry's family listened to music at home, no additional musical engagement was reported.

Natalie

Natalie remained part of the study for its entirety. She displayed a great deal of social maturity at the end of the 3 years of observation, developing into a confident member of the Center's culture. She has an older sibling, which is evident in the abundance of ingredients of popular culture (e.g., characters from television shows and music played on commercial radio) that were the basis for much play, conversation, and singing, but no member of her family has formal musical training. She was a frequent and confident singer, producing a large number of songs throughout the 3 years.

Heidi

Heidi was a young girl with an older brother and an aunt who sometimes worked at the Center as a casual staff member. At the beginning of the study, Heidi was a quiet child who attached very easily to adults in the Center. After 3 years, she left the Center to attend school as an assertive child, who, toward the end of the study, seemed to enjoy shocking the observer and staff with her vocalizations and actions. Music was part of Heidi's family life in the form of listening and viewing within popular culture.

Robert

Robert was a confident singer and had a well-defined group of playmates. He was assertive, yet rarely aggressive, and had very supportive parents who were eager to provide the best opportunities for him. Music played no particularly strong part in Robert's experiences outside the Center. During the 2 years that Robert participated in the study, he was observed in a variety of play episodes that became more socially oriented as time progressed. He was a prolific, spontaneous singer, with music forming a big part of his play and appearing to make significant contributions to those play episodes.

Anthony

Anthony was an energetic child who often ran from place to place, even inside, and displayed a generally cheerful disposition. A confident child who always rose to a challenge, he remained part of the study for 2 years. Anthony enjoyed the company of his peers and was frequently involved in socially based play. He often sang during play and was eager to explore the world around him, but did not engage in particularly musical experiences beyond this at home.

Helen

Helen was an affable, strong-willed child, who frequently talked about her older sister. She was the only girl who left the study at the end of the first 2 years, also to attend school. She demonstrated quite a high level of social/emotional growth over the 2 years she participated in the study, moving from being a child who had some difficulty separating from her parents in the morning, to a socially confident person with well-established peer networks.

Helen was one of the less frequent spontaneous singers in the group. Observations and anecdotal information from Center staff suggested the frequency with which Helen sang songs when asked was much higher than the frequency with which she sang spontaneously. Music was not a particular emphasis in Helen's life outside the Center.

Sean

Sean was a child of reasonably small physical stature, who attended the Center with his older sister. He was often deeply involved in play activities that focused on pursuits involving a high degree of investigation. Sean's confidence grew during the 2 years he was involved in the study, after which he left to attend another preschool. He frequently sang during play and often played with others, although rarely as a dominant member of the group. Before his sister left to begin kindergarten at school, she would often be part of a group that included Sean. At other times, just she and Sean would play together.

Julie

With two professional musicians as parents, Julie's brother also attended the Center during the early part of the study, before leaving to go to kindergarten at school. Julie was encouraged to develop independence in both thought and actions from an early age. She had a highly active imagination and was a very affectionate child, who would sometimes need extra individual attention, especially in the early mornings in the early part of the study, when separation from parents proved difficult from time to time.

Over the 3 years, Julie sang a number of songs in a wide range of circumstances. She enjoyed singing and creative explorations, both in music and other domains. Julie's social confidence grew over the life of the study, which seemed to afford ever-increasing opportunities to use songs in a number of circumstances; a challenge which she appeared comfortable and eager to take.

Data Collection and Analysis

The children were videotaped monthly for one hour during morning play, except when they were absent from the Center. Wherever possible, an extra visit was made to the Center to compensate for children's absences due to illness and the like. After the observation periods, the camera tapes were reviewed and spontaneous songs that had been recorded were identified for further study and analysis. The songs produced during each observation period were manually transcribed using traditional Western notation, modified with diacritical markings (e.g., "+" or "–" adjacent to a notehead to indicate microtonal pitch changes of less than a semitone) where necessary to represent the children's songs as accurately as possible (Abraham

& von Hornbostel, 1994; Gerson-Kiwi, 1953). To maintain a sociocultural perspective and accurately represent the characteristics, contexts, and occurrences of the children's songs, each song was coded for base data (e.g., age, date of observation), musical aspects, and social aspects.

Musical Elements of the Coding Protocol

Song type. Songs were given an overall label of "type" as detailed in Table 3.1.

Melody. Melodic details were coded according to a modified version of Davidson's (1985) system of contour schemes in order to guard against organization according to adult norms of tonality and intervals. These prescalar structures were developed to describe "children's growing understanding of both intervals and contours" (p. 363) and do "not assume that the child used fixed pitches, measured intervals in scalar terms, or organized performances based on keys or on melodic contours" (p. 363). The magnitude of the melodic contours was extended to encompass those found in the songs. No upper boundary was placed on the range; each contour was still coded as skip type or step type, with the interval size denoting the numeric value of the scheme's label. Examples of contour schemes are provided in Table 3.2.

Rhythm. Rhythmic details were coded using the 5-point rating scale outlined in Table 3.3, based on Bamberger (1991), and Wilson and Wales (1995). The points should not be seen as equidistant from each other, but rather descriptive terms along a continuum.

Structural organization. An overall measure of variety in each song was calculated according to Dowling's (1984) phrase-contour type/token ratio (TTR). The ratio is calculated by dividing the total number of phrases in a song by the number of original phrases present. Songs with no repetition of phrasal contours that consist entirely of new material were allocated a TTR of 1. Decreasing originality is indicated by a decrease in TTR.

TABLE 3.1 Song Types

Type	Indications
Standard	Child sings or attempts to sing a known song. Performance is not necessarily perfect, but the apparent intention is to reproduce the known song to the best of their ability at that particular point.
Standard variation	Child sings a song that begins as a standard song but ends up as something different. The change may be to another standard song, or material that is improvised spontaneously.
Improvised	Child sings a song that bears no resemblance to any known repertoire or style thereof.

TABLE 3.2 Examples of Contour Schemes

Range	Contour type — Skip type	Contour type — Step type
Contour schemes of a third	3a high-low motion with unfilled space between boundaries.	3b 3a boundary with intervening space filled with stepwise motion.
Contour schemes of a fourth	4a 3a with a step added (to top or bottom).	4b 4a boundary with intervening space filled with stepwise motion
Contour schemes of a fifth	5a some combination of 1a and/or 2a that outlines interval of fifth.	5b 5a boundary with intervening space filled with stepwise motion
Contour schemes of a sixth	6a some combination of levels 1a and/or 2a that outlines interval of a sixth.	6b 6a boundary with intervening space filled with stepwise motion

TABLE 3.3 Levels of Temporal Organization

Temporal level	Indications
Free-form	Rhythmic elements appear to be organized singularly, apparently devoid of temporal organization, similar to plainsong and Moorhead and Pond's (1977) description of the rhythm of "song." There is no evidence of motivic or metrical organization.
Approaching motivic	Mainly free-form, with some rhythmic phrases evident.
Motivic	Rhythmic elements display some form of temporal organization, with rhythmic phrases evident through the song. There is no apparent metrical organization.
Approaching metric	Mainly motivic, but some sections with an underlying beat beyond a phrase.
Metric	Rhythmic elements are organized according to an underlying beat, with rhythmic phrases produced accordingly.

The TTR is calculated using whole numbers, based on the notion that a phrase is either the same as or different from others. A phrase that is the same as another can have additional aspects such as passing notes, but has an equivalent underlying structure. The songs that were collected in this study revealed a third category. These phrases contained too many similarities with the first occurrence to be deemed different, but also too many changes beyond passing notes and apparent decorative features to be the same. In order to acknowledge the presence of these phrases, they were treated as variants of the original and allocated a value of 0.5 when calculating the TTR.

Social Elements of the Coding Protocol

The social aspects of the data were subdivided into two categories: overall social category of play and the apparent sociomusical components of the play episode. The social category of play was based on the works of Parten (1932), Saracho (1984), and Wyver and Spence (1995). Each episode was coded according to the taxonomy presented in Table 3.4.

Sociomusical categories of the data were rated according to the models of Bjørkvold (1990) and Adachi (1994). Song function was gauged according to Bjørkvold's (1990) functional model of children's singing during play, which is outlined in Table 3.5.

TABLE 3.4   Social Categories of Play

Category	Indications
Solitary	Play activities are undertaken alone, using toys and equipment that are unlike those in use by children within speaking distance.
Onlooker	Most of the time is spent observing peers play, sometimes suggesting or questioning, but making no overt attempts to enter into the play episode.
Parallel	Occupied in activity similar to children within speaking distance, using similar toys and equipment. The child appears to be pursuing personal goals and does not attempt to modify or influence the activities or behavior of children nearby. No attempts are made to control entrance to and departure from the group.
Associative	Actively involved with other children in a group activity, with members sharing ideas, materials, and common goals. All children engage in similar or identical behavior, with no division of labor. Individuals' interests are not treated as subordinate to those of the group, with each child acting as they wish.
Cooperative	Similar to but more organized than associative play. There is a hierarchical division of labor, with efforts of one child being supplemented by those of others. Each child is allotted specific activities, roles, and responsibilities, with control of the group in the hands of one or two of its members.

TABLE 3.5 Song Function

Functional level	Indications
Sound play	Imitation of physical movements with sound. Representation of emotions with musical monologues.
Musical speech acts	Using song as a communicative tool e.g., question and answer, teasing, information exchange
Song accompaniment	Singing while involved in another task and appears secondary to that task.

TABLE 3.6 Role of the Knowledgeable Other

Role	Indications
Transmitter	Musical signs (e.g., pitches, intervals, self-correction of pitch) transmitted from knowledgeable other to child and later formed part of independent music-making.
Practice partner	Child involved in same play situation with different person, substituted their role with that of the knowledgeable other, as perceived by the child in the initial play episode.
Co-player	Adult and child co-construct the intersubjectivity.

Adachi's analysis of the role of social elements was based on Vygotsky's (1978, 1986) notion of the zone of proximal development. Behaviors indicating various roles of the knowledgeable other in these interactions are presented in Table 3.6.

Additional comments about the beginning and end of each song were also recorded. These were open-ended jottings regarding observed behaviors, in an attempt to provide an insight into possible patterns for the onset and termination of singing during play.

Data consisted of an assortment of fixed and open-ended types and were stored in a relational database developed using Microsoft Access. Analysis was undertaken using NUD•IST software. The data stored in the database were imported into NUD•IST using a mixture of automated and manual procedures, with the coding of fixed data (categories for which a finite value had been stored in the database) undertaken automatically by the software. Remaining codes, such as those pertaining to narrative observations, were manually entered into the appropriate part of the NUD•IST system.

When all data were located in the NUD•IST system, manual exploration allowed for the teasing out of themes and unfolding of the structures of social and musical circumstances that were revealed as part of the children's singing. This analysis was undertaken in a recursive process, with individual topic coding, followed by organizing the data into categories, and finally sorting for patterns.

Four tactics championed by Lincoln and Guba (1985) were employed to maximize the realization of sound data and truthful findings. "Prolonged engagement" was accomplished by 3 years of twice-weekly data collection, allowing the researcher to understand daily life in the Center. Concurrent data collection, interpretation, and developing analysis allowed the researcher to undertake "persistent observation." Extended observation periods, including routines and mealtimes as well as free play, resulted in details that contextualized the collection of data and brought to fruition the third tactic: "referential adequacy." Finally, "peer debriefing" was undertaken through discussing data collection and emerging analysis with professionals experienced in the field but removed from the immediate environment of this study.

RESULTS

Spontaneous singing was a common, unbridled component of the play environment, which formed the backdrop to this study and was treasured by the children and adults in the Center. The 8 children involved sang frequently and used their songs for a range of purposes, including communicating with others, accompanying play, experimenting with sound, and just singing apparently for its own sake. The 140 hours of video recordings realized 443 spontaneous songs for analysis. The girls sang 209 of these (66, 60, 52, 31 respectively), while 234 were sung by the boys (69, 67, 52, 46) respectively.

Song Type and Function

All participants made use of spontaneous song in a number of purposeful ways, with all but one child singing spontaneous songs more frequently than standard songs. By far, the most frequently sung songs were of the improvised type, with standard and standard-variation accounting for a small number. The distribution of song type can be seen in Table 3.7.

TABLE 3.7 Distribution of Song Type

Type	Number of songs
Standard	58
Standard variation	22
Improvised	363

Children communicated with songs, they accompanied play with songs, incorporated songs as sound effects in play, and they sang songs for their apparent intrinsic value. Communicating and accompanying were the two most commonly employed functions, with communication accounting for 59% of all songs, and song accompaniments for 21%. Songs as sound play accounted for 7% of the songs collected, with the remaining 13% being sung for no apparent purpose beyond their own intrinsic value.

Songs to Communicate

All participants produced musical speech acts. In general, these were the shortest of all song types encountered in the study. They were usually sung confidently and were rhythmically organized in terms of displaying a constant pulse, at least at the phrase level. Motivically organized songs accounted for 113 examples (43%) of total musical speech acts, 39 songs (15%) were rated as approaching metric, and 68 songs (26%) rated as metric. The remaining 41 songs were divided between free-form (27 songs or only 10.34% of the total) and approaching motivic (just 14 songs or 5.36%).

Musical speech acts (e.g., Figure 3.1) were used for such purposes as transmitting and exchanging information with others (whether to a specifically targeted audience or as a general broadcast to all within earshot), gaining the attention of others, and responding to the overtures of others. Not all songs in this category had readily identifiable audiences; some were general broadcasts to all within close proximity.

Songs to Accompany

Song was used to accompany play activities in 93 cases. The definitive element of these incidents was that the song was in some way subordinate to the play in which the singer was involved. It was rare for standard or standard-variation songs to be used for this purpose. In fact, only seven standard (7.5%) and five standard variation songs (5%) were sung to accompany play, compared with 81 improvised songs (87%). This is not surprising, since the song was always the subordinate partner in these pursuits. Songs specifically created for a particular circumstance have a much greater chance of fitting neatly into the activity and being driven by the children's play.

A prominent feature of song accompaniments collected in this study was their text. Just over half were wholly sung in the children's mother tongue

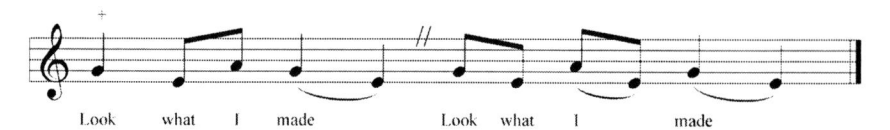

Figure 3.1 Musical speech act

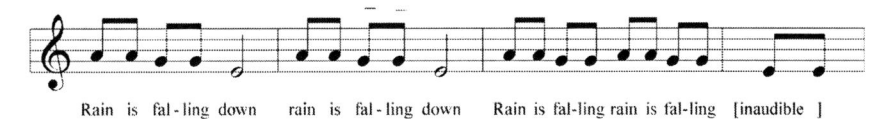

Rain is fal-ling down   rain is fal-ling down   Rain is fal-ling rain is fal-ling   [inaudible]

Figure 3.2 Song accompaniment using mother tongue.

Na la ba   nan e   da lu pa   la   la ba   ba   ba la ba

Figure 3.3 Song accompaniment using apparently nonsense syllables.

(Figure 3.2), leaving approximately 46% consisting of apparently nonsense syllables (Figure 3.3) or a mixture of mother tongue and nonsense.

There are two possible explanations of these texts; first, the area of selective attention. Perhaps the existence of apparently nonsensical text is a filtering tool, brought into play to impede the assault of ambient noise in the play environment, or to ward off intrusive approaches of others. This could afford the singer a privileged cognitive workspace in which to become immersed in the task at hand. A range of methods by which people selectively focus attention in order to filter unwanted information have been proposed (e.g., Cherry, 1953; Moray, 1959; Norman, 1968; Treisman, 1960). In this case, song could be used in this manner.

Locating apparently nonsensical song accompaniments within the theoretical frameworks of systemic language and cognitive load permits strong speculation for the children's choice of language in these songs. The systemic theory of language (Halliday, 1976, 1978) views language as a social phenomenon that is learned by engaging with others (Painter, 1985). Both Halliday and Painter explain how very young infants are ready to act symbolically but are unable to do so through their mother tongue because they do not yet have control of it. Instead, the children develop an early symbol system known as a protolanguage, which has meanings shared with close cultural members (e.g., a primary caregiver) consisting of verbal utterances, gestures, or combinations thereof.

The song accompaniments collected in the current study were produced by children who had progressed beyond the use of a protolanguage, but there were some striking phonemic similarities between the texts of their song accompaniments and the verbal signs that one could typically expect as elements of a hypothetical protolanguage. It is reasonable to assume that the children had not yet fully mastered their mother tongue. When they were engaged in an activity of a reasonably high cognitive load (e.g., a difficult puzzle or a particularly involved art activity), it may be that their working memory was taxed to the point where improvising songs in their (developing) mother tongue was not possible, hence they resorted to a form of language that did not place further load on working memory.

Rhythmic Aspects

The temporal organization of the songs ranged from completely free-form to highly metric. It was not unexpected that there were a number of metric songs, as approximately 13% of the total songs were classified as standard songs from the culture. Of the remaining songs, the majority (167) was classified as motivic, displaying evidence of some rhythmic phrases, but with no underlying beat beyond a phrase. Considering the ages and experience of the children, this is not extraordinary, as the early preschool years appear to be a time when children begin to imitate parts of songs around them (Moog, 1976a). It is interesting to note that most of the free-form songs were performed with neutral syllables and no recognizable text.

A common pattern emerged when the temporal organization of the children's songs was considered. Over time, the children incorporated more metrical qualities in their songs. Sometimes this trend was accompanied by a downturn in the production of less metrically organized songs, and at other times, it was in addition to the production of temporal levels such as free-form. Regardless of whether other levels changed or not, in general, the children's songs were characterized by an increase in the use of a regular beat beyond a phrase; a characteristic of songs that surrounded them in their wider culture and also of songs sung by Center staff.

Melodic Aspects

The children's songs proved quite surprising in terms of melodic attributes. While changes in temporal organization can be supported with evidence from prior studies, this was not so with the melodies. The children created quite sophisticated songs that could not always be considered pre-scalar, with many consisting of a range of notes wider than those previously reported in the literature. The lowest note used was G_1; the highest C^2. Some repertoire consisted of ranges of between 1 and 19 semitones; others were narrower but not quite as varied, while other songs were made up of ranges that were smaller still. Regardless of this wide variety of ranges, the majority of songs fell within a range around 6 to 9 semitones. Approximately 66% of songs consisted of a melodic contour that included every note between the limits of the song's range. Just under 33% of songs consisted of melodic contours that included gaps, and a small number (23) had a bitonal range only.

While temporal organization increased over time, a similar melodic trend was not evident. Although some children's improvised songs were characterized by slight increases in melodic range, these are not noteworthy as they were two semitones at most.

The children used melodic contours in very different ways throughout the study. It was in this area that departures from a single model were most apparent. A wide range of melodic contour patterns is evident across the whole sample of songs. Changes in the frequency of use of each type of melodic contour are apparent, and a range of relationships between the frequency of use of the two types is also clear. Even with eight children, four different patterns of contour use emerged over the 3 years. For all but one of the children, the use of skip-type contours was prevalent. Improvised songs consisting of step-type contours were rare, except for one child who sang mainly standard songs. It could be speculated that this child was attempting to standardize her improvised songs, and in so doing, was incorporating musical characteristics that appeared valued by the culture that she was assimilating. However, one could equally argue that the children, for whom melodic characteristics were not shifting toward a predetermined mold, were making valuable contributions to a co-constructed culture by continuing to explore beyond boundaries.

Chant

A number of the children's songs were reminiscent of chants collected by Bjørkvold (1990), Moorhead and Pond (1977), and Veldhuis (1992). Figure 3.4 provides an example of these songs, which were characterized by a falling minor third and a rising perfect fourth, with some rhythmic and melodic embellishments. Bjørkvold (1990) maintained that the musical characteristics of chant are but some of its defining attributes, with a social

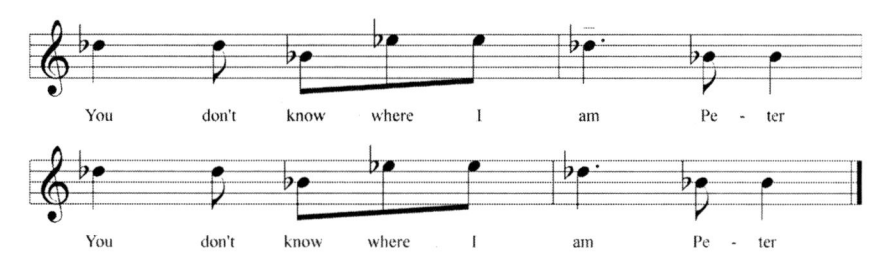

Figure 3.4 Chant with rhythmic embellishment.

function of communication as an important component. The children in the current study often used these types of songs as musical speech acts.

Phrase Boundaries

The children seemed to have a somewhat well-developed sense of Western musical structure. It was not uncommon for children who were engaged in some form of communicative activity to terminate their message at the end of a phrase. Similarly, interrupting a peer's singing was often executed at the end of a phrase, as shown in Figure 3.5.

The final songs of interest here were shared constructions. These songs were sung by more than one child and linear in nature, with children taking turns at singing. In a type of vocal hocket, some of these songs involved one child taking over from another and completing the song; some involved one taking over and then the original singer reclaiming the song again. Regardless of the type of song sharing, points at which the song was exchanged are of most interest. Exchanges marked by phrase endings (e.g., Figure 3.6) could indicate some structural understanding on the part of the singers. This is particularly true of those exchanges that occurred without temporal indicators, such as general pauses that could act as a warning to the children that the other singer had finished and it was their turn to take over.

In her discussion of musical intuitions, Bamberger (1999) proffers three "generative primitives from which musical development builds and grows" (p. 50). These are the ability to make sense of music in terms of structural elements such as phrases; the ability to respond to contextual functions of music; and the ability to perceive music kinesthetically, as though one were playing it on an instrument.

The first two points in this list are of particular interest to the current study. Bamberger views phrases as examples of "structurally meaningful...units of perception" (p. 49) and asserts that it is units such as these

Figure 3.5 Interruption at phrase end.

[Sheet music notation]

Figure 3.6 Shared song, shifting singers at phrase boundaries.

on which novices concentrate their perception of music, just as we focus on words or groups of words when reading, rather than on individual letters. This view is in accord with topological mapping preceding digital mapping as children engage with various symbol systems (Gardner & Wolf, 1983). Bamberger's second point entails bestowing contextual functions on these meaningful musical entities. That is, functions that could be construed as culturally specific, such as tension and release in the Western tonal tradition, are linked with structural entities such as phrases. A phrase to Western listeners, for example, can sound unfinished (a sense of tension) or finished (a sense of resolution).

In the current study, children seemed able to ensure that the end of their song coincided with the end of a phrase in Western tonal terms. This was especially important when a child's singing was interrupted by another or the purpose of the song was communication. In most cases the singers managed to terminate their songs at a phrase ending. Likewise, the children's playmates also timed their interruptions to coincide with the end of a phrase. These nodes not only marked musical configurations, but also indicated an emerging sense of semantic structure, as the children displayed their ability to enmesh meaningful structural entities from both musical and linguistic realms.

CONSTRAINTS OF THE END STATE

These descriptions of children's spontaneous singing could support models of musical development characterized by predetermined acquisition of musical signs. There are similarities with models resulting from prior research, and individual differences could be explained as deviations from a norm. However, more contemporary perspectives refocus development and culture as generative, adaptive phenomena—concepts that are strongly supported by data from the current study.

Corsaro (2005) provides a framework within which to locate such a view of musical and other development. This explanation of interpretive reproduction holds the child as the central focus of their development and views their involvement in cultural formation as interpretation rather than linear reproduction. Corsaro maintains that children "interpret" rather than "internalize" existing cultures and in so doing, also produce a range of their own cultures.

An interesting tension apparently arises when the nature of interpretive reproduction is considered along with the restrictions of teleology. It has been established that children's musical development occurs in a social setting; that interactions with other members of a culture are the agents and channels through which development is mediated (Adachi, 1994; Gardner & Wolf, 1983; Sloboda, 1985). Children interact with others, constructing, transmitting and using a range of cultural symbols or signs. This study has concentrated on musical signs and highlighted the considerable differences that can occur because of the multitude of ways in which these children engaged with other members of their cultures. Transmission and acquisition of signs and hence human development is necessarily a joint process, involving not just an individual, but an assortment of members of a culture. Corsaro (2005) presents the following inventory of three specific types of collective action that constitute the concept of interpretive reproduction: "children's creative appropriation of information and knowledge from the adult world; children's production [of] and participation in a series of peer cultures; and children's contribution to the reproduction and extension of the adult culture" (p. 41). He offers this list not only as an explanation of the collective actions that shape interpretive reproduction, but also arranges these in a form of chronological taxonomy. Without suggesting that there is a rigid timeline for the occurrence of these collective actions, Corsaro does state that the order in which the above list is presented is the sequence in which one is most likely to find the actions played out. He believes that the production of a culture is facilitated by appropriation and is also an important conduit for reproduction and change.

On first glance, it would seem that this model has now returned to a teleological base; one of the very entities that the examination of the data in this study is attempting to move beyond. Appropriation leading to production, and ultimately change, seems to imply stages that are working toward an end state. How then can this path be reconciled within the flexibility of interpretive reproduction? Corsaro (2005) uses the analogy of a spider web to explain his model. This "orb web" has at its center the child and his/her family. The spirals that emanate from the center of the web, representative of the peer cultures created in a society, are crossed by radii representing fields of institutional interaction. These social institutions (e.g., family, community, economic, educational, political) are played out in a range of relevant locations. For example, education can be located in preschool playrooms, school classrooms, and community orchestra rehearsal halls.

The more traditional linear path assumes that children develop as individuals, moving from beginning to end by proceeding through a series of clearly delineated stages, each of which is preparatory for the next, until arriving at a stage of maturity. Corsaro's (2005) orb web represents the varied array of cultural establishments in which interaction transpires, and consequently, transmission of signs takes place. Importantly, children age in a linear fashion: they are born young and get older. It is this journey that can endow some perplexity on the nonlinear argument. However, as children do get older, they develop not as individuals, in a linear fashion, but as individuals within a group. That is, they do not merely internalize a preexisting world, but struggle to make sense of it. In so doing, a collective production of a range of cultures transpires. Evidence for this slant on development is readily available from the data collected for the current study, as a range of musical signs were afforded various importance by different children, and a multiplicity of approaches to transmission and acquisition of these signs was documented.

Even though the appropriation-production-reproduction arrangement appears to negate modular pathways, children are driven by chronology to some extent. It is the range of experiences in numerous contexts that facilitate interpretive reproduction in a fashion that suits individual groups in individual circumstances. A number of more traditional linear blueprints of development have been proposed in a range of musical areas, including song acquisition (Bentley, 1966; Davidson, McKernon, & Gardner, 1981; Moog, 1976a, 1976b; Welch, 1986), rhythm and meter (Cox, 1977; Davidson & Scripp, 1992; Petzold, 1966; Thackray, 1972; Zimmerman, 1985), and tonality (Dowling, 1988; Krumhansl & Keil, 1982). These models generally taxonomize the acquisition of musical signs and indicate that the incidence of particular skills and knowledge can be quite readily aligned with certain ages and/or stages of development. In contrast, a nonlinear approach to the notion of development is more appropriate, because it allows musical signs that are transmitted and acquired during the children's day-to-day activities to realize a co-constructed culture. Such cultures are characterized by signs deemed valuable by participants; the signs are suited to those who belong to the culture. The signs are not regarded as important simply because conventions maintain they should fit into a preexisting framework. The current study provided evidence of how complex and mature a culture can be if viewed within a paradigm where children are agents of cultural construction.

IMPLICATIONS

The data reported herein contribute to a growing understanding of children's musical development and provide insight into the emerging musical cultures of a group of preschoolers. The songs of these eight children charted a range of developmental trajectories, supporting musical development and cultural construction as generative phenomena, modular in nature and specific to members. The data do not support a "one size fits all" approach to normalizing the children and their musicking. It seems that such teleological models of development may be inadequate to fully describe the complex nature of these young children's musical cultures and development.

The songs indicate that the children are capable of producing sophisticated music. They sang songs demonstrating a range of musical signs from their cultures, many of which were produced with increasing levels of accuracy as the study progressed. The children sang purposefully for a variety of reasons. The ability to produce sophisticated songs has a vital implication for teachers of young children. The image of the teacher as direct instructor is immediately dismantled if the children's musical constructions are taken as focal points in the teaching-learning process. Teachers of young children need to understand the rich musical cultures that those children construct and the complex ecologies within which they operate. This is imperative for the implementation of contemporary, quality, child-centered pedagogies using the children's repertoire and emerging musical understandings as starting points in an emergent curriculum (Jones & Nimmo, 1994).

The children showed that they can make important contributions to the construction of their cultures. Overall, practitioners need to value these. They should not expect children to assimilate a preexisting culture, created and shaped by adults. Rather, these should be co-constructed as shared entities. The cultural signs that children generate and reproduce as part of their everyday lives should become an integral part of the ethos of the group, practiced by all members, including those regarded as more culturally experienced or mature.

The notion of cultures and the manner in which they are defined and constructed has quite serious implications for early childhood classrooms.

It has been established that high quality programs for prior-to-school-aged children have as their nucleus a child-centered, authentic approach to planning teaching and learning experiences based on detailed knowledge of the children (Hutchin, 2006; Lambert & Clyde, 2000; Nutbrown, 2006). This in turn requires that teachers undertake systematic observation of children in order to determine the most appropriate type of learning experiences for individuals. The range of available frameworks within which to locate teachers' observations has been limited largely to linear developmental models (Corsaro, 2005; Thelan & Smith, 1994). Such models are based on actualization of an end state that is often determined by cultural members other than the child in question. In the current study, the children demonstrated that there are multiple pathways along which to travel in order to reach cultural maturity, rather than one predetermined corridor through which all members of a culture pass and arrive at an inexorable finishing line. If teachers acknowledge that children can follow various paths as they mature, then child-centered programming can be tailored much more for individuals as parts of a group, rather than just individuals somewhere on a single pathway toward a predetermined end-state.

Further research is needed to confirm that the patterns of musical development displayed by the children in the current study were not a result of a sheltered cultural microcosm. Mapping early musical development and co-construction of musical cultures, acknowledging development as a dynamic system (Thelan & Smith, 1994), an orb web (Corsaro, 2005), or an ecological system (Bronfenbrenner, 2005) would provide a sound basis for comparison and extension of knowledge.

REFERENCES

Abraham, O., & von Hornbostel, E. M. (1994). Suggested methods for the transcription of exotic music. *Ethnomusicology, 38*(3), 425–456.

Adachi, M. (1994). The role of the adult in the child's early music socialization: A Vygotskian perspective. *The Quarterly Journal of Music Teaching and Learning, V*(3), 26–35.

Alford, D. L. (1966). *Emergence and development of musical responses in preschool twins and singletons: A comparative study.* Unpublished doctoral dissertation, Florida State University, Tallahassee.

Bamberger, J. (1991). *The mind behind the musical ear.* Cambridge, MA: Harvard University Press.

Bamberger, J. (1999). Learning from the children we teach. *Bulletin of the Council for Research in Music Education, 142,* 48–74.

Bentley, A. (1966). *Musical ability in children and its measurement.* London: Harrap.

Bjørkvold, J. R. (1990). Canto-ergo sum: Musical child cultures in the United States, the Soviet Union and Norway. In F. R. Wilson & F. L. Roehmann (Eds.), *Music* and *child development: Proceedings of the 1987 biology of music making conference* (pp. 117–135). St Louis, MO: MMB Music.

Bronfenbrenner, U. (2005). *Making human beings human: Bioecological perspectives on human development.* Thousand Oaks, CA: Sage.

Broström, S. (2006). Children's perspectives on their childhood experiences. In J. Einarsdottir & J. T. Wagner (Eds.), *Nordic childhoods and early education* (pp. 223–255). Greenwich, CT: Information Age Publishing.

Burton, S. (2002). An exploration of preschool children's spontaneous songs and chants. *Visions of Research in Music Education, 2.* Retrieved July 19, 2003, from http://musicweb.rutgers.edu/vrme/v2n1/index.htm.

Cherry, E. C. (1953). Some experiments on the recognition of speech, with one and with two ears. *Journal of the Acoustical Society of America, 25,* 975–979.

Corsaro, W. A. (2005). *The sociology of childhood* (2nd ed.). Thousand Oaks, CA: Pine Forge Press.

Cox, M. O. (1977). *A descriptive analysis of the response to beat, meter and rhythm pattern by children in grades one to six.* Unpublished doctoral dissertation, University of Wisconsin, Madison.

Dahlberg, G., & Moss, P. (2005). *Ethics and politics in early childhood education.* Abingdon, Oxfordshire, UK: Routledge.

Davidson, L. (1985). Tonal structures of children's early songs. *Music Perception, 2*(3), 361–374.

Davidson, L. (1994). Songsinging by young and old: A developmental approach to music. In R. Aiello & J. Sloboda (Eds.), *Musical perceptions* (pp. 99–130). New York: Oxford University Press.

Davidson, L., McKernon, P., & Gardner, H. (1981). The acquisition of song: A developmental approach. In J. Mason (Ed.), *Documentary report of the Ann Arbor symposium / National Symposium on the Applications of Psychology to the Teaching and Learning of Music* (pp. 301–315). Reston, VA: Music Educators National Conference.

Davidson, L., & Scripp, L. (1988). Young children's musical representations: Windows on music cognition. In J. A. Sloboda (Ed.), *Generative processes in music: The psychology of performance, improvisation and composition* (pp. 195–230). Oxford, UK: Oxford University Press.

Davidson, L., & Scripp, L. (1989). Education and development in music from a cognitive perspective. In D. J. Hargreaves (Ed.), *Children and the arts.* Milton Keynes, MA: Open University Press.

Davidson, L., & Scripp, L. (1992). Surveying the coordinates of cognitive skills in music. In R. Colwell (Ed.), *Handbook of research on music teaching and learning* (pp. 392–413). New York: Schirmer.

Dowling, W. J. (1984). Development of musical schemata in children's spontaneous singing. In W. R. Crozier & A. J. Chapman (Eds.), *Cognitive processes in the perception of art* (pp. 145–163). Amsterdam: Elsevier Science Publishers B.V.

Dowling, W. J. (1988). Tonal structure and children's early learning of music. In J. Sloboda (Ed.), *Generative processes in music.* Oxford, UK: Clarendon Press.

Gardner, H., & Wolf, D. (1983). Waves and streams of symbolization: Notes on the development of symbolic capacities in young children. In D. Rogers & J. A.

Sloboda (Eds.), *The acquisition of symbolic skills* (pp. 19–42). New York: Plenum Press.

Gerson-Kiwi, E. (1953). Towards an exact transcription of tone-relations. *Acta Musicologica, 25*(1), 80–87.

Halliday, M. A. K. (1976). *System and function in language: Selected papers.* London: Oxford University Press.

Halliday, M. A. K. (1978). *Language as social semiotic: The social interpretation of language and meaning.* Baltimore, MD: University Park Press.

Hutchin, V. (2006). Meeting individual needs. In T. Bruce (Ed.), *Early childhood: A guide for students* (pp. 29–42). London: Sage.

James, A., & Prout, A. (Eds.). (1997). *Constructing and reconstructing childhood: Contemporary issues in the sociological study of childhood* (2nd ed.). New York: Falmer Press.

Jones, E., & Nimmo, J. (1994). *Emergent curriculum.* Washington, DC: National Association for the Education of Young Children. (ERIC Document Reproduction Service No. ED382343).

Kelle, U. (1997). Theory-building in qualitative research and computer programs for the management of textual data. *Sociological Research Online, 2*(2). Retrieved June 1, 2007, from http://www.socresonline.org.uk/socresonline/2/2/1.html

Kjørholt, A. T. (2002). Small is powerful: Discourses on "children and participation" in Norway. *Childhood, 9*(1), 63–82.

Krumhansl, C. L., & Jusczyk, P. W. (1990). Infants' perception of phrase structure in music. *Psychological Science, 1*(1), 70–73.

Krumhansl, C. R., & Keil, F. C. (1982). Acquisition of the hierarchy of tonal functions in music. *Memory and Cognition, 10,* 243–251.

Lambert, E. B., & Clyde, M. (2000). *Rethinking early childhood theory and practice.* Katoomba, NSW, AU: Social Science Press.

Lincoln, Y. S., & Guba, E. G. (1985). *Naturalistic inquiry.* Newbury Park, CA: Sage.

McKernon, P. E. (1979). The development of first songs in young children. In H. Gardner & D. Wolf (Eds.), *Early symbolization. New directions for child development* (Vol. 3, pp. 43–58). San Francisco: Jossey-Bass.

Miles, M. B., & Huberman, A. M. (1994). *Qualitative data analysis* (2nd ed.). Thousand Oaks, CA: Sage.

Moog, H. (1976a). The development of musical experience in children of preschool age. *Psychology of Music, 4*(2), 38–45.

Moog, H. (1976b). *The musical experience of the preschool child.* London: Schott & Co. (Original work published 1968)

Moorhead, G. E., & Pond, D. (1977). *Music of young children.* Santa Barbara, CA: Pillsbury Foundation for Advancement of Music Education.

Moray, N. (1959). Attention in dichotic listening: Affective cues and the influence of instructions. *The Quarterly Journal of Experimental Psychology, 11,* 56–60.

Morse, J. M., & Richards, L. (2002). *Readme first for a user's guide to qualitative methods.* Thousand Oaks, CA: Sage.

Norman, D. A. (1968). Toward a theory of memory and attention. *Psychological Review, 75,* 522–536.

Nutbrown, C. (2006). *Threads of thinking* (3rd ed.). London: Sage.

Painter, C. (1985). *Learning the mother tongue.* Geelong, VIC, AU: Deakin University.
Parten, M. (1932). Social participation among pre-school children. *Journal of Abnormal and Social Psychology, 27,* 143–263.
Petzold, R. G. (1966). *Auditory perception of musical sounds by children in the first six grades. Cooperative research project number 1051.* Madison, WI: University of Wisconsin.
Saracho, O. N. (1984). Construction and validation of the play rating scale. *Early Child Development and Care, 17,* 199–230.
Sloboda, J. (1985). *The musical mind: The cognitive psychology of music.* Oxford, UK: Oxford University Press.
Thackray, R. (1972). *Rhythmic abilities in children.* Seven Oaks, CA: Novello.
Thelan, E., & Smith, L. B. (1994). *A dynamic systems approach to the development of cognition and action.* Cambridge, MA: MIT Press.
Treisman, A. M. (1960). Contextual cues in selective listening. *The Quarterly Journal of Experimental Psychology, 12,* 242–248.
Veldhuis, H. A. (1984). Spontaneous songs of preschool children. *The Arts in Psychotherapy, 11,* 15–24.
Veldhuis, H. A. (1992). *Singing of preschool children in two contexts.* Unpublished doctoral dissertation, The Fielding Institute, Santa Barbara, CA.
Vygotsky, L. S. (1978). *Mind in society: The development of higher mental processes.* Cambridge, MA: Cambridge University Press.
Vygotsky, L. S. (1986). *Thought and language* (A. Kozulin, Trans.). Cambridge, MA: MIT Press.
Welch, G. (1986). A developmental view of children's singing. *British Journal of Music Education, 3,* 295–302.
Werner, H. (1917). *Comparative psychology of mental development.* New York: Science Editions.
Wilson, S. J., & Wales, R. J. (1995). An exploration of children's musical compositions. *Journal of Research in Music Education, 43*(2), 94–111.
Wyver, S. R., & Spence, S. H. (1995). Cognitive and social play of Australian preschoolers. *Australian Journal of Early Childhood, 20*(2), 42–46.
Zimmerman, M. P. (1985). State of the art in early childhood music and research. In J. Boswell (Ed.), *The young child and music: Contemporary principles in child development and music education.* Reston, VA: Music Educators National Conference.

CHAPTER 4

PRESERVICE TEACHERS' PERCEPTIONS AND PERSPECTIVES ON EARLY CHILDHOOD MUSIC EDUCATION

A Comparative Analysis of the United States and Korea

Jinyoung Kim
The College of Staten Island
City University of New York

Seung Yeon Lee
Ewha Womans University

ABSTRACT

The purpose of this study was to examine and compare how early childhood preservice teachers in two different cultures (the United States and Korea) perceive their musical competence and what their attitudes are toward classroom teachers' musical competence and music education in early childhood education. Participants included 315 preservice teachers (156 from the United States and 159 from Korea) in early childhood education programs from urban universities in the United States and Korea. A survey was used to ascertain participants' (a) self-perceptions of their own musical competence, (b) perspectives on classroom teachers' musical competence, and (c) perspectives toward early childhood music education. The results indicated that preservice teachers of early childhood education programs in the two countries have significant differences in their perceptions and perspectives toward early childhood music education, even though there was a strong consensus on the importance of music education for young children.

INTRODUCTION

The purpose of this study was to examine early childhood preservice teachers from the United States and Korea regarding their perceptions of musical competence and perspectives on early childhood music education. Children's musical growth and growth through music have been a matter of concern to early childhood educators as well as music educators both in the United States and Korea (Han, 1999; Levinowitz, 1999; McDonald & Simons, 1989; Neelly, 2002). Consequently, how teachers are prepared so that they, in turn, can provide children with appropriate musical experiences has become a vital part of curriculum in teacher education. Research in this area has focused on (a) ways to provide appropriate music education in an early childhood setting, (b) characteristics that early childhood music educators should exhibit, and (c) mechanisms for addressing/providing subject knowledge in education (Chang, 2007; Neelly, 2002; Scott-Kassner, 1999).

MENC: The National Association for Music Education has published standards in music education that describe appropriate musical experiences and competencies for PreK–12 learners (MENC, 1994). These standards have challenged preservice music teacher education programs, both in the United States and Korea, to provide future teachers with the skills to teach music to children. Teacher education programs help preservice teachers not only understand music, but they also help future teachers understand the processes of teaching and learning (Abrahams, 2000; Conkling, 2007; Wiggins, 2007). Little research, however, has focused on musical content knowledge and skills for early childhood classroom teachers, even though subject-matter knowledge is considered to be a part of instructional knowledge (Chang, 2007; Saracho, 1993; Shulman, 1986). Teachers' attitudes or dispositional characteristics, rather than subject-matter competence, have received more research attention and recognition as important components of effective early childhood teaching (Cartwright, 1999). The reasoning is that (a) proficiency in traditional academic subjects is not required for children considering their developmental level, and (b) children's learning experience should be more process-oriented and integrated respecting their interests (Cartwright, 1999, 2004).

The importance of content knowledge cannot be overlooked in teacher education. Learning content is necessary for presenting academic subjects in a traditional way to children, and for responding to children's musical needs in an integrated curriculum (Park & Kim, 2003). Classroom teachers need to be able to expand and/or divide subject-matter topics within different disciplines in order to actualize the benefits of integrative curricula, as well as help children use subject knowledge to solve real-world problems (Campbell, 1995; Nielson, 1989). A continuing and unresolved issue, despite the importance of subject matter in a teacher's preparation, is how teacher education programs should provide for early childhood preservice teachers who are not necessarily musicians and have diverse musical backgrounds (Kim, 2004).

Several studies have suggested that classroom teachers may have limited confidence in teaching music, especially when using the music content standards as outlined by MENC (Barry, 1992; Byo, 2000; Kim & Choy, 2005b; MENC, 1994; Mullins, 1993). This lack of confidence may be related to their own subject matter competence. Kim and Choy (2005a), for example, studied preservice teachers' self-perceptions of their own musical knowledge and self-efficacy. They found that most of the early childhood preservice teachers in their study did not have extensive knowledge of music prior to taking a music education course that was required in their program. Kim and Choy suggested that preservice teachers' musical knowledge was strongly correlated to self-efficacy in teaching music.

Teachers' perceptions and perspectives may also be influenced by specific cultural values and educational systems (Clark-Steward, Lee, Allhusen, Kim, & McDowell, 2006). Culture shapes the content, methods, structure, and process of development and school learning (Grant & Ladson-Billings, 1997). An individual's learning style and preference are areas where cultural differences show up clearly because, as Nieto (2000) asserts, "culture does matter" in learning and teaching (p. 152). Furthermore, the way people perceive, feel, and learn music and develop attitudes toward music education vary across cultures (Ramsey & Williams, 2003).

Comparative cross-cultural studies broaden our knowledge of different populations, including the diversity of their cultural backgrounds (Cheung, 2008; Coley, 2000). They also help us understand which culturally specific features or sociocultural factors concretely affect ideas and shape people's perceptions (Barton, 2001). Consequently, comparative cross-cultural studies can help educators understand and develop more appropriate instructional approaches to use with students of differing needs.

The National Association of Early Childhood Specialists in State Departments of Education (NAECS/SDE, 2008) and the National Association of Early Childhood Teacher Educators (NAECTE) in the United States have recommended sets of guidelines for early childhood teacher certification. In their joint position statement on early childhood teacher certification, music is included as a part of "Integrated Perspectives of Knowledge Bases." In the United States, however, teacher certification requirements are controlled by each individual state, regardless of professional position statements or policy recommendations. This is reflected in the variation of requirements for early childhood teacher certification in each state. For example, one music course is required in an educational sequence in a New York State approved teacher preparation program, as highlighted in Table 4.1. Alternate pathways for candidates seeking certification, but who do not complete a preapproved teacher preparation program in New York State, do not require a specific course in early childhood music education. In Korea, on the other hand, two courses—music in early childhood education and movement in early childhood education—are included among the 15 elective courses that preservice teachers must take to get a teaching certifi-

TABLE 4.1 Course Requirements for Initial Certificate in Early Childhood Education

U.S. (New York State Requirements)[a]	Korea (National Requirements)[b]
Pathway 1: Completion of a NYS Approved Teacher Preparation Program An example of program requirements[c] *General Education* (12 credits) Scientific Analysis Social Scientific Analysis The Contemporary World Textual, Aesthetic, and Linguistic Analysis Pluralism and Diversity *Major Requirements* (34–36 credits) Natural Sciences and Mathematics Humanities Social Sciences *Elective Courses in Science, Letters, and Society* (24–46 credits) *Education Sequence* (30 credits) Psychological Foundations of Early Childhood Education Social Foundations of Early Childhood Education	*Pedagogical Theory* (14 credits) Introduction to Education (2) Curriculum and Evaluation (2) Educational Methods & Technology (2) Sociology of Education (2) Educational Psychology (2) Philosophy & History of Education (2) Educational Administration & Management (2) Counseling & Guidance (2) *Pedagogical Practice* (4 credits) Education of Exceptional Children (2) Understanding of School Culture & Educational Setting (2) *Student Teaching* (4 credits) Core Courses for Major (8 credits) Material Development & Teaching Methods in Early Childhood Education (2–3) Theoretical Foundation of Teaching Early Childhood Education (2–3) Logics and Writing (2–3)

U.S. (New York State Requirements)[a]	Korea (National Requirements)[b]

Affective Development of the Child
Language Development in Young Children and the Education Process
The Teaching of Reading and Writing
Music in Early Childhood
Workshop in Mathematics and Science for Early Childhood
Fieldwork in Preschool Classroom
Workshop in Social Studies
 	
Student Teaching (4 credits)
 	
Pathway 2: Individual Evaluation[d]
 	
General Core in Liberal Arts and Science (30 S.H.)
   Artistic Expression
   Communication
   Information Retrieval
   Humanities
   Language other than English
   Written Analysis and Expression
   Concepts in Historical and Social Sciences
   Scientific Processes
   Mathematical Processes
 	
Content Core-Liberal Arts & Science (30 S.H.)
 	
Pedagogical Core (21 S.H.)
   College Coursework at Student Developmental Level (6 S.H.)
   Human Development and Learning
   Teaching Students with Disabilities & Special Health-Care Needs
   Teaching Literacy Skills Methods (3 S.H.)
   Teaching Literacy Skills (3 S.H.)
   Curriculum, Instruction, and Assessment
   Foundations of Education
 	
Student Teaching (40 Days)
	Elective Courses for Major (42 credits)
	Introduction to Early Childhood Education (3)
	Curriculum for Early Childhood Education (3)
	Early Childhood Development and Education (3)
	The Theories of Play and Education (3)
	Observation Methods and Practice for Early Childhood Education (3)
	Language Arts in Early Childhood Education (3)
	Social Studies in Early Childhood Education (3)
	Science in Early Childhood Education (3)
	Mathematics in Early Childhood Education (3)
	Visual Arts in Early Childhood Education (3)
	Music in Early Childhood Education (3)
	Movements in Early Childhood Education (3)
	Parent Education and Participation (3)
	Administration and Management in Early Childhood Education (3)
	Child Welfare (3)
	Other Early Childhood Courses

[a] New York State Education Department, http://eservices.nysed.gov/teach/certhelp/CertRequirementHelp.doc
[b] Ministry of Education & Human Recourses Development, 2007
[c] http://www.csi.cuny.edu/catalog/pdfs/FINAL2007-2009%20Catalog.pdf#degree_requirements
[d] The individual evaluation pathway is for candidates who have not completed a preapproved teacher preparation program or whose application is not based on a valid teaching certificate from a reciprocal state. This pathway is also for candidates applying for supplementary permits or teaching assistant credentials.

cate. According to Nam (2006), all early childhood teachers in Korea are required to complete early childhood music education courses in their preservice programs. In addition, Han (1999) states that early childhood programs in Korean universities and colleges offer an average of three courses related to early childhood music education. Frequent among these offerings are music in early childhood education, physical movement in early childhood education, musical instruments for early childhood education, and traditional Korean music education for young children. Similarly, Park and Hong (2005) analyzed the curricula of early childhood teacher education programs at 3-year junior colleges in Korea and found that music-related courses are most emphasized, comprising 24% of all subject-related education courses.

In addition, it is usual for Korean girls to learn to play musical instruments such as piano and violin in their childhood. This is seen as a part of their studies or as a "must-do" thing rather than an activity pursued for fun or enjoyment. According to Kim (2006), it is usual for young children in Korea to start learning the piano at 3 or 4 years of age. Hence, almost all preservice teachers in Korea are able to play at least one musical instrument and have a basic knowledge of music. By contrast, according to Kim and Choy (2005a), less than 20% of the preservice teachers in an early childhood education program at an urban university in the United States reported that they were able to play at least one musical instrument.

According to Kim, Min, Yang, Lee, Jang, Ju, and Choi (2002), who conducted a comparative analysis of music curriculum in six countries, music is a compulsory course up to the 6th grade in the United States. In Korea, it is required up to the10th grade. In addition, the curriculum for music education in the United States focuses on basic musical concepts and highlights diversity and creativity in and through music. On the other hand, the curriculum for music education in Korea focuses on detailed musical knowledge and highlights the acquisition of musical skills.

Because of the lack of research on early childhood music teacher education, a comparative study between the United States and Korea on preservice teachers' perceptions and perspectives would broaden researchers' and educators' perspectives on early childhood music education and shed light on improving curricula and teaching methods in early childhood teacher education in both countries. The purpose of this study is to examine and compare how early childhood preservice teachers in two different cultures (the United States and Korea) perceive their musical competence and what their attitudes are toward classroom teachers' musical competence and music education in early childhood education. The following served as specific study interests regarding the participants' thinking: (a) self-perceptions of their own musical knowledge, skills, and attitudes; (b) perspectives on classroom teachers' musical knowledge, skills, and attitudes; and (c) perspectives on early childhood music education.

METHOD

Participants

Participants included 315 early childhood preservice teachers: 156 from the United States and 159 from Korea. To make the backgrounds of the participants of the two countries comparable, three selection criteria were used. First, in terms of area, a major city of each country was selected: New York City in the United States and Seoul in Korea. The two cities share many similarities, especially in terms of scale, education, living conditions, and diversity. Second, universities and departments were limited to undergraduate early childhood programs in 4-year universities. Third, in terms of the academic status of the participants, preservice students in the second or third year of undergraduate early childhood programs were selected. These participants had taken early childhood foundation courses such as psychological foundations of early childhood and introduction to early-childhood education, but had not taken any early childhood music education courses. The average age of the preservice teachers from the United States was 26 and 21 from Korea.

Data Collection and Analysis

To investigate early childhood preservice teachers' perceptions toward early childhood music education, a survey was used. Survey research is not only one of the most widely used methods in educational research, but it is also useful in measuring attitudes, opinions, and perceptions of people (Wiersma, 2000). Section 1 focused on ascertaining personal information, such as age and status. Section 2 focused on participants' self-perceptions of their own musical knowledge, skills, and attitudes. Section 3 focused on the participants' perspectives on classroom teachers' musical knowledge, skills, and attitudes. Section 4 focused on participants' perspectives toward early childhood music education. Throughout, participants were asked to respond using a 5-point Likert-type scale based upon the extent to which they agreed or disagreed with the statement. The number 5 was used to indicate "strongly agree," with 1 indicating "strongly disagree." A total of 61 statements were used. The entire survey was based upon, but modified from, a study by Kim and Choy (2005a) and was written and presented in English and Korean (see Table 4.2).

TABLE 4.2 Selected Questions from the 61-Item Questionnaire

Statements	Rating scale
Section I: General Information	
Section II: Self-perceptions	
I like music	SD D N A SA
I am good at music	SD D N A SA
I know musical concepts such as:	
a. Timbre	SD D N A SA
b. Rhythm/Beat	SD D N A SA
c. Tempo	SD D N A SA
d. Dynamic	SD D N A SA
I can teach children musical concepts such as:	
a. Timbre	SD D N A SA
b. Rhythm/Beat	SD D N A SA
c. Tempo	SD D N A SA
d. Dynamic	SD D N A SA
I can play musical instruments such as:	
a. String, such as violin	SD D N A SA
b. Wind, such as flute	SD D N A SA
c. Keyboard, such as piano	SD D N A SA
d. Percussion, such as drum	SD D N A SA
Section III: Perspectives on classroom teachers' musical knowledge and skills	
I think classroom teachers should be musical	SD D N A SA
I think classroom teachers should be able to teach music to children	SD D N A SA
I think classroom teachers should play a musical instrument	SD D N A SA
Section IV: Perspectives on music integration	
I think music should be taught to children so that music can:	
a. help learning other subjects, such as the ABC song to teach alphabet	SD D N A SA
b. be integrated into "theme" or "unit"	SD D N A SA
c. be taught for musical concepts themselves	
I think it would be better to have a music teacher in early childhood or elementary schools.	SD D N A SA

Two bilingual university professors analyzed the statements of the survey and reviewed it for content validity. The Cronbach alpha reliability coefficient for the survey was .92.

Descriptive statistics (mean and standard deviation) and independent *t*-tests were used to analyze the data and compare the perceptions and perspectives of preservice teachers from the United States and Korea.

RESULTS

Perceptions of Preservice Teachers' Own Musical Knowledge, Skills, and Attitudes

To examine how early childhood preservice teachers in the United States and Korea perceive their own musical knowledge, skills, and attitudes, independent *t*-tests were conducted. As shown in Table 4.3, significant differences between the United States and Korea were found in musical skills (*t* = –4.90, *p* < .001) and attitudes (*t* = 5.93, *p* < .001). While Korean preservice teachers indicated more agreement with the statement on their musical skills, U.S. preservice teachers agreed more on their musical attitudes.

The analysis of the subquestions also showed interesting results (see Table 4.4). In terms of knowledge, more U.S. preservice teachers than Korean preservice teachers agreed with the statement that they are musically knowledgeable (U.S. M = 3.05; Korea M = 2.86). However, Korean preservice teachers indicated a strong agreement in their knowing musical concepts, such as timbre, rhythm, pitch, and so forth (U.S. 3.08; Korea 3.53). In terms of skills, U.S. preservice teachers strongly agreed with the statement, "I can dance or move to rhythm or beat" (U.S. 4.15; Korea 3.31), while Korean preservice teachers indicated a strong agreement in "singing songs in tune" (U.S. 2.99; Korea 3.78) and "reading musical notes" (U.S. 2.31; Korea 3.79). Moreover, Korean preservice teachers agreed more with the statement that they can play musical instruments, especially keyboard (e.g., piano; U.S. 2.00; Korea 3.63).

In terms of attitudes, U.S. preservice teachers strongly agreed with the statement that they like music (U.S. 4.67; Korea 4.13). In addition, U.S.

TABLE 4.3 Preservice Teachers' Perceptions of Their Musical Knowledge, Skills, and Attitudes

Category	Country	M	SD	t
Knowledge	U.S.	2.59	0.66	–1.18
	Korea	2.68	0.46	
Skills	U.S.	2.89	0.55	–4.90***
	Korea	3.18	0.47	
Attitudes	U.S.	3.79	0.51	5.93***
	Korea	3.44	0.53	

*** *p* < .001

TABLE 4.4 Preservice Teachers' Perceptions on Their Musical Knowledge, Skills, and Attitudes: Subquestions

Category	Sub-questions	U.S. M(SD)	Korea M(SD)
Knowledge	I am musically knowledgeable	3.05(1.05)	2.86(0.74)
	I know musical concepts	3.08(0.89)	3.53(0.64)
	I am familiar with music teaching methods	1.66(0.70)	1.64(0.64)
Skills	I can teach music to children	3.46(0.69)	3.11(0.73)
	I can teach children musical concepts	2.76(0.92)	3.05(0.63)
	I am good at music	2.93(1.04)	2.96(0.85)
	I can sing songs in tune	2.99(1.09)	3.78(0.79)
	I can read musical notes	2.31(1.21)	3.79(0.78)
	I can play a musical instrument	1.72(0.74)	2.22(0.65)
	I can dance or move to rhythm or a beat	4.15(0.65)	3.31(0.84)
Attitudes	I like music	4.67(0.59)	4.13(0.69)
	I am musical	2.97(1.11)	3.20(0.83)
	I can feel or respond to music	4.15(0.75)	3.60(0.74)
	I am comfortable teaching music to children	3.39(0.77)	2.83(0.69)

preservice teachers showed their agreement in "feeling and responding to music" (U.S. 4.15; Korea 3.60) and "feeling comfortable in teaching music to children" (U.S. 3.39; Korea 2.83).

Perspectives on Classroom Teachers' Musical Knowledge, Skills, and Attitudes

In the comparison between the U.S. and Korean preservice teachers' perspectives on early childhood classroom teachers' musical knowledge, skills, and attitudes, significant differences were found only in musical skills ($t = -7.89$, $p < .001$; see Table 4.5). Korean preservice teachers showed higher expectations on early childhood teachers' competence in musical skill (M = 3.87, SD = 0.48) than the U.S. preservice teachers did (M = 3.34, SD = 0.69).

As shown in Table 4.6, the analysis of the subquestions also showed similar results of preservice teachers' perceptions on their own musical knowledge, skills, and attitudes. The U.S. preservice teachers showed higher expectations toward early childhood classroom teachers' competence in "dancing or moving to rhythm or beat" (U.S. 3.75; Korea 3.48) and "liking music" (U.S. 4.30 ; Korea 3.96) than Korean preservice teachers. Yet, Korean preservice teachers showed higher expectations on early childhood classroom teachers' competence, espe-

TABLE 4.5 Preservice Teachers' Perspectives on Classroom Teachers' Musical Knowledge, Skills, and Attitudes

Category	Country	M	SD	t
Knowledge	U.S.	3.64	0.74	1.79
	Korea	3.51	0.55	
Skills	U.S.	3.34	0.69	−7.89***
	Korea	3.87	0.48	
Attitudes	U.S.	4.00	0.58	1.57
	Korea	3.90	0.56	

*** $p < .001$

TABLE 4.6 Preservice Teachers' Perspectives on Classroom Teachers' Musical Knowledge, Skills, and Attitudes: Subquestions

Category	Subquestions	U.S. M(SD)	Korea M(SD)
Knowledge	CT should be musically knowledgeable	3.70(0.92)	3.77(0.67)
	CT should know musical concepts	3.57(0.86)	3.81(0.65)
	CT should be familiar with music teaching methods	3.67(0.91)	2.95(0.88)
Skills	CT should be able to teach music to children	3.82(0.86)	4.11(0.70)
	CT should be good at music	3.22(0.93)	3.16(0.84)
	CT should be able to sing songs in tune	3.24(1.06)	3.98(0.74)
	CT should be able to read musical notes	2.83(1.07)	4.12(0.66)
	CT should play a musical instrument	2.70(1.04)	4.07(0.73)
	CT should dance or move to rhythm or beat	3.75(0.86)	3.48(0.81)
Attitudes	CT should like music	4.30(0.70)	3.96(0.67)
	CT should be musical	2.97(1.11)	3.20(0.83)
	CT should feel or respond to music	3.99(0.78)	3.89(0.72)
	CT should be comfortable in teaching music to children	4.08(0.80)	4.08(0.70)

cially in "teaching music to young children" (U.S. 3.82 ; Korea 4.11), "singing songs in tune" (U.S. 3.24; Korea 3.98), "reading musical notes" (U.S. 2.83; Korea 4.12), and "playing a musical instrument" (U.S. 2.70; Korea 4.07).

Perspectives toward Early Childhood Music Education

Both U.S. and Korean preservice teachers indicated that it is important for young children to learn music. However, there were statistically sig-

TABLE 4.7 Preservice Teachers' Perspectives toward Early Childhood Music Education

Category	Country	M	SD	t
Importance of music education for young children	U.S.	4.44	0.63	.39
	Korea	4.42	0.63	
Use of music				
For helping to learn other subjects	U.S.	4.63	0.50	10.22***
	Korea	3.90	0.76	
For helping to relate to a theme	U.S.	4.40	0.65	3.58***
	Korea	4.14	0.64	
For learning musical concepts	U.S.	4.00	0.77	5.26***
	Korea	3.49	0.94	
Having a music teacher	U.S.	4.34	0.73	13.49***
	Korea	3.01	0.98	

*** $p < .001$

nificant differences in their perspectives toward the use of music in early childhood education (see Table 4.7). Overall, the U.S. preservice teachers showed higher mean scores (4.63, 4.40, 4.00 respectively) than Korean preservice teachers (3.90, 4.14, 3.49 respectively). Yet, data suggest that the U.S. preservice teachers highlighted the use of music to help learn other subjects the most, while Korean preservice teachers emphasized the use of music as a way of relating to themes or units the most, with the goal of an integrated curriculum. Finally, the U.S. preservice teachers strongly preferred having music teachers in early childhood institutions, while Korean preservice teachers showed neutral responses.

DISCUSSION AND CONCLUSIONS

This chapter examined early childhood preservice teachers from the United States and Korea regarding their perceptions of musical competence and perspectives on early childhood music education. There was a strong consensus on the importance of music education for young children among the preservice teachers in the United States and Korea. However, there were also significant differences between U.S. preservice teachers and Korean preservice teachers in their perceptions of their musical competence, their perspectives toward classroom teachers' musical competence, and the use of music in early childhood education.

Overall, early childhood preservice teachers in Korea indicated strong agreement with the statements about their own musical skills and higher expectations of early childhood teachers' musical skills. On the other hand, those in the United States showed strong agreement with the statements about their musical attitudes such as "I like music" and so forth. This result seems to originate from cultural and educational differences. For example, learning to play the piano and/or other musical instruments in childhood is very common in Korea. Therefore, most early childhood preservice teachers in Korea have basic knowledge of musical concepts and practical musical skills such as "reading musical notes" or "singing songs in tune." Consequently, Korean preservice teachers' self-perceptions and perspectives toward classroom teachers' musical competence could be different from those of the United States. At the same time, U.S. early childhood preservice teachers showed strong agreement with the statements regarding their attitudes toward music and music teaching. This result suggests that preservice teachers' having musical skills is not directly proportional to their attitudes toward music and early childhood music teaching. In other words, general musical skills such as "reading notes" or "playing musical instruments" alone do not influence early childhood preservice teachers' attitudes toward music and music teaching directly.

Another interesting result of this study was the difference in perspectives toward early childhood music education (see Figure 4.1). Even though early childhood preservice teachers of both countries stated that it is important for young children to learn music, they differed in their perspectives on the use of music and having a music teacher. U.S. preservice teachers agreed with statements that music in early childhood education should be used for various purposes, such as helping to learn other subjects, helping to relate to a theme, and learning musical concepts. On the other hand,

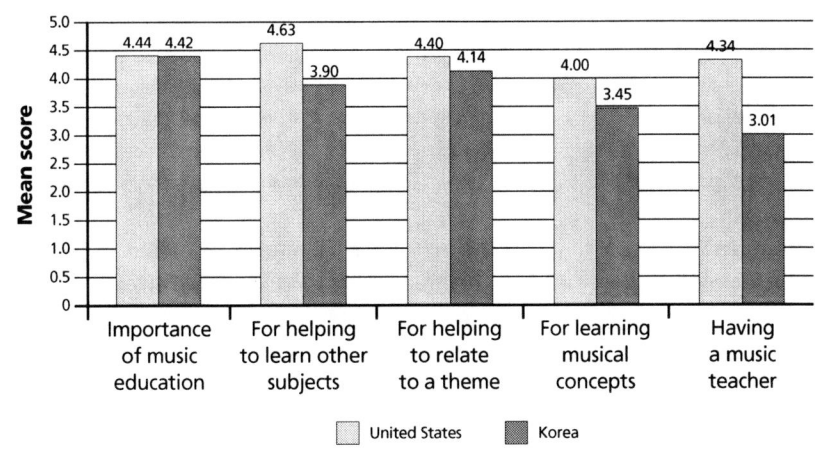

Figure 4.1 A comparison of preservice teachers' perspectives toward early childhood music education between the United States and Korea.

Korean preservice teachers considered the use of music mainly as a tool for integrated curriculum. In addition, U.S. preservice teachers strongly preferred to have music teachers, while Korean preservice teachers showed neutral responses. This result may relate to how early childhood preservice teachers in two countries perceive their own musical competence, have expectations toward classroom teachers' musical competence, and see the purpose of the use of music for early childhood education. However, more in-depth studies would be needed to find out cultural differences in early childhood preservice teachers' preferences for having music teachers.

IMPLICATIONS

The results of this study have implications for early childhood teacher educators in both countries. Teacher educators need to think about how to prepare early childhood teachers so that they can gain appropriate knowledge of music to teach young children in their classes. Although there was a slight difference between U.S. and Korean preservice teachers regarding their own perceptions of musical knowledge, the results suggest that preservice teachers in both countries may not think they have enough knowledge for teaching music. One might say that U.S. preservice teachers need knowledge of musical concepts and musical skills such as playing musical instruments to be musically more knowledgeable. However, looking at the case of preservice teachers in Korea carefully, one notices that preservice teachers do not think that they are musically knowledgeable, even though they know musical concepts or skills such as playing musical instruments. What early childhood preservice teachers need to know is how to transfer the knowledge they have to teach children in developmentally appropriate ways. Early childhood preservice teachers in both countries not only have the same basic need to gain musical knowledge but also have different needs. For example, U.S. preservice teachers need to gain knowledge of musical concepts and skills, while those in Korea need to develop their confidence by practicing how to utilize the musical knowledge and skills they have.

This study also has implications for expectations of early childhood classroom teachers. Since the MENC (1994) standards provide guidelines for music content skills and abilities children should have, early childhood classroom teachers should be expected to understand the musical content knowledge and skills indicated in the standards. The results of this study show that preservice teachers' expectations toward classroom teachers' musical knowledge and skills were higher than their perceptions on their own knowledge and skills. In other words, there is a gap between what they can do now and what they should do in the future. It would be a challenge for teacher educators to bridge the gap between the "now" and the "future" of early childhood preservice teachers. The question of the level of musical competency that should be expected for early childhood classroom teachers might need to be addressed according to the needs of each population.

Undoubtedly, there is a need for more studies on music teachers in early childhood education. It is not easy to conclude that there is a need for music teachers in early childhood education in United States but not in Korea simply on the basis that the U.S. preservice teachers indicated that they prefer to have music teachers.

Comparative studies help us broaden knowledge about different populations from diverse cultural backgrounds, understand which factors shape people's perceptions, and learn from each other. In this study, we investigated the perspectives of two different populations on music and music education. The findings of this study lead us to believe that preservice teachers should be equipped with positive attitudes toward music and music teaching as well as with adequate musical knowledge and skills through preservice teacher education. The investigation of early childhood preservice teachers' perceived strengths and shortcomings would be the first step for teacher educators to develop in music education courses. Considering early childhood preservice teachers' musical needs, teacher educators can better prepare early childhood preservice teachers to teach and incorporate music into their future classrooms.

REFERENCES

Abrahams, F. (2000). National standards for music education and college preservice music teacher education: A new balance. *Art Education Policy Review, 102*(1), 27–31.

Barry, N. H. (1992). Music education in the elementary music method class. *Journal of Music Teacher Education, 2*(1), 16–23.

Barton, K. C. (2001). A sociocultural perspective on children's understanding of historical change: Comparative findings from Northern Ireland and the United States. *American Educational Research Journal, 38*(4), 881–913.

Byo, S. J. (2000). Classroom teachers' and music specialists' perceived ability to implement the national standards for music education. *Arts Education Policy Review, 101*(5), 1063–2913.

Campbell, M. R. (1995). Interdisciplinary projects in music. *Music Educators Journal, 82*(2), 37–45.

Cartwright, S. (1999). What makes good early childhood teachers? *Young Children, 54*(1), 4–7.

Cartwright, S. (2004). Young citizens in the making. *Young Children, 59*(5), 108–109.

Chang, E. J. (2007). *Developing of the early childhood music education program model for in-service teachers*. Unpublished doctoral dissertation, Ewha Womans University, Seoul, Korea.

Cheung, H. Y. (2008). Teacher efficacy: A comparative study of Hong Kong and Shanghai primary in-service teachers. *The Australian Educational Researcher, 35*(1), 103–123.

Clarke-Steward, K. A., Lee, Y., Allhusen, V. D., Kim, M., & McDowell, D. J. (2006). Observed differences between early childhood programs in the U.S. and Korea: Reflections of "Developmentally Appropriate Practice" in two cultural contexts. *Journal of Applied Developmental Psychology, 27*(5), 427–443.

Coley, J. D. (2000). On the importance of comparative research: The case of folkbiology. *Child Development, 71*(1), 82–90.

Conkling, S. W. (2007). The possibilities of situated learning for teacher preparation: The professional development partnership. *Music Educators Journal, 93*(3), 44–48.

Grant, C. A., & Ladson-Billings, G. (1997). *Dictionary of multicultural education*. Phoenix, AZ: Oryx Press.

Han, K. Y. (1999). *A study on music related curriculum for early childhood teacher education in the universities and colleges in Seoul*. Unpublished master's thesis, Ewha Womans University, Seoul, Korea.

Kim, H. W. (2006, May 10). Super hot housing boom in very early education: The realities and issues. *Hankookilbo*, 14.

Kim, J. (2004). *The musical teacher: Preparing teachers to use music in the childhood classroom*. Dubuque, IA: Kendall/Hunt.

Kim, J., & Choy, D. (2005a). An investigation of preservice teachers' self perception on musical knowledge and teaching efficacy. *International Journal of Early Childhood Education, 11*(2), 81–98.

Kim, J., & Choy, D. (2005b). Preservice teachers' efficacy in teaching music. *Academic Exchange Quarterly, 9*(4), 134–138.

Kim, W., Min, K., Yang, J., Lee, N., Jang, K., Ju, D., & Choi, E. (2002). An analysis of school music curriculum in Korea by way of international comparative research. *Music and People, 24*, 317–353.

Levinowitz, L. M. (1999). Importance of music in early childhood. *Music Educators Journal, 86*(1), 17–18.

McDonald, D.T., & Simons, G. M. (1989). *Musical growth and development: Birth through six*. New York: Schirmer Books.

MENC. (1994). *Perspectives on implementation: Arts education standards for U.S.'s students*. Reston, VA: Music Educators National Conference.

Ministry of Education & Human Resources Development, Republic of Korea. (2007). *The National guide of Teacher's Certificate*.

NAECS. (2008). *Executive summary: Early childhood teacher certification*. NAECS/SDE Position Papers. Retrieved on December 15, 2008, from http://naecs.crc.uiuc.edu/position/ecteachr.html

Nam, S. H. (2006). *In-service teachers' perceptions on early childhood music education course in early childhood teacher education curriculum*. Unpublished master's thesis, Ewha Womans University, Seoul, Korea.

Neelly, L. P. (2002). Practical ways to improve singing in early childhood classrooms. *Young Children, 57*(4), 80–83.

Nielson, M. E. (1989). Integrative learning for young children: A thematic approach. *Educational Horizons, 68*(1), 19–24.

Nieto, S. (2000). *Affirming diversity: The sociopolitical context of multicultural education* (3rd ed.). New York: Longman.

Park, E. H., & Kim, S. H. (2003). *Characteristics of subject contents in early childhood educational institutes and professionalism.* Paper presented at the 6th annual meeting of the Korea Association for Childhood Education International, Seoul, Korea.

Park, H., & Hong, H. (2005). An analysis of major early childhood teacher education programs at 3-year junior college. *Korean Journal of Early Childhood Education, 25*(1), 147–169.

Ramsey, P. G., & Williams, L. R. (2003). *Multicultural education: A source book* (2nd ed.) New York: RoutledgeFalmer.

Saracho, O. N. (1993). Preparing teachers for early childhood programs in the United States. In B. Spodek (Ed.), *Handbook of research on the education of young children* (pp. 412–426). New York: Macmillan.

Shulman, L. S. (1986). Those who understand: Knowledge growth in teaching. *Educational Researcher, 15*(2), 4–14.

Scott-Kassner, C. (1999). Developing programs for early childhood programs. *Music Educators Journal, 86*(1), 19–25.

Wiersma, W. (2000). *Research methods in education: An introduction* (7th ed.). Boston: Allyn & Bacon.

Wiggins, J. (2007). Authentic practice and process in music teacher education. *Music Educators Journal, 93*(3), 36–42.

CHAPTER 5

AN INVESTIGATION OF THE 2 × 2 ACHIEVEMENT GOAL FRAMEWORK IN THE CONTEXT OF INSTRUMENTAL MUSIC

Peter Miksza
University of Colorado, Boulder

ABSTRACT

This study examined the 2 × 2 achievement goal framework (Elliot, 1999) in the context of instrumental music. A researcher adaptation of the 12-item achievement goal questionnaire (Elliot & McGregor, 2001) was administered to 228 HS band students. Confirmatory factor analyses were performed to empirically compare several theoretical models: (a) a 4-factor model (mastery-approach, mastery-avoid, performance-approach, performance-avoid); (b) a 3-factor model (performance-approach, performance-avoid, and a single mastery factor); (c) a second 3-factor model (mastery-approach, performance-approach, and an overall avoidance factor); (d) a 2-factor model (overall mastery and performance factors); and (e) a second 2-factor model (overall approach and avoidance factors). The findings from this study generally support those in academics and sports in that the 4-factor structure was the best model fit to the data.

INTRODUCTION

Understanding how, why, and to what extent children are motivated to engage and persist in music is a serious concern for all who have vested interests in music education. In a review of related music education research, Asmus (1995) claims that as much as 20% of student achievement can be explained by motivation. It is imperative that music teachers be able to determine what types of instructional emphases, incentives, and environmental conditions will be most likely to result in optimal student learning. Accordingly, motivation is a topic that continues to receive much attention in music education research forums as well as practice-focused trade publications. Insight has been gained from studies designed to examine motivation from theoretical perspectives such as attribution theory (e.g., Asmus, 1986), self-efficacy (e.g., McCormick & McPherson, 2003), self-concept (e.g., Austin & Vispoel, 1998), self-regulation (e.g., McPherson & Zimmerman, 2002), and locus of control (e.g., Sandene, 1997).

Most recently, researchers in educational psychology have identified the achievement-goal approach as an important theoretical framework to consider when exploring learning-related dispositions and behaviors. Achievement goals describe how an individual is motivated to pursue competence in a given domain (e.g., task mastery, performance relative to others). Achievement goals have been shown to be predictive of critical adaptive (e.g., academic achievement, amount of study time, deep- vs. surface-cognitive processing, organized vs. disorganized study habits) and maladaptive (e.g., fear of failure, self-handicapping, test anxiety) learning issues in general academics and sports that have parallel manifestations in music education (e.g., performance achievement, practice time, performance anxiety) (Elliot, 1999; Moller & Elliot, 2006). Given the potential for achievement goals to explain learning-related behaviors, it is important that music education researchers critically examine whether contemporary achievement goal frameworks can be validated in music education contexts.

Advances in research regarding achievement goal motivation constructs have resulted in the development of the 2 × 2 achievement goal framework (Elliot & McGregor, 2001). In contrast to previous models that incorporate dichotomous (e.g., mastery, performance) (e.g., Ames & Archer, 1987) or trichotomous (mastery, performance-approach, performance-avoid) (e.g., Elliot & Church, 1997) frameworks, the 2 × 2 model consists of approach and avoid distinctions for both mastery and performance goal orientations. Mastery goal orientations can be defined as those in which an individual is motivated to achieve competence for the sake of one's own satisfaction or maximization of potential. In contrast, performance goal orientations can be defined as those in which an individual is motivated to achieve in order to demonstrate competence relative to other individuals. Elliot (1999) suggests that approach and avoid distinctions be considered a function of "valence," in that approach orientations refer to behaviors that are directed by a positive outcome, whereas avoid orientations refer to behaviors that are directed by a negative outcome (p. 170). Therefore, mastery-approach goals are those directed toward achieving self-referential competence, whereas mastery-avoid goals are those directed toward avoiding self-referential incompetence. Accordingly, performance-approach goals are directed toward demonstrating norm-referenced competence, whereas performance-avoid goals are directed toward avoiding demonstrations of norm-referenced incompetence (Elliot, 2005). The four motivation orientations included in the 2×2 framework have typically been measured with a 12-item, self-report, Likert-type questionnaire.

Several researchers have tested the construct validity of the 2×2 achievement goal framework by using confirmatory factor analyses to compare the 2×2 model with competing trichotomous and dichotomous models (e.g., Conroy, Elliot, & Hofer, 2003; Elliot & McGregor, 2001; Finney, Pieper, & Barron, 2004; Wang, Biddle, & Elliot, 2007). In each case cited above, results have indicated that the 2×2 framework was the superior model (significantly better model fit) when compared with dichotomous (e.g., mastery/performance; approach/avoidance) or trichotomous (e.g., mastery/performance-approach/performance-avoid; mastery-approach/performance-approach/avoidance) models. These results remained consistent regardless of whether the samples used were college students (Elliot & McGregor, 2001; Finney et al., 2004), secondary-school students (Wang et al., 2007), or adult recreational athletes (Conroy et al., 2003). The results were also consistent regardless of whether the items were worded to reflect general academic achievement (Finney et al., 2004), academic course-specific achievement (Elliot & McGregor, 2001), or achievement in sports/physical education (Conroy et al., 2003; Wang et al., 2007). As far as can be determined, no studies have yet to test the validity of the 2×2 framework in the context of music education.

Studies of the predictive validity of the 2×2 model have generally found that mastery-approach and performance-approach orientations tend to be related to positive and/or adaptive learning outcomes, whereas mastery-avoid and performance-avoid orientations tend to be related to negative and/or less adaptive learning outcomes (see Moller & Elliot, 2006 for a detailed review of such results). For example, when studying the academic tendencies of undergraduate chemistry students, Karabenick (2003) found that students with stronger mastery- and performance-approach goal orientations were more likely to report seeking help when necessary. Conversely, students with stronger mastery- and performance-avoid orientations tended to report avoidance of help-seeking and were more likely to perceive help-seeking as a shortcoming or threat. Similar relationships between help-seeking tendencies and achievement goal orientations were found by Karabenick (2004) in a later study with a separate sample of undergraduate chemistry students. Furthermore, researchers have reported positive relationships between mastery- and performance-approach motivation orientations and the math achievement scores of French children (Cury, Elliot, Da Fonseca, & Moller, 2006), as well as with academic exam scores of undergraduate psychology students (Elliot & McGregor, 2001). It is important to investigate whether similar relationships would be found between motivation orientations and musical learning outcomes such as practice habits/behaviors and performance achievement.

Results regarding the reliability of the 2×2 goal orientation subscales as well as correlations among the goal orientations are not as consistent across studies. For example, Elliot and McGregor (2001) reported internal consistency coefficients for the subscales ranging from .83 to .92, whereas Finney et al.(2004) reported a range of coefficients from .68 to .88, and Wang et al.(2007) reported a range of coefficients from .66 to .84. In addition, Conroy et al.(2003) reported test-retest reliability coefficients ranging from .45 to .80 when investigating the stability of the subscale responses over various lengths of time (i.e., 2, 5, 6, 14, 19, and 21 day periods).These mixed reliability results may be due to the limited number of items each subscale consists of (i.e., 3 items each), and the consequently limited degree of variability present in the scores. Correlations reported between the mastery-approach and mastery-avoid subscales have also varied across studies. Significant relationships detected between the mastery-approach and mastery-avoid orientations have ranged from as low as .28 with a sample of college students (Finney et al., 2004) to as high as .65 with a sample of secondary-school students from Singapore (Wang et al., 2007). These contrasting findings suggest that the discriminant validity of the 2×2 framework may vary with age or cultural background. Further research with varied samples is required to determine the generalizability of the 2×2 achievement goal model.

Although motivation has been a popular topic among music education researchers (e.g., Asmus, 1995), only a few studies have examined the role of achievement goal motivation in music learning. Those studies that have investigated achievement goal motivation with respect to music have employed measures based only on dichotomous (Schmidt, 2005; Schmidt, Zdzinski, & Ballard, 2006) or trichotomous (Smith, 2002) models. In a study with 7th- through 12th-grade band students, Schmidt (2005) found that mastery and performance scales loaded onto two separate factors suggesting an underlying dichotomy. Schmidt (2005) also found that scales designed to measure approach success and avoid failure orientations loaded on the same factor as the performance scale suggesting that the approach/avoid distinction may not be valid with 7th- through 12th-grade band students. Furthermore, correlational analyses revealed that the approach success and avoid failure subscales were highly related (.76). In addition, Schmidt, Zdzinski, and Ballard (2006) found a similar correlation between approach success and avoid failure subscales (.74) with a sample of college music students. Smith (2002) examined the relationships between achievement goal motivation and the practicing of college musicians. Smith also found a strong correlation (.74) between the performance-approach and performance-avoid subscales used in his study. Given the findings of these studies, it is clear that the construct validity of the 2 × 2 achievement goal framework needs to be examined further before it is known whether it could be applied in the context of music education.

The current study is a partial replication and extension of research conducted by Finney, Peiper, and Barron (2007), which examined the 2 × 2 achievement goal framework in a collegiate, general academic context (e.g., without reference to a particular discipline or class). The purpose of this study was to examine the 2 × 2 achievement goal framework in the context of instrumental music. The specific research questions addressed were: (a) Does the 2 × 2 model replicate in the context of high school instrumental music (e.g., band class)? (b) Will the internal consistency for each subscale continue to be at least .70? (c) Will the correlations among the 2 × 2 subscales show evidence of discriminant validity? and (d) Will the motivation orientations be significantly related to subjects' self-reports of practice habits (e.g., time per day, informal/formal practicing, ratings of practice efficiency)?

METHOD

The subjects in this study were volunteer high school band students ($N = 228$) from four different American public high schools, varying widely in demographic characteristics (e.g., school size, number of curricular bands offered, number of directors, district expenditure per student, rural/suburban/urban location). One of the schools is on the East Coast, one is in the Midwest, and the remaining two are located in the Southwest. Volunteers from the school on the East Coast and one of the schools in the Southwest included the entire make-up of the band programs at the respective schools. The sample consisted of 116 males and 112 females from grades 9 through 12 and ranged in age from 14 to 18 years ($M = 15.78$, $SD = 1.25$). Brass (28.8%), woodwind (61.8%), and percussion (9.6%) students were included in the sample. Approximately one-half of the subjects reported taking private lessons at some point (52%). Of those subjects, most reported studying privately for one to two years (77.2%). The data were collected across the 2006–2007 and 2007–2008 school years during the subjects' usual band classes or study hall times.

A researcher adaptation of the Elliot and McGregor (2001) 2 × 2 achievement goal questionnaire was used. The original questionnaire consists of 12 items, with 3 items designated to measure each motivation orientation; mastery-approach, mastery-avoid, performance-approach, and performance-avoid. For the purposes of this study, the items were reworded by the researcher to reflect the specific context of instrumental music (see Questionnaire). For example, the item, "It is important for me to do well when compared to others in this class" was reworded to "It is important for me to do well when compared to others in band." The subjects responded to each item using a 7-point Likert-type rating scale ranging from 1 (not at all true of me) to 7 (very true of me). The items were presented in random order. Elliot and McGregor (2001) reported reliability results for the original orientation subscales ranging from $\alpha = .82$ to .96 in a series of studies with several samples of college students. As discussed previously, studies examining the construct validity of the 2 × 2 achievement goal model in the context of academics or sports have typically found the four motivation orientations to be relatively discrete and stable dimensions (e.g., Conroy et al., 2003; Elliot & McGregor, 2001; Finney et al., 2004; Wang et al., 2007).

Subjects in this study also completed a brief practice habit and background questionnaire. Subjects were asked to report (a) length of average practice session in minutes, (b) the average number of practice sessions they participated in per day, (c) percentage of time spent on informal practicing (i.e., with no specific musical or technical goal in mind), and (d) percentage of time spent on formal practicing (i.e., with a specific musical or technical goal in mind). Lastly, subjects were asked to rate their average daily practice efficiency on a scale of 1 (extremely inefficient) to 10 (extremely efficient).

RESULTS

Descriptive analyses carried out at the item level revealed the highest means for the mastery-approach items, "I desire to completely master the material presented in band" and "I want to learn as much as possible about playing my instrument," with means of 5.00 and 4.96, respectively. A relatively high mean was also found for the performance-avoid item, "I just want to avoid doing poorly in band" ($M = 4.75$). In contrast, the lowest means were found for the mastery-avoid items, "I am concerned that I may not learn all that

QUESTIONNAIRE

Researcher adaptation of the Elliot and McGregor (2001) Achievement Goal Questionnaire

Directions: Read each statement carefully then indicate the extent to which you agree or disagree by circling a number following each statement. There are no "right" or "wrong" answers. You will probably agree with some items and disagree with others. If you find that the numbers to be used in answering do not adequately reflect your own opinion, use the one that is ***closest*** to the way you feel.

GIVE YOUR OPINION ON EVERY STATEMENT

The scale represents responses ranging from "1"—Not at all true of me to "7"—Very true of me

1. I want to learn as much as possible about playing my instrument.   1 2 3 4 5 6 7
2. It is important for me to understand the content of this class as thoroughly as possible.   1 2 3 4 5 6 7
3. I desire to completely master the material presented in band.   1 2 3 4 5 6 7
4. I am concerned that I may not learn all that I possibly could in band.   1 2 3 4 5 6 7
5. Sometimes I'm afraid that I may not understand the musical material as thoroughly as I'd like.   1 2 3 4 5 6 7
6. I am often concerned that I may not learn all that there is to learn in band.   1 2 3 4 5 6 7
7. It is important for me to do better than other students.   1 2 3 4 5 6 7
8. It is important for me to do well when compared to others in band.   1 2 3 4 5 6 7
9. My goal in band is to get a better evaluation than most of the other students.   1 2 3 4 5 6 7
10. I just want to avoid doing poorly in band.   1 2 3 4 5 6 7
11. My goal in this class is to avoid performing poorly.   1 2 3 4 5 6 7
12. My fear of performing poorly in this class is often what motivates me.   1 2 3 4 5 6 7

Note: Mastery Approach = items 1 through 3; Mastery Avoid = items 4 through 6; Performance Approach = items 7 through 9; Performance Avoid = items 10 through 12

Note: Items presented to subjects in random order (e.g., not the order shown above)

I possibly could in band" and "I am often concerned that I may not learn all that there is to learn in band," with values of 3.00 and 3.06, respectively. Standard deviations indicated a moderate amount of variability across the sample on each item (SD = 1.61 to 2.02). Skewness and kurtosis results suggested that, with the slight exception of kurtosis values for items 5, 7, 8, and 12, the score distributions were relatively normal.

Pearson correlations determined among the items indicated significant relationships ($p < .05$) between many item pairs (Table 5.1). However, as might be expected, the strongest correlations were detected among the 3-item groupings designed to measure each motivation orientation (i.e., 1 to 3; 4 to 6; 7 to 9; 10 to 12). The range of correlations among each motivation item grouping were as follows: (a) mastery-approach, items 1 to 3, $r = .49$ to .54; (b) mastery-avoid, items 4 to 6, $r = .32$ to .71; (c) performance-approach, items 7 to 9, $r = .55$ to .65; and (d) performance-avoid, items 10 to 12, $r = .32$ to .56.

Five theoretical achievement goal models were estimated and compared in this study: (a) a 4-factor model consisting of latent variables representing mastery-approach, mastery-avoid, performance-approach, and performance-avoid motivation orientations; (b) a 3-factor model including performance-approach, performance-avoid, and a single mastery factor; (c) a 3-factor model including mastery-approach, performance-approach, and an overall avoidance factor; (d) a 2-factor model including overall mastery and performance factors; and (e) a 2-factor model with overall approach and avoidance factors. Confirmatory factor analyses were determined using LISREL 8.72 (Jöreskog & Sörbom, 2007). Given the slight departure from normality indicated by the kurtosis values for four of the questionnaire items, an asymptotic covariance matrix was calculated, and the robust maximum likelihood method was used to estimate all parameters. The robust maximum likelihood procedure is a more conservative estimation method in that it results in standard errors adjusted to compensate for departures from multivariate normality.

Absolute and incremental goodness-of-fit indices were considered when evaluating model fit (see Table 5.2) (Hu & Bentler, 1999). The minimum fit function, χ^2, is an absolute index that assesses whether the model-derived covariance matrix is a perfect replication of the covariance matrix derived from the observed data. The significant ($p < .001$) result of this test for each model suggests that the models did not perfectly fit the data. However, this test has been shown to be extremely sensitive to sample size and is apt to lead to model rejection, even when only small differences exist between the model and observed covariance matrices. As a result, it is customary to report additional "absolute fit" indices such as the root mean square error of approximation (RMSEA) and the standardized root mean square residual (SRMR) (Kaplan, 2000). RMSEA values below .05 are considered

TABLE 5.1 Item-Level Correlations and Descriptive Statistics

Item	1	2	3	4	5	6	7	8	9	10	11	12
1	1.00	.52***	.54***	.31***	.11	.28**	.25**	.27**	.28**	.07	.15*	.16*
2		1.00	.49***	.34***	.09	.25**	.08	.21**	.19**	.06	.15*	.16*
3			1.00	.20**	.16*	.14*	.22**	.28**	.30***	.15*	.30***	.16*
4				1.00	.32***	.71***	.24**	.27**	.26**	.09	.19**	.26**
5					1.00	.47***	.08	.08	.11	.28**	.14*	.18**
6						1.00	.20**	.22**	.24**	.10	.09	.16*
7							1.00	.55***	.65***	.16*	.26**	.24**
8								1.00	.60***	.28**	.31***	.23**
9									1.00	.38***	.44***	.33***
10										1.00	.56***	.32***
11											1.00	.41***
12												1.00
M	4.96	4.54	5.00	3.00	4.00	3.04	3.90	4.36	3.90	4.75	4.58	3.51
SD	1.77	1.81	1.61	1.79	1.89	1.90	1.89	1.87	1.84	1.90	1.84	2.04
Skew	-.61	-.41	-.58	.66	.01	.66	-.02	-.16	.00	-.52	-.42	.19
Kurt	-.59	-.78	-.28	-.54	-1.15	-.74	-1.16	-1.06	-.98	-.70	-.80	-1.25

Note: Mastery Approach = items 1 through 3; Mastery Avoid = items 4 through 6; Performance Approach = items 7 through 9; Performance Avoid = items 10 through 12 (See Questionnaire).
* $p < .05$, ** $p < .01$, *** $p < .001$

"close fit," whereas values between .05 and .08 are considered "fair fit," and values between .08 and .10 are indicative of "mediocre fit" (Kaplan, 2000). Hu and Bentler (1999) suggest that SRMR values below .08 are indications of "adequate fit." In the current study, the 4-factor model is the only model that resulted in acceptable values, RMSEA (.05) and SRMR (.06).

The incremental comparative fit index (CFI) was considered in addition to the absolute fit indices reported above (i.e., χ^2, RMSEA, SRMR). The CFI compares the hypothesized model with a baseline model in which all the variables present are hypothesized to be uncorrelated. Values higher than .95 are considered indicative of good fit (Hu & Bentler, 1999). The only model with an acceptable CFI value was the 4-factor model (CFI = .98). Lastly, the models were empirically compared by evaluating the difference between the chi square value (i.e., $\Delta\chi^2$) obtained from the 4-factor model and those obtained from the other models. The results indicated that the 4-factor model proved to be a significantly better fit than each alternative model (see Figure 5.1). The model comparison results are in accordance with those reported by Conroy et al. (2003), Elliot and McGregor (2001), Finney et al. (2004), and Wang et al. (2007) in that the 4-factor model fit significantly better than the alternative dichotomous and trichotomous models. Path diagrams for the competing dichotomous and trichotomous models can be found in Figures 5.2–5.5.

Adequate internal consistency was found for the mastery-approach ($\alpha = .76$), mastery-avoid ($\alpha = .75$), and performance-approach ($\alpha = .82$) subscales. However, only marginal reliability was found for the performance-avoid subscale ($\alpha = .69$). These results are highly similar to those reported

TABLE 5.2 Fit Statistics for All Models Tested

Model	χ^2	df	p	RMSEA	p Close	CFI	SRMR	$\Delta\chi^2$	Δdf
Four-factor model	97.86	48	<.001	.05	.38	.98	.06	—	
Trichotomous model 1	238.28	51	<.0001	.12	<.0001	.87	.10	140.40	3
Trichotomous model 2	251.00	51	<.0001	.13	<.0001	.85	.12	153.14	3
Dichotomous model 1	305.06	53	<.0001	.12	<.0001	.82	.11	207.20	5
Dichotomous model 2	387.25	53	<.0001	.15	<.0001	.75	.14	289.39	5

Note: χ^2= Minimum fit function chi square; RMSEA = Root mean square error of approximation; CFI = Comparative fit index; SRMR = Standardized root mean square residual; $\Delta\chi^2$ = Difference between 4-factor chi square value and each comparative models.

Note: Four-factor model = mastery approach, mastery avoid, performance approach, performance avoid; Trichotomous model 1 = mastery, performance approach, performance avoid, Trichotomous model 2 = mastery approach, performance approach, avoidance; Dichotomous model 1 = mastery, performance; Dichotomous model 2 = approach, avoidance.

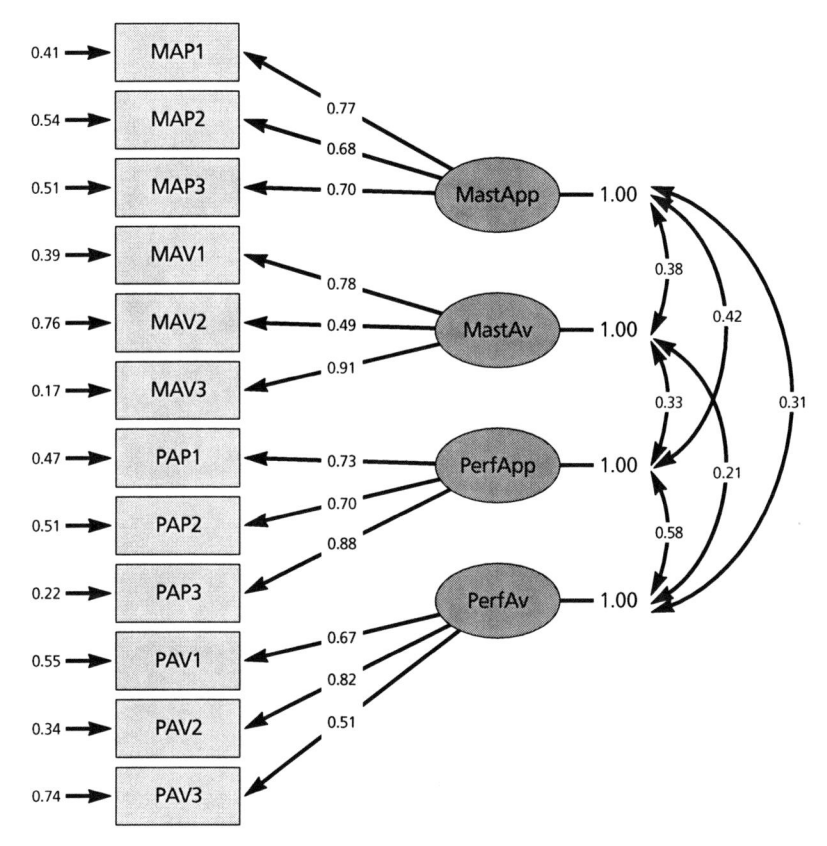

Figure 5.1 Four-factor achievement goal model.
Note: MastApp (MAP) = mastery-approach; MastAv (MAV) = mastery-avoid; PerfApp (PAP) = performance-approach; PerfAv (PAV) = performance-avoid; All coefficients are standardized.

by Finney et al.(2004) and Wang et al.(2007), who found similar alpha coefficients (e.g., .71 to .88) for the mastery-approach, mastery-avoid, and performance-approach subscales and alpha coefficients less than .70 for the performance-avoid subscale. Descriptive analyses revealed the highest mean for the mastery-approach subscale ($M = 14.44$) followed in descending order by the performance-avoid ($M = 12.75$), performance-approach ($M = 12.16$), and mastery-avoid ($M = 9.98$) subscales. These results are somewhat parallel to those conducted at the item-level analyses in that the sample rated mastery-approach goals the highest and mastery-avoid goals the lowest. The range of standard deviations determined indicated similar degrees of variability across the responses on each subscale ($SD = 4.27$ to 4.78).

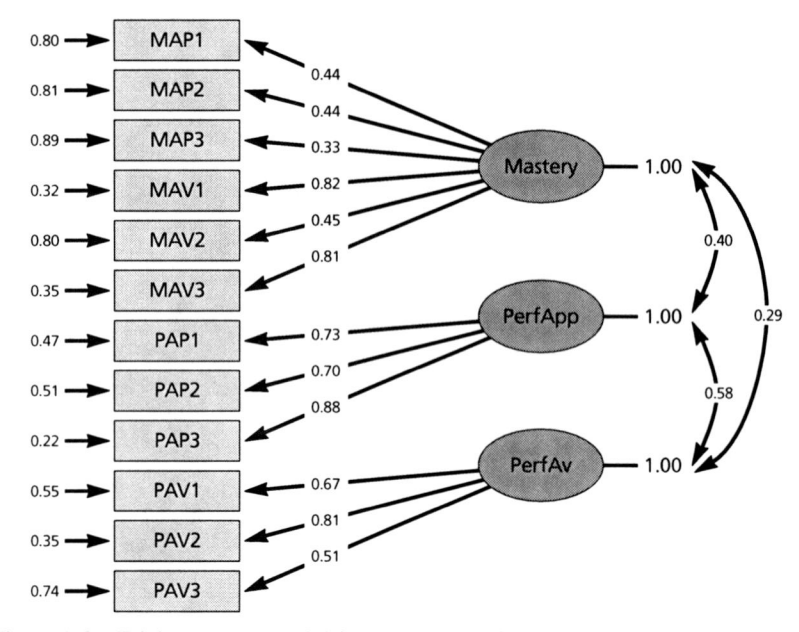

Figure 5.2 Trichotomous model 1 = mastery, performance-approach, performance-avoid.

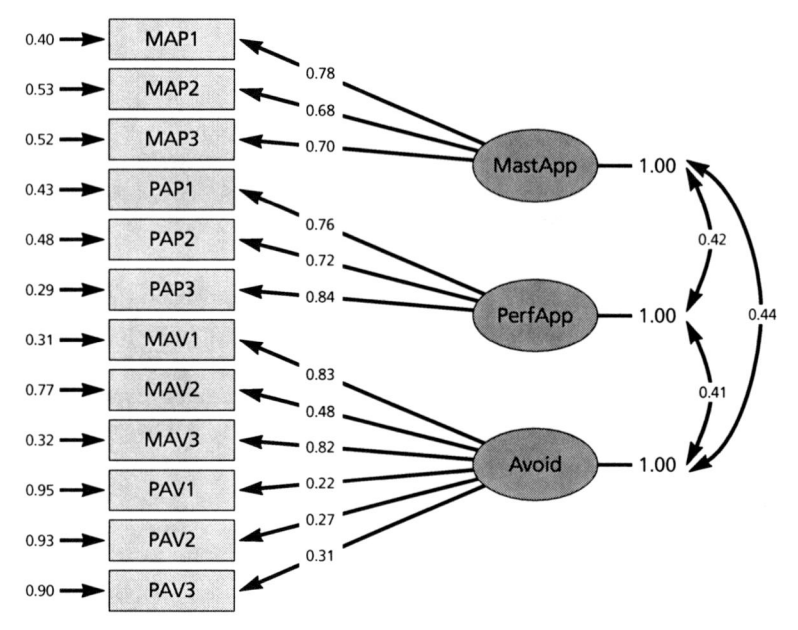

Figure 5.3 Trichotomous model 2 = mastery-approach, performance-approach, avoidance.

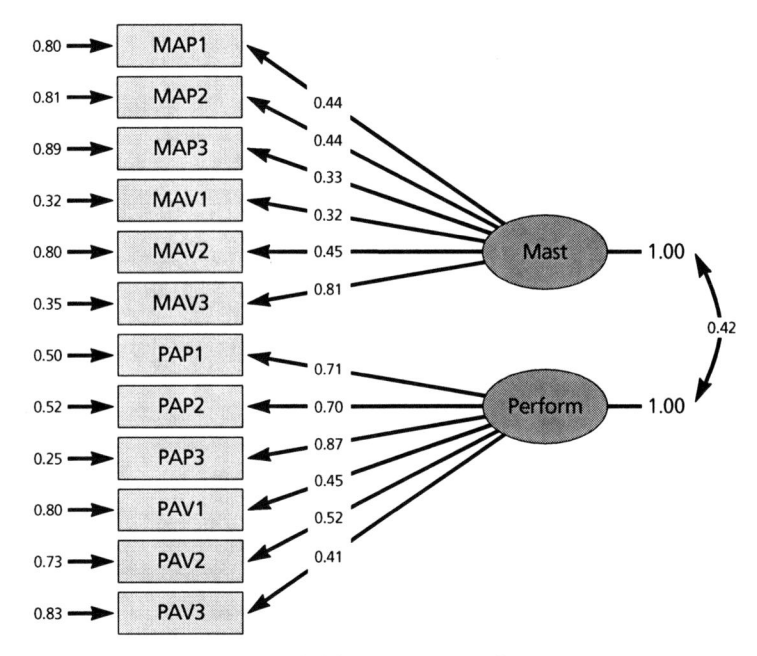

Figure 5.4 Dichotomous model 1 = mastery, performance.

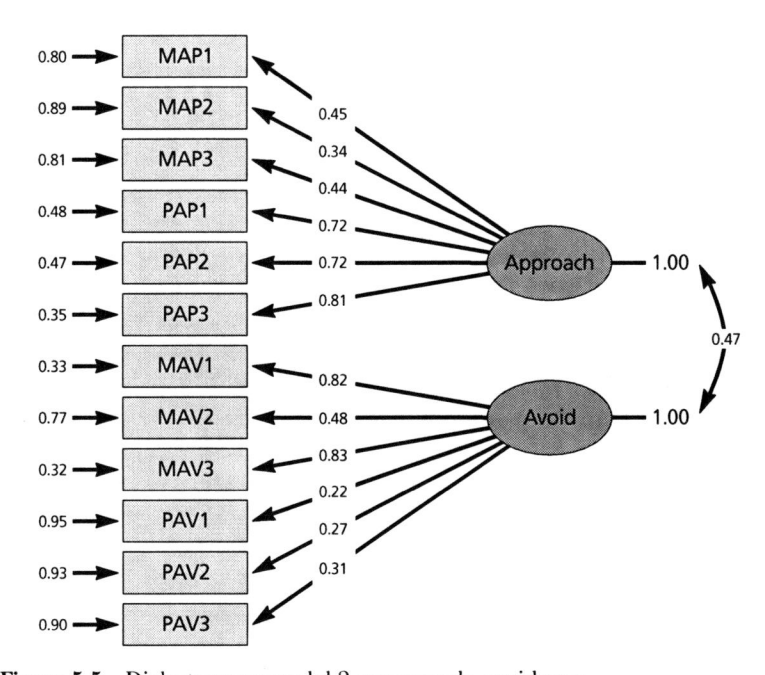

Figure 5.5 Dichotomous model 2 = approach, avoidance.

TABLE 5.3 Descriptive Statistics for Motivation Subscales and Self-Reported Practice Habit Items

	M	SD	Skew	Kurt
Mastery-approach	14.50	4.27	−.52	−.27
Mastery-avoid	10.05	4.55	.36	−.71
Performance-approach	12.17	4.78	−.04	−.80
Performance-avoid	12.83	4.53	−.20	−.63
Length of average practice session	30.70	20.85	1.41	3.47
Average number of practice sessions per day	.95	.61	1.17	5.62
% of time spent on *informal* practice	34.67	28.60	.61	−.55
% of time spent on *formal* practice	54.58	30.84	−.34	−.95
Average daily practice efficiency[a]	5.68	2.19	−.65	−.32

[a] Scale = "1—Extremely Inefficient" to "10—Extremely Efficient."

TABLE 5.4 Pearson Correlations among Motivation Subscales

	MastApp	MastAv	PerfApp	PerfAv
Mastery-approach	1.00	.31***	.32***	.23**
Mastery-avoid		1.00	.27**	.26**
Performance-approach			1.00	.43***
Performance-avoid				1.00

* $p < .05$, ** $p < .01$, *** $p < .001$

Pearson correlations determined among the achievement goal motivation orientations are presented in Table 5.4. Significant positive correlations ($p < .01$) were detected between all pairs of orientations. The strongest relationship was found between the performance-approach and performance-avoid dimensions with a coefficient of .43. This result suggests that the sample may not have perceived a large difference between the approach and avoid dimensions when responding to the performance items. All of the other significant correlations found were small, accounting for less than 10% of shared variance between each respective variable pair. Overall, the correlation coefficients determined among the motivation orientations in the current study (.23 to .43) are slightly larger than those reported by Elliot and McGregor (2001) (−.05 to .40) with a sample of college students. However, the findings of the current study are similar to those reported by Wang et al.(2007) (.34 to .65) with a sample of secondary-school students from Singapore. It may be that the discriminant validity of the motivation orientations is somewhat less pronounced with younger samples.

Descriptive analyses of the self-reported practice habit items are presented in Table 5.3. Subjects reported an average of approximately one practice session per day and 30 minutes spent practicing per session. The length of reported practice time per day was quite varied across the sample ($SD = 20.85$). Mean percentages of time spent on formal and informal practicing were 54.58% and 34.67%, respectively, indicating that the subjects may spend more time playing with a specific musical goal in mind than without a specific musical goal in mind. However, standard deviations suggest that the reports of formal and informal practice were extremely varied as well. The mean practice efficiency rating for the sample was 5.68, suggesting that on average the subjects did not necessarily consider themselves to be efficient in their practicing.

Spearman correlations between the motivation orientation subscales and self-reported practice habits indicated several small, yet statistically significant relationships (see Table 5.5). The strongest correlations were found between the mastery-approach subscale and reports of length of average practice session ($rho = .25$, $p < .01$) and reports of average daily practice efficiency ($rho = .31$, $p < .01$). These findings suggest that those who tended to report greater amounts of practice and greater efficiency in practicing also tended to indicate a stronger mastery-approach motivation orientation. Interestingly, four significant correlations were detected between both mastery- and performance-approach subscale scores and practice reports, whereas only two were detected between mastery-avoid subscale scores and practice reports, and none were detected between performance-avoid subscale scores and practice reports. Although this trend is thought provoking, the significant correlations indicated in Table 5.5 are each small in magnitude and may have minimal practical significance.

TABLE 5.5 Spearman Correlations between Motivation Subscales and Self-Reported Practice Habits

	MastApp	MastAv	PerfApp	PerfAv
Length of average practice session	.25**	.15*	.17*	−.07
Average number of practice sessions per day	.19**	.10	.14*	.12
% of time spent on *informal* practice	−.05	−.08	−.05	−.02
% of time spent on *formal* practice	.20**	.15*	.22**	.10
Average daily practice efficiency	.31***	−.03	.19**	.08

* $p < .05$, ** $p < .01$, *** $p < .001$

DISCUSSION

This study explored the possibility of adapting the 2×2 achievement goal framework in the context of instrumental music with the intention of developing a better understanding of why and how students are motivated to pursue competence in music. Previous research in academics and sports have demonstrated that the 2×2 achievement goal framework has great potential with regard to explaining and predicting learning-related behaviors. More specifically, it seems that mastery-approach and performance-approach goal structures may be particularly effective in encouraging students to strive for and achieve competence (Moller & Elliot, 2006). Although some researchers have explored similar constructs with respect to music learning (e.g., Schmidt, 2005; Smith, 2002), none have investigated whether the 2×2 achievement goal framework is valid in the context of music education. The primary research questions of the current study addressed (a) the validity of the 2×2 model with respect to factor stability, subscale intercorrelation, and the prediction of self-reported practice habits; and (b) the reliability of the achievement goal subscales with respect to internal consistency.

The results of this study generally support the previous studies in academics and sports in that the 4-factor model resulted in a better fit than any of the competing dichotomous or trichotomous models. However, the fit indices indicated that the 4-factor model was only a fair fit to the observed data (e.g., Hu & Bentler, 1999; Kaplan, 2000). This suggests that while the 4-factor model was the best comparative fit, it may not be the only viable model. Furthermore, the correlations among the achievement goal orientation subscales suggested that the discriminant validity of the four orientations might not be extremely robust when applied in an instrumental music education context. For example, some subjects may not have perceived a large difference between the items worded to reflect approach and avoid distinctions. These findings are similar, albeit less pronounced, when compared with those of Schmidt (2005), Schimdt, Zdzinski, and Ballard (2006), and Smith (2002), who also found significant positive relationships between approach and avoid motivation constructs. The correlations also indicated that some subjects might not have perceived a large difference between items written to reflect performance and mastery orientations. The elements of public performance inherent in instrumental music education may serve to weaken the distinctions between approach and avoid or mastery and performance orientations. For example, when performing among peers on a regular basis, distinctions between whether an individual is motivated by a personal desire to improve may be intimately entwined with one's desire to perform well in reference to others. As a result, some students may have developed achievement goal motivational beliefs that are better described as a single construct representing degree of motivation, high or low. Alternatively, given the similar correlations reported by Wang et al.(2007), it may be that the discriminant validity of the 2 × 2 model may vary with age of the sample. Younger individuals may not have had the time or experiences to develop the fine distinctions captured in the 2 × 2 framework. Clearly, more research is needed to determine the validity of the 2 × 2 achievement goal framework in an instrumental music context.

The marginal reliability coefficient found for the performance-avoid subscale suggests that the psychometric properties of that scale in particular may be suspect. That similar findings have been reported by previous researchers supports this claim. Creating additional items may be one method to increase the reliability of the goal orientation subscales. Adding items to each scale would likely increase the variability among the scores and as a result decrease the amount of measurement error present. The resulting increase in variability gained from adding more items to each subscale may also tend to increase the degree of correlation among the subscales and therefore have a significant effect on assessments of discriminant validity among the goal orientation constructs.

Limitations of the 2 × 2 achievement goal model aside, the descriptive analyses of the questionnaire items and subscales have yielded several compelling results. Primarily, that the sample rated mastery-approach goals the highest and mastery-avoid goals the lowest. The mastery-approach results suggest that the subjects are primarily motivated to achieve for the sake of satisfying personal expectations and maximizing their experience in band. In contrast, the mastery-avoid results suggest that concern for not maximizing personal achievement was not a major issue for this sample. These findings may hold practical importance for music teachers. For example, teachers could try to focus class activities and learning outcomes on mastery-approach oriented goals by perhaps including self-referential forms of assessment and encouraging their students to work toward meeting personal goals. However, more research is needed to confirm whether similar patterns of achievement goal orientations would be found in other samples of high school band students.

The trend of significant correlations found between self-reports of practice habits and approach goal orientations as compared with avoid goal orientations is consistent with findings reported by researchers who have investigated relations between achievement goal orientations and academic learning (e.g., Cury et al., 2006; Karabenick, 2003, 2004). Although the magnitude of the relationships found in the current study was overall quite small, it seems logical that there may be benefits of adopting approach-directed motivation orientations to music learning. For example, students who are concerned with mastery-approach goals such as personal improvement and self-referential competence may be more likely to practice for longer amounts of time and may be more efficient in their practicing. However, the practice habits examined in this study are clearly limited from a methodological standpoint in that they are purely self-report. It is important that researchers compare achievement goal motivations with actual observed practice behaviors and objective measures of performance achievement. It would also be informative to conduct intervention-based studies that might determine whether achievement goal motivation orientations could be truly predictive of adaptive learning outcomes and achievement in music.

This study represents an initial investigation into the validity of the 2 × 2 achievement goal framework in the context of music education. More research is needed that focuses on (a) testing the construct validity of the 2 × 2 framework with more varied musician populations (composers, strings, vocalists, etc.); (b) testing the 2 × 2 framework with musicians from various age groups or experience levels; (c) improving the reliability of the goal orientation subscales; and (d) examining the predictive validity of the 2 × 2 achievement goal model with respect to observed behaviors and musical achievement/competence. Given the findings regarding relationships between learning outcomes and achievement goal motivation in research devoted to academics and sports (see Moller & Elliot, 2006), it is logical to assume that more knowledge about the relationships between achievement goals and music learning outcomes would be beneficial.

Music education researchers must continue to explore the nature of student motivation. However, it is equally important that researchers critically examine the validity of applying innovative theoretical models to practice. The 2 × 2 achievement goal framework holds promise with regard to understanding what drives music students to engage and persist in music learning. Through careful and rigorous testing and development, the 2 × 2 achievement goal framework may be used to explain student behavior and inform instructional design. Ultimately, insights gained from the application of this model have the potential to improve music education practice and result in greater student learning.

REFERENCES

Ames, C., & Archer, J. (1987). Mothers' belief about the role of ability and effort in school learning. *Journal of Educational Psychology, 79,* 409–414.

Asmus, E. P. (1986). Student beliefs about the cause of success and failure in music: A study of achievement motivation. *Journal of Research in Music Education, 34*(4), 262–278.

Asmus, E. P. (1995). Motivation in music teaching and learning. *The Quarterly Journal of Music Teaching and Learning, V*(4), 5–32.

Austin, J. A., & Vispoel, W. P. (1998). How American adolescents interpret success and failure in classroom music: Relationships among attributional beliefs, self-concept, and achievement. *Psychology of Music, 26*(1), 26–45.

Conroy, D. E., Elliot, A. J., & Hofer, S. M. (2003). A 2 × 2 achievement goal framework for sport: Evidence for factorial invariance, temporal stability, and external validity. *Journal of Sport and Exercise Psychology, 25*, 456–476.

Cury, F., Elliot, A. J., Da Fonseca, D. D., & Moller, A. C. (2006). The social-cognitive model of achievement motivation and the 2 × 2 achievement goal framework. *Journal of Personality and Social Psychology, 90*(4), 666–679.

Elliot, A. J. (1999). Approach and avoidance motivation and achievement goals. *Educational Psychologist, 34*(3), 169–189.

Elliot, A. J. (2005). A conceptual history of the achievement goal construct. In A. J. Elliot & C. S. Dweck (Eds.), *Handbook of competence and motivation* (pp. 52–72). New York: Guilford.

Elliot, A. J., & Church, M. (1997). A hierarchical model of approach and avoidance achievement motivation. *Journal of Personality and Social Psychology, 72*, 218–232.

Elliot, A. J., & McGregor, H. A. (2001). A 2 × 2 achievement goal framework. *Journal of Personality and Social Psychology, 80*(3), 501–519.

Finney, S. J., Pieper, S. L., & Barron, K. E. (2004). Examining the psychometric properties of the achievement goal questionnaire in a general academic context. *Educational and Psychological Measurement, 64*(2), 365–382.

Hu, L., & Bentler, P. M. (1999). Cutoff criteria for fit indices in covariance structure modeling: Conventional criteria vs. new alternatives. *Structural Equation Modeling, 6*, 1–55.

Jöreskog, K., & Sörbom, D. (2007). LISREL 8.72. Chicago: Scientific Software International.

Kaplan, D. (2000). *Structural equation modeling: Foundations and extensions.* Thousand Oaks, CA: Sage.

Karabenick, S. A. (2003). Seeking help in large college classes: A person-centered approach. *Contemporary Educational Psychology, 28*, 37–58.

Karabenick, S. A. (2004). Perceived achievement goal structure and college student help seeking. *Journal of Educational Psychology, 96*(3), 569–581.

McCormick, J., & McPherson, G. E. (2003). The role of self-efficacy in a musical performance examination: An exploratory structural equation analysis. *Psychology of Music, 31*(1), 37–51.

McPherson, G. E., & Zimmerman, B. J. (2002). Self-regulation of musical learning: A social cognitive perspective. In R. Colwell & C. Richardson (Eds.), *The new handbook of research on music teaching and learning* (pp. 327–347). New York: Oxford University Press.

Moller, A. C. & Elliot, A. J. (2006). The 2 × 2 achievement goal framework: An overview of empirical research. In A. V. Mitel (Ed.), *Focus on educational psychology* (pp. 307–326). Hauppauge, NY: Nova Science Publishers, Inc.

Sandene, B. A. (1997). An investigation of variables related to student motivation in instrumental music. *Dissertation Abstracts International, 58* (10), 3070. (UMI No. 9315947).

Schmidt, C. P. (2005). Relations among motivation, performance achievement, and music experience variables in secondary instrumental music. *Journal of Research in Music Education, 53*(2), 134–147.

Schmidt, C. P., Zdzinski, S. F., & Ballard, D. L. (2006). Motivation orientations, academic achievement, and career goals of undergraduate music education majors. *Journal of Research in Music Education, 54*(2), 138–153.

Smith, B. (2002). The role of selected motivational beliefs in the process of collegiate instrumental music practice. *Dissertation Abstracts International, 63* (2), 536. (UMI No. 3042170)

Wang, C. K., Biddle, S. J. H., & Elliot, A. J. (2007). The 2 × 2 achievement goal framework in a physical education context. *Psychology of Sport and Exercise, 8*, 147–168.

CHAPTER 6

IN-SERVICE MUSIC TEACHERS' PERCEPTIONS OF PROFESSIONAL DEVELOPMENT

William I. Bauer
Case Western Reserve University

Jere Forsythe and Daryl Kinney
Ohio State University

ABSTRACT

The purpose of this study was to describe music teachers' perceptions of professional development. In-service teachers ($N = 783$) completed an online survey that collected data related to (a) demographics, (b) graduate study as professional development, (c) the perceived value of types of nondegree professional development, (d) motivation for pursuing professional development, and (e) delivery systems for and approaches to professional development. The participants' highest ranked reasons for pursuing a master's degree were for personal satisfaction and to become a better teacher. Motivations for nondegree professional development were to become a better teacher, improve musicianship, and renew the teaching license. Professional music conferences were the most desirable professional development experience for these teachers, followed by music in-services in their school districts, and multiple-day summer workshops. Professional development topics of most interest varied according to area of specialization. Significant differences in professional development topic preferences were found between newer and more experienced teachers.

INTRODUCTION

The professional development of teachers in all disciplines has received the attention of researchers. Important findings from these studies have indicated that when professional development is subject-specific and grounded in student learning, instructional practices, and the improvement of teacher's understanding of the content of their discipline, it will be most effective (Resnick, 2005). In a recent analysis of the professional development literature in general education as it applies to music education, Hammel (2007) discussed issues related to (a) professional development and school reform, (b) the disconnect between administrators and teachers regarding professional development needs, (c) the varying types of professional development desired by different types of teachers, (d) analyses of diverse delivery formats for professional development, (e) the relationship between professional development and teacher collegiality and collaboration, and (f) investigations that have examined professional development programs perceived as exemplary. However, the role of professional development in the careers and lives of music educators has been researched less extensively than in other areas of education (Bauer, 2007).

Hookey (2002) provided a summary of the literature on the professional development of music teachers. Bauer (2007) analyzed and discussed the *research* literature specifically. Readers are encouraged to examine those sources for more extensive coverage of this literature. Only research most closely associated with the present study will be discussed here, including studies examining professional development topics of interest to music teachers, approaches utilized in delivering professional development to music educators, and professional development that meets the needs of all music teachers.

Professional Development Topics

Several researchers have examined professional development topics desired by, and of interest to, music teachers. Bowles (2003) received survey responses from 456 members of a state music education association in the upper Midwest. The top professional development topics of interest to those teachers were technology, assessment, and instrumental/choral literature. Tarnowski and Murphy (2003) developed a questionnaire that was completed by 281 elementary music educators who were members of music education associations in Wisconsin and Minnesota. The highest ranked subjects in which these teachers were interested in furthering their learning included Orff, technology, and assessment. In a statewide study of music teaching in Illinois (Rosenthal, 2005), nearly all teachers indicated that they had pursued professional development, with the top areas of study including technology, methods, and curriculum. Finally, Bush (2007) surveyed music educators ($n = 108$) in Arizona, asking them what types of workshops they would like to attend. Overall, these teachers' top choices were new music/repertoire, technology, and assessment. However, Bush also examined the data according to primary area of teaching responsibility (band, strings, choral, or general music) and found that the rankings differed according to area of specialization.

Approaches to Professional Development

One common type of professional development is attendance at conferences. Price and Orman (1999, 2001) conducted a content analysis of the Music Educators National Conference (now known as MENC: The National Association for Music Education) biennial in-service conferences between 1984 and 2000. They categorized the conferences' content, with educational clinics, lectures, and demonstrations comprising the majority of the sessions. When Friedrichs (2001) queried California high school instrumental music teachers ($n = 242$) as to their top professional growth experiences, they indicated preferences for (a) having a guest clinician work with them, (b) being able to observe other rehearsals, (c) participating in music conferences, and (d) attending concerts. In contrast, they did not find in-school in-services, county education workshops, district-level workshops, or nonmusic workshops to be effective.

In the previously described study by Bowles (2003), participants indicated a preference for intensive, consecutive-day, summer professional development experiences. Approximately 40% of the study participants desired opportunities for professional development within 100 miles of their residence and 42% liked collegiate settings as locations. Forty-two percent of the participants indicated they would be interested in studying via electronic correspondence. In a longitudinal study of a 1-week (30 hours) professional development workshop on music instructional technology (Bauer, Reese, & McAllister, 2003), researchers found sustained increases in teachers' self-reported knowledge, comfort, and frequency of use of technology. Bush (2007) reported teachers' preferred professional development opportunities as including (a) informal discussions with fellow music teachers, (b) summer or weekend courses/workshops, (c) state music educators annual in-service conference, (d) Internet resources, and (e) professional journals. The relative rank of these and other experiences varied by area of music teaching specialization.

Varying Professional Development Needs of Music Teachers

It appears that a "one-size-fits-all" approach to professional development for music educators, let alone teachers in general (Hammel, 2007; Resnick, 2005), is not effective. Killian, Baker, and Johnson (2006) found that the perceived value of various professional development activities varied between preservice and early-career music educators. As previously discussed, Bush's (2007) analysis of responses from teachers revealed that band, orchestra, choir, and general-music teachers differed in both the content and delivery mechanisms they preferred for professional development. Researchers (Friedrichs, 2001; Conway, 2008) have found that music teachers do not find nonmusic/music education in-service experiences to be valuable. Finally, similar to Killian, Baker, and Johnson's findings, Conway (2008) has observed that the professional development needs of music educators may vary according to the stage of their careers.

Need for the Study

The research literature on the professional development of music teachers is relatively small. Extant studies in both general education and music education give rise to a number of questions regarding the professional development preferences and needs of in-service music educators. Evidence indicates that these needs and preferences may vary according to teaching responsibilities and career stage. The purpose of this study was to describe Ohio in-service music teachers' perceptions of professional development.

METHOD

Based on a review of the related literature and the researchers' personal experiences in delivering and receiving professional development, an online survey was developed to collect data related to (a) demographics, (b) graduate study as professional development, (c) the perceived value of types of nondegree professional development (music/music education specific and nonmusic) in which teachers had been engaged, (d) motivation for pursuing professional development, and (e) delivery systems for and approaches to professional development. Members of the Executive Committee of the Ohio Society for Music Teacher Education (OSMTE) examined the survey for readability, accuracy, and content validity. A small group of in-service teachers were recruited to pilot-test the survey. Based on feedback from the OSMTE group and the pilot-testers, minor changes were made to the wording and format of the survey. Both the OSMTE committee and the individuals who helped to pilot-test the instrument believed the content was appropriate and adequate.

The survey was placed online using the SurveyMonkey (http://www.surveymonkey.com/) survey tool. Although SurveyMonkey allows surveys to be password protected, no protection was utilized in this study for the following reasons: so as not to create additional hurdles for potential respondents (e.g., possibly mistyping a password, not gaining access to the survey and then giving up) that could potentially lower the response rate; and because given the nature of the survey and our belief in the reliability of the e-mail addresses we were given by the Ohio Music Education Association (OMEA) office, we did not perceive there to be a need to protect the instrument in this way. All K–12 members ($N = 2{,}797$) of the Ohio Music Education Association were contacted through (a) direct e-mail; (b) communications from the state, district, and region officers; and (c) notices placed in *TRIAD*, the OMEA state journal. In addition, teachers were requested to seek out colleagues who were not members of the state association and ask them also to participate in the study. Two weeks after the initial e-mail, a second follow-up message was sent requesting the teachers who had not yet completed the survey to do so. After another two weeks had passed, a third and final e-mail was sent urging those who had not yet responded to take part in the investigation.

RESULTS

Characteristics of the Sample

A total of 783 teachers (61% female, 39% male), who taught at all grade levels (K–12) and had been teaching between 1 to 40 years ($M = 17.87$; $SD = 10.14$), completed the survey. The participants, the vast majority who were OMEA members (94%), taught in suburban (46%), rural (30%), and urban (24%) settings; and in public (90%) and private (10%) schools. A majority of respondents were full-time teachers (94%), while the remaining 6% were part-time. Ethnicity was predominantly white (97%), followed by African American (2%). A small number of teachers who were of Hispanic ($n = 3$), Asian ($n = 1$) and multi-racial ($n = 1$) ethnicities were also participants.

About one-half of the respondents reported teaching exclusively in the area of band (22%), orchestra (4%), choir (9%) or general music (16%). The remainder indicated multiple areas of teaching responsibility, including choir/general music (23%), band/general music (12%), band/strings (4%), band/choir (1%), or strings/general music (1%). Eight percent of participants identified three or more areas of teaching. In addition to their responsibilities in the areas reported above, a small percentage of the educators (18%) specified teaching responsibilities in other areas of music (e.g., music theory, music appreciation, music technology). Only 3% of respondents reported teaching in an academic area outside of music in addition to their music responsibilities.

Teachers reported their highest degree earned as bachelor's (41%), master's (58%) or doctor's (1%). In order to compare trends in teachers' avenues to master's degree completion, respondents were divided into those who had already completed their master's ($n = 461$) and those who were currently pursuing their degree ($n = 75$). Of those participants who had already completed the master's, a majority reported their cognate area was in music, including music education (55%), performance (11%), conducting (2%), or another area such as music history, theory, jazz studies, or sacred music (2%). Several teachers specified areas of emphasis outside of music: 24% in general education (e.g., curriculum and development, administration) and 3% in counseling. Only 3% of master's degrees were outside the area of education altogether (e.g., technology, business). Avenues to degree completion varied among those who had already completed the degree, with most seeking to complete the master's on a part-time basis in evening and summer classes (see Figure 6.1).

Likewise, of those currently pursuing a master's degree, a majority of respondents' cognate area was in music. However, most teachers sought degrees in music education (65%) as compared with performance (1%) or conducting (3%). No other cognate areas in music were reported. Again, several participants reported areas of emphasis outside of music: 30% in general education (e.g., curriculum and development, administration) and 1% in counseling. None were pursuing master's degrees outside the area of education altogether. Avenues to degree completion demonstrated greater percentages of respondents seeking degrees exclusively through summer and online courses (see Figure 6.2).

On a Likert-type scale ranging from 1 (strongly disagree) to 4 (strongly agree), participants indicated that their reasons for pursuing a master's degree were for personal satisfaction ($M = 3.63$, $SD = .69$), to become a better teacher ($M = 3.61$, $SD = .65$), to earn a higher salary ($M = 3.52$, $SD = .75$) and to become a better musician ($M = 2.95$, $SD = 1.11$). General disagreement

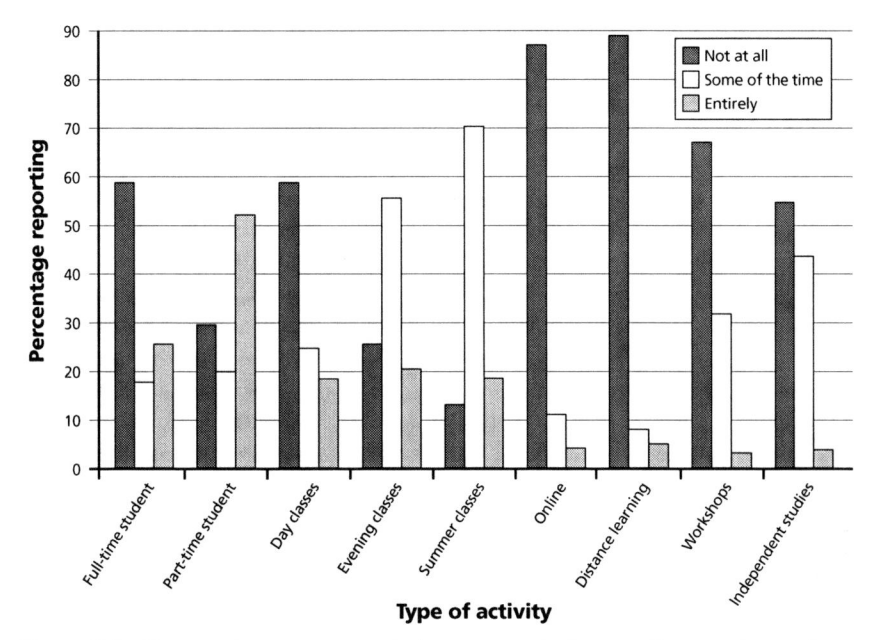

Professional Development Practices and Needs ■ **107**

Figure 6.1 Reported route to completing a master's degree of respondents who had already completed a master's.

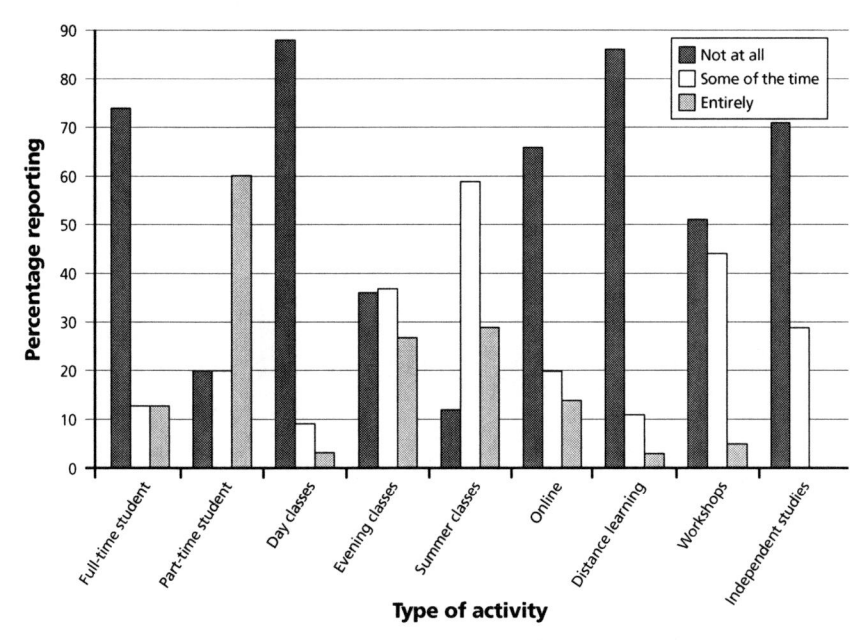

Figure 6.2 Reported route to completing a master's degree of those currently pursuing a master's.

was evidenced for wanting to pursue a doctorate ($M = 1.80$, $SD = .99$), being required to earn a master's by their school district ($M = 1.91$, $SD = 1.09$) and wanting to learn how to do research ($M = 1.99$, $SD = .93$). Respondents' opinions about earning the master's in order to maintain licensure were relatively neutral and highly variable ($M = 2.60$, $SD = 1.24$), perhaps reflecting the degree to which state laws concerning licensure and certification have changed over time.

Doctoral degrees ($n = 20$) were earned or currently being pursued in the areas of music education ($n = 12$), music performance ($n = 2$), conducting ($n = 2$), general education ($n = 2$), music theory/composition ($n = 1$), or ministry ($n = 1$). Figure 6.3 illustrates the routes by which respondents sought to complete their doctorate. Here, full-time status and part-time status were more evenly divided among participants, along with the number of respondents reporting taking day, evening, and summer classes at least some of the time.

Teachers agreed that their reasons for pursuing a doctorate were for personal satisfaction ($M = 3.80$, $SD = .52$), to become a better teacher ($M = 3.50$, $SD = .95$), to teach at the collegiate level ($M = 3.35$, $SD = .81$), to become a better musician ($M = 3.15$, $SD = .99$) and to learn to do research ($M = 3.15$, $SD = 1.09$). Disagreement was evidenced for being required to earn a doctorate by their school district ($M = 1.10$, $SD = .31$) and being required to earn a doctorate to maintain their teaching license ($M = 1.30$,

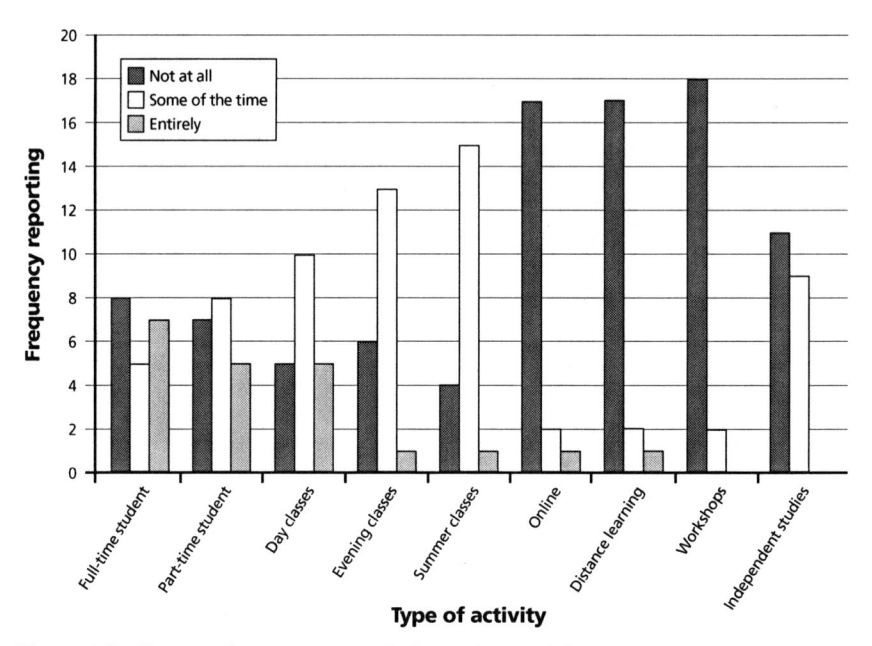

Figure 6.3 Reported route to completing a doctoral degree.

SD = .66). Responses were mixed regarding pursuing a doctorate to earn a higher salary (M = 2.35, SD = 1.18).

Professional Development

A majority of teachers (95%) reported that their districts have Local Professional Development Committees (LPDC), and 72% of respondents indicated that they have an Individual Professional Development Plan (IPDP) on file with their district. Of those reporting a LPDC, 88% found them somewhat to very valuable. More than one-half of the participants reported that their school district required an average of three or more professional development days per year. District-required professional development days relating specifically to music varied over all response categories, with respondents reporting zero (15%), one (15%), two (31%), three (20%), four (5%), or five or more (14%) required days.

On a scale of 1 (strongly disagree) to 4 (strongly agree), participants agreed that their motivation for seeking professional development was to become better teachers (M = 3.81, SD = .45), to become better musicians (M = 3.27, SD = .86) and because it was required to maintain their certification/licensure (M = 2.90, SD = 1.22). Participants were collectively more neutral in their responses regarding motivating factors such as increasing their salary (M = 2.62, SD = 1.10) and being a requirement of their school district (M = 2.41, SD = 1.13). Other motivating factors reported in open responses included networking with other music teachers, visiting with colleagues, interaction with presenters who are leaders in their field, to stay current, and to "reenergize."

Respondents indicated their preferred approaches to professional development using a 4-point Likert-type scale ranging from 1 (undesirable) to 4 (very desirable). The most desired approach to professional development was attending professional music conferences such as the OMEA conference, followed by music in-services held at the respondent's school district and intensive 3- to 5-day summer workshops (see Table 6.1). Least desirable professional development approaches were nonmusic in-services held in the respondent's school district and distance learning that did not involve utilizing the Internet (e.g., a cohort of teachers who meet regularly to view and discuss videos for a class they are taking at a remote university). Opinions were relatively neutral regarding approaches based on professional conferences other than music, summer courses at a college/university, short-term online workshops, after-school workshops at colleges, and online coursework. Some participants reported that district conferences sponsored by OMEA were also a preferred mode of professional development. Others reported that those planning professional development events

TABLE 6.1 Rankings of Most Preferred to Least Preferred Mode of Professional Development[a]

Type of Activity	M	SD
Professional Music Conferences (such as Ohio conference)	3.72	.60
Music in-services held at my school district	3.25	.90
Summer workshops (intensive 3–5 days long)	3.09	.88
Professional conference focused on other aspects of teaching besides music	2.71	.94
Summer college/university formal courses	2.65	.96
Short-term online workshops	2.50	1.08
After-school workshops at a college or university	2.47	.93
Online courses	2.45	1.07
Distance learning (not Internet based)	1.86	.93
Nonmusic in-services held at my school district	1.75	.82

Note: Likert scale ranged from 1 (undesirable) to 4 (very desirable).
[a] N = 783.

TABLE 6.2 Rankings of Most Valuable to Least Valuable Professional Development Experiences

Type of Professional Development Experience	n	M	SD
Ohio State Conference	738	3.60	.65
Other music/music education conferences beyond Ohio or MENC	442	3.41	.86
Summer workshops sponsored by a college or university	641	3.35	.78
MENC National Conference	338	3.14	.95
Ohio district-level workshop/conference	497	3.13	.83
School district music in-service	457	2.82	1.01
Online learning activities	427	2.37	1.02
Other nonmusic/music education conference	409	2.34	1.06
School district nonmusic in-service	745	1.82	.84

Note: Likert scale ranged from 1 (not at all valuable) to 4 (extremely valuable).

should consider summer and weekend conflicts attributable to ensemble performance schedules.

Finally, participants rated the value they placed on specific professional development events they had experienced on a Likert-type scale ranging from 1 (not at all valuable) to 4 (extremely valuable). Experiences found to be highly valued by respondents included the OMEA professional conference, other professional music conferences (e.g., the Midwest Band and Orchestra Clinic, American Choral Directors Association), summer workshops at a college, the MENC national conference, and OMEA district conferences (see Table 6.2). Least value was placed on nonmusic conferences being held at a local school district. Those who had experienced these types of professional development activities regarded school district music in-services, online learning activities, and other nonmusic conferences as somewhat valuable.

Preferred Professional Development Topics

Respondents' interests in specific professional development topics are shown in Table 6.3. Here, mean scores were calculated from Likert-type scale responses ranging from 1 (no interest) to 4 (very interested). In order to achieve a better understanding of participants' interest relative to their teaching responsibilities, respondents were grouped according to their primary teaching area. Overall, teachers were most interested in the topics of rehearsal techniques, literature, music technology, and classroom management. Least interest occurred for strings, jazz/show choir, marching band, and jazz ensemble. These overall ratings must be qualified by teaching area, however. Specifically, all subgroups favored topics in their specialization, while reporting little interest in professional development activities that were outside of their area. For example, band teachers were most interested in rehearsal techniques, concert band, literature, conducting, and pedagogy, and least interested in jazz/show choir, early childhood music, choral topics, and strings. Choral teachers were most interested in choral topics, rehearsal techniques, literature, and classroom management, and least interested in marching band, strings, concert band, and jazz ensemble. General-music teachers reported interests in elementary general music, special learners, early childhood music, music technology, and standards-based learning, and little interest in marching band, jazz ensemble, concert band, and strings.

To determine if newer teachers preferred professional development topics that were different from those of more experienced teachers, respondents were divided into those with three years or less of teaching experience and those with four or more years of teaching experience. Because of the specialty area differences evidenced above, only professional development topics outside of specialty areas were compared to protect against bias. Examining mean scores (Table 6.4) revealed that newer teachers were most interested in topics of classroom management, literature, conducting, teaching improvisation, administrative duties associated with music teaching, pedagogy, and working with special learners. More experienced teachers were most interested in music technology, literature, classroom management, pedagogy, and conducting.

Comparing mean scores for professional development topics using Multivariate Analysis of Variance (MANOVA) procedures revealed significant dif-

TABLE 6.3 Means and Rank Orders of Degree of Interest in Professional Development Topics by Teaching Area[a]

Professional Development Topic	Overall Mean	Overall Rank	Band Mean	Band Rank	Strings Mean	Strings Rank	Choir Mean	Choir Rank	General Music Mean	General Music Rank	Choral/General Music Mean	Choral/General Music Rank	Two or More Mean	Two or More Rank
Rehearsal Techniques	3.30	1	3.67	1	3.74	2	3.43	2	2.38	19	3.27	2	3.44	1
Literature	3.15	2	3.34	3	3.32	4	3.26	3	2.69	14	3.13	4	3.21	3
Music Technology	3.14	3	3.09	6	2.90	9	3.01	6	3.16	4	3.14	3	3.26	2
Classroom Management	3.01	4	2.96	8	3.23	5	2.69	9	3.15	6	3.06	5	3.02	6
Pedagogy	2.97	5	3.14	5	3.19	6	3.06	4	2.35	21	3.02	6	3.08	4
Conducting	2.88	6	3.29	4	3.35	3	3.03	5	2.06	24	2.76	13	3.01	7
Assessment	2.80	7	2.61	13	2.94	7	2.63	12	3.08	7	2.90	9	2.75	11
Teaching Improvisation	2.76	8	2.89	10	2.81	10	2.29	19	2.88	10	2.63	16	2.84	8
Advocacy	2.74	9	2.85	11	2.94	8	2.68	10	2.71	13	2.59	17	2.79	9
Wellness	2.62	10	2.41	16	2.68	13	2.68	11	2.80	12	2.69	15	2.61	12
Special Learners	2.62	11	2.24	19	2.58	15	2.26	20	3.34	2	2.81	12	2.49	17
Multicultural Music Education	2.60	12	2.17	21	2.32	18	2.56	14	3.08	8	2.92	8	2.47	20
World Music	2.59	13	2.24	20	2.19	20	2.60	13	2.99	9	2.85	10	2.50	16

Standards-Based Teaching	2.59	14	2.31	18	2.29	19	2.40	18	3.16	5	2.72	14	2.49	18
Music Administration	2.58	15	2.84	12	2.77	11	2.46	15	2.09	23	2.44	22	2.77	10
Career Development	2.54	16	2.48	14	2.65	14	2.43	17	2.63	16	2.48	21	2.61	13
Grant Writing	2.52	17	2.42	15	2.71	12	2.46	16	2.61	17	2.59	18	2.49	19
Teaching Composition	2.50	18	2.41	17	2.42	16	2.17	21	2.65	15	2.56	20	2.57	15
Choral Topics	2.40	19	1.38	27	1.42	25	3.83	1	2.28	22	3.57	1	2.00	26
Elementary General Music	2.37	20	1.39	25	1.61	24	1.53	24	3.80	1	2.94	7	2.26	23
Secondary General Music	2.35	21	1.77	24	1.74	22	2.86	8	2.38	20	2.82	11	2.33	22
Reading in the Content Area	2.31	22	2.09	23	2.10	21	2.17	22	2.83	11	2.43	23	2.17	25
Concert Band	2.28	23	3.63	2	1.23	28	1.17	27	1.42	27	1.24	28	3.06	5
Research Applications	2.25	24	2.13	22	2.39	17	2.15	23	2.52	18	2.22	25	2.24	24
Early Childhood Music	2.04	25	1.35	28	1.65	23	1.38	25	3.27	3	2.40	24	1.85	27
Jazz Ensemble	2.02	26	2.99	7	1.35	26	1.32	26	1.40	28	1.38	26	2.46	21
Marching Band	1.97	27	2.89	9	1.10	29	1.15	29	1.38	29	1.20	29	2.59	14
Jazz/Show Choir	1.92	28	1.35	29	1.32	26	2.92	7	1.76	25	2.59	19	1.68	29
Strings	1.58	29	1.38	26	3.84	1	1.15	28	1.48	26	1.30	27	1.85	28

Note: Likert scale ranged from 1 (no interest) to 4 (very interested).

[a] N = 783.

TABLE 6.4 Means and Rank Orders for Degree of Interest in Professional Development Topics by Teaching Experience

Professional Development Topic	1–3 Years Teaching Experience[a] Mean	Rank	4 or More Years Teaching Experience[b] Mean	Rank
Classroom Management	3.37	1	2.99	3
Literature	3.24	2	3.14	2
Conducting	3.20	3	2.85	5
Teaching Improvisation	3.03	4	2.74	7
Music Administration	3.03	5	2.54	14
Pedagogy	3.02	6	2.96	4
Special Learners	3.00	7	2.59	10
Music Technology	2.95	8	3.16	1
Career Development	2.92	9	2.51	16
Advocacy	2.85	10	2.73	8
Multicultural Music Education	2.81	11	2.59	11
World Music	2.81	12	2.58	13
Assessment	2.80	13	2.80	6
Teaching Composition	2.73	14	2.49	17
Wellness	2.71	15	2.62	9
Standards-Based Teaching	2.63	16	2.59	12
Research Applications	2.58	17	2.23	19
Grant Writing	2.46	18	2.52	15
Reading in the Content Area	2.46	19	2.30	18

Note: Likert scale ranged from 1 (no interest) to 4 (very interested).
[a] $n = 59$
[b] $n = 724$

ferences between teachers of varying experience levels: $F(19, 764) = 2.79$, $p < .001$, $\eta^2 = .06$. Subsequent univariate F tests showed that newer teachers reported significantly greater interest in topics pertaining to classroom management: $F(1, 781) = 10.26$, $p = .001$, $\eta^2 = .01$; administrative aspects of music teaching: $F(1, 781) = 13.22$, $p < .001$, $\eta^2 = .02$; working with special learners: $F(1, 781) = 9.12$, $p = .003$, $\eta^2 = .01$; and career development: $F(1, 781) = 9.49$, $p = .002$, $\eta^2 = .01$. Younger teachers also rated "applications of research" significantly higher than more experienced teachers: $F(1, 781) = 6.84$, $p = .009$, $\eta^2 = .01$; although this item was rated (and subsequently ranked) low for both groups (see Table 6.4). No other significant differences were evidenced between groups.

Non-OMEA Members

Demographic information for non-OMEA members ($n = 48$) indicated that most taught general music ($n = 21$) or general music/choir ($n = 11$), followed by band ($n = 8$), two or more music subjects ($n = 6$), or choir ($n = 2$). A majority taught in urban school districts ($n = 27$), while 13 taught in suburban and 8 in rural settings. Non-OMEA members were primarily full-time teachers ($n = 42$), fairly evenly divided across years of teaching experience (0–5 years, $n = 8$; 6–10 years, $n = 11$; 11–15 years, $n = 6$; 16–20 years, $n = 8$; 21–25 years, $n = 7$; 26+ years, $n = 8$). Forty-five had earned their undergraduate degree in music education, while two had earned undergraduate degrees in music performance and one in elementary education. Of the 48, 23 had earned a master's degree and seven were currently pursuing a master's. Cognate areas for the master's included music education ($n = 13$), performance ($n = 2$), conducting ($n = 1$), and general education ($n = 14$).

In order to determine if those teachers who did not belong to OMEA held different opinions about professional development, their responses regarding professional development topics, attitudes toward professional development, and the types of professional development activities they valued were compared with OMEA members. Preferred professional development topics mirrored previous findings, with non-OMEA and OMEA respondents' interest gravitating to their cognate area. Comparing mean scores for common professional development topics using Multivariate Analysis of Variance (MANOVA) procedures revealed significant differences between groups: $F(19, 764) = 3.19$, $p < .001$, $\eta^2 = .09$. Subsequent univariate F tests showed that non-OMEA members reported significantly greater interest in topics pertaining to multicultural education: $F(1, 781) = 7.33$, $p = .007$, $\eta^2 = .02$; world music: $F(1, 781) = 6.03$, $p = .01$, $\eta^2 = .01$; and working with special learners: $F(1, 781) = 6.98$, $p = .006$, $\eta^2 = .02$. Non-OMEA members reported significantly less interest in topics of pedagogy: $F(1, 781) = 6.18$, $p = .009$, $\eta^2 = .01$; conducting: $F(1, 781) = 8.23$, $p = .004$, $\eta^2 = .02$; and literature: $F(1, 781) = 8.29$, $p = .004$, $\eta^2 = .02$.

Examining reasons for pursuing professional development activities revealed no significant differences between OMEA and non-OMEA members. Similar to previous analyses, both OMEA and non-OMEA members rated wanting to become a better teacher and better musician highest among the reasons for pursuing professional development. Several significant differences were found for preferred type of professional development activities, however. Here, non-OMEA members preferred the professional conference in music significantly less than OMEA members [non-OMEA: $M = 3.40$, $SD = .79$; OMEA: $M = 3.74$, $SD = .57$; $F(1, 781) = 13.11$, $p < .001$, $\eta^2 = .04$]. On the other hand, non-OMEA members indicated significantly greater preference for after-school workshops at a college or university [non-OMEA: $M = 2.82$, $SD = .98$; OMEA: $M = 2.45$, $SD = .91$; $F(1, 781) = 6.91$, $p = .009$, $\eta^2 = .03$] and nonmusic in-service workshops in their school district [non-OMEA: $M = 2.09$, $SD = 1.04$; OMEA: $M = 1.72$, $SD = .80$; $F(1, 781) = 8.52$, $p = .004$, $\eta^2 = .03$]. Paralleling these findings, non-OMEA members rated the value of the OMEA professional conference significantly lower than OMEA members [non-OMEA: $M = 3.32$, $SD = .88$; OMEA: $M = 3.62$, $SD = .63$; $F(1, 736) = 7.86$, $p = .005$, $\eta^2 = .02$], and rated the value of nonmusic in-service professional development in their school district significantly higher than OMEA members [non-OMEA: $M = 2.16$, $SD = 1.03$; OMEA: $M = 1.80$, $SD = .82$; $F(1, 743) = 7.46$, $p = .006$, $\eta^2 = .02$]. No other significant differences between groups were evidenced for preferred professional development activities or respondents' opinions as to the value of activities they had experienced personally.

DISCUSSION

This study relied upon volunteer participants who elected to complete an online questionnaire, yielding a rather large number of responses ($N = 783$). The reader is urged to interpret these results cautiously since the respondents are only a portion of the total number of OMEA members and an even smaller percentage of all music teachers in Ohio. It is possible that nonrespondents' perceptions of professional development may differ from those teachers who did participate in the study. Nevertheless, as will be discussed, the demographics represented suggest that some implications and generalizations may be drawn from these data with measured confidence. In addition, limited, insightful analysis and thoughtful comparisons with prior studies can be made.

Demographic Analysis

Overall, the demographics of the respondents in this survey suggest a sample of music teachers who were not very diverse racially (97% white, 2% African-American, 1% other), were mostly female (61%), had a wide range of years of teaching experience (from 1 to 40 years), and who taught in suburban (46%), rural (30%), and urban (24%) settings. Around one-half of the participants reported teaching exclusively in one area (band, orchestra, choir, or general music), while the other one-half had two or more areas of teaching responsibility. A relatively recent study by the Ohio State Board of Education, *Condition of Teacher Supply and Demand in Ohio* (Levin, Driscoll, & Fleeter, 2005), reported demographics of all Ohio teachers. Although separate data for music teachers were not included in this report, demographic data for Ohio's music teachers were made available (M. Danzuso, Data Administrator, Ohio Center for Teaching Profession, personal communication, August 15, 2007). These two documents allow for some comparisons of the study sample with other teachers. The Center for Teaching Profession (CTP) data indicated that during the 2006–2007 school year, there were 4,737 music teachers in Ohio, with a music teacher being defined as anyone who taught at least a single music course. Personnel in each school district report these data annually; reliability of the data may vary, according to the CTP. No recent study of music teacher demographics in the United States was found in the literature. Clearly there is a need for periodic national data on music teacher demographics.

Levin et al. (2005) reported the percentage of African-American teachers in Ohio to be 4.76%, an amount that is slightly larger than the survey sample (2%). The CTP data indicated that in 2006–2007, 94% of the music teachers in Ohio were white, slightly less than the survey sample, and that 5.3% were African American, a larger percentage than completed the current survey. Compared with the findings of Levin et al., the percentage of female music teachers in the survey sample (61%) is notably lower than data for all female Ohio teachers (74.52%), but nearly as high as the CTP's data for all female music teachers in Ohio (64%). Thus, the gender representation and racial demographics of the survey sample, while similar, do not exactly match the presumed demographics of Ohio music educators. It should be noted that Levin et al. also cited a decline (28.62%) in African American teachers in Ohio from 1999 to 2005, but it is not known if a similar trend has occurred for music teachers.

Of interest was the distribution of years of teaching experience in the present study compared with the population of all Ohio teachers (Levin et al., 2005). Music teachers in Ohio appear to be more experienced than teachers in general (see Table 6.5). It is gratifying to see this career longevity among so many Ohio music educators. Of course, this longevity has the

TABLE 6.5 Years of Teaching Experience of Ohio Music Teachers

Years of Teaching	0–5	6–10	11–20	21–30+
Music Teachers	14%	16%	28%	42%
All Teachers[a,b]	26%	20%	26%	22%

[a] From Levin, Driscoll, & Fleeter (2005).
[b] Data reflect 6% not reporting/missing.

consequent effect of creating fewer openings for newer teachers, thus the observed lower percentage of music teachers with fewer years experience in the study sample.

Corresponding to Ohio's demographic combination of a number of large cities with surrounding suburbs, numerous medium-sized cities, smaller towns, and rural communities, teachers reported a distribution of positions in suburban (46%), rural (30%) and urban (24%) settings. The division of teaching responsibilities reported by respondents was as expected, considering the traditional nature of the music curriculum in Ohio and the certification and licensure standards in the state that have been extant for many years. The Ohio Department of Education has maintained its commitment to a multi-age teaching license in music, without specialization. This allows music educators to provide instruction at all grade levels and in all areas of music. However, traditional curriculum areas of specialization—band, choir, strings, and general music—remain prominent in the state. Participants' teacher preparation and current teaching responsibilities reflected both licensure patterns and curricular traditions, as slightly more than one-half of respondents reported teaching in one area exclusively, presumably in their area of interest and special competence, while the remaining participants taught in multiple areas.

Graduate Study as Professional Development

Most respondents in the survey possessed a master's degree (58%), a percentage that is notably higher than that indicated by the CPT data for Ohio's music teachers (49.8%), and also higher than all Ohio teachers (52.97%) (Levin et al., 2005). The teachers in this study, representing a wide range of years of teaching experience, reported multiple routes to completion of graduate degrees. The most common approach was through part-time study and summer classes. With the master's degree becoming the standard for permanent licensure in Ohio (completion of a master's degree or 30 semester hours of graduate credit in classroom teaching and/or the area of licensure is required for the *second* renewal of a professional teacher license), the demand for master's programs is likely to increase. Music teacher education programs are responding to these needs by providing options for pursuing the master's, most notably through traditional residential programs, "summers-only" programs, and online programs. The data from the current survey are not able to confirm whether the summers-only option is becoming the favored route, however, analysis of teachers who reported that they are currently pursuing the master's indicated that 30% ($n = 23$) are doing so through a summers-only program. This compares with 18% ($n = 84$) of those already possessing the master's who reported completing the degree through this type of program.

The purported demand for more online courses and/or degree programs, as well as other distance learning options, also received some illumination through the current study. Among those who currently possess a master's degree, only 3% did so through an online approach. However, of those who reported currently pursuing their master's, 13% ($n = 10$) indicated an online program as their exclusive approach to obtaining the degree. Interestingly, of those following this approach, six reported pursuing a general education program and four reported a music education program. Further research should be conducted to confirm or deny the emergence of notable trends in the pursuit of master's degrees in music education. If online learning continues to grow, it will be important to study the approaches utilized to arrive at a set of pedagogies that will best prepare music educators for their work in classrooms.

Teachers reported that their reasons for seeking the master's degree were largely for personal satisfaction, to become a better teacher, and to earn a higher salary. With the respondents primarily being teachers with more experience, and presumably older, the master's degree was perhaps not a requirement for permanent licensure/certification when they obtained it. The recent requirement of the master's or its equivalent may explain the mixed results when respondents were asked whether they pursued the degree to maintain licensure. These older teachers' reasons for pursuing the master's would be less confounded by the technicality that it was required. Therefore, teachers who received a master's prior to its being required may have seen graduate study as professional development more than those who now see it as a credential requirement. A deeper study of this question would be needed to test this hypothesis.

Nondegree Professional Development

In a number of ways, results from this study are similar to, and often support, findings from other research regarding music teachers' motivations for pursuing professional development, preferences for approaches to professional development and professional development topics, and the need for professional development to be suited to specialized interests, curricular areas, and career stages (e.g., Bush, 2007; Conway, 2008). It was gratifying that these teachers engaged in professional development primarily to become better teachers and musicians. The reality of having to engage in professional development in order to renew their teaching license was, of course, also a primary reason for many teachers. In total, it appears that these teachers' motivation for pursuing professional development is healthy and appropriate.

Overall, professional music conferences were the most desirable professional development experience for these teachers, followed by music in-services in their school districts, and multiple-day summer workshops. In addition, the participants rated the OMEA conference as their most valuable professional development experience. The yearly professional conference in Ohio is large and offers clinic sessions and performances in all areas. Anecdotally, it has a very strong reputation both within Ohio and throughout the country for being a fine conference. Since the majority of these respondents were OMEA members, it is not surprising that they held this event in high regard. The least desirable and valued approach for these teachers was nonmusic in-services, a finding supported throughout the literature (e.g., Bush, 2007; Conway, 2008; Friederichs, 2001; Hammel, 2007; Resnick, 2005). Not surprisingly, these generic workshops are not generally seen as relevant or useful to music teachers. Most music educators desire to utilize their professional development time in ways that are clearly related to music and music pedagogy.

The participants indicated preferences for professional development closely related to their areas of specialization. This corresponds to findings by Bush (2007). It seems logical that the types of professional development appropriate for specific teaching areas and responsibilities would vary. Further study of the specific needs of band, choir, orchestra, and general-music teachers is needed.

A finding of the present study that corroborates the work of other researchers (e.g., Conway, 2008; Killian, Baker, & Johnson, 2006) concerned the differing preferences for professional development topics between new and more experienced teachers. Newer teachers rated their interest in classroom management, administrative aspects of music teaching, working with special learners, career development, and the applications of research significantly higher than more experienced teachers. It makes sense that at different stages of one's career, different professional development topics would be of greater interest and value. Yet, professional development experiences are not usually tailored to the specific needs of an individual teacher.

Non-OMEA Members

Although the small number of non-OMEA members in this study makes it difficult to arrive at any definitive conclusions, comparison of their responses with teachers who belonged to OMEA does raise some interesting questions. Many of the non-OMEA teacher perceptions mirrored those of the OMEA members; however, there were some significant differences found between the groups. Among these was the non-OMEA educators' lower perception of the value of the state's annual professional development conference. Since it is a requirement to belong to OMEA to attend the conference, perhaps that is a reason why these teachers do not belong to the association. If they perceive the ability to attend the conference as a primary benefit of being an OMEA member, an activity that they do not highly value, they may not choose to join if they feel the other membership benefits (e.g., journal subscriptions) are not worth the cost. Efforts to study further the professional development perceptions and needs of music teachers who do not belong to their primary professional association should be made.

CONCLUSIONS AND IMPLICATIONS

Those charged with developing professional development experiences for music educators, whether those experiences entail pursuit of a graduate degree or nondegree activities, must clearly consider teachers' expressed preferences for topics and modes of delivery. The data gathered in this study, when considered with results of previous research, seem to point toward some common characteristics of the professional development of music educators.

1. Teachers desire professional development that is oriented to their specific needs and areas of teaching responsibility.
2. As music educators progress through their careers, it appears their professional development requirements and interests evolve.
3. Although some nonmusic in-service meetings at the local school or district level may be necessary, in general this type of professional development is not valued (and hence, probably not too effective) and should be kept to a minimum.
4. Sustained professional development appears to have a greater impact on teaching practice than short-term sessions.

One strategy to deal with this situation would be to have teachers prepare a yearly professional growth plan that highlights their learning goals and describes the means they will use to achieve them. Teachers in Ohio do this and reported that they find it a valuable practice. Ideally, the professional growth plans would be tightly focused and oriented toward deeper levels of sustained learning about one or more topics. School administrators should then be charged with providing the resources (i.e., time and funding) to assist teachers in accomplishing their objectives. In addition, it seems that professional organizations would better serve their members, while possibly attracting individuals who are not currently members, if they periodically surveyed their constituents to ascertain if their needs were being met. Then these organizations and others who organize conferences might begin to rethink the typical conference paradigm of numerous 50-minute sessions on a smorgasbord of topics. Perhaps smaller, focused symposia that allow for more discussion-oriented, active approaches to learning that are sustained over a longer period of time would result in more meaningful in-service education, resulting in changes to teaching practice.

Researchers need to continue to examine both overall professional development issues as well as aspects of professional growth and renewal relevant to varying music teacher populations. A number of specific research topics have been suggested in the preceding discussion. Professional development in music education should be investigated through a variety of research lenses; well-designed quantitative, qualitative, and mixed-methods studies all hold the possibility of revealing unique insights into the challenge of helping teachers grow professionally. One population that is extremely underresearched at present is music educators who do not belong to a professional association such as MENC: The National Association for Music Education. How are these teachers' professional development perceptions, needs, and motivations the same or different from music teachers who are formally affiliated with other professionals? Through thoughtful consideration and continued study of this complex phenomenon by researchers, the in-service education of music educators may become more meaningful for them, ultimately benefiting the learning of their students.

REFERENCES

Bauer, W. I. (2007). Research on the professional development of experienced music teachers. *Journal of Music Teacher Education, 17*(1), 12–21. Retrieved January 4, 2008, from http://www.menc.org/mbronly/publication/JMTEFall2007.pdf

Bauer, W. I., Reese, S., & McAllister, P. A. (2003). Transforming music teaching via technology: The role of professional development. *Journal of Research in Music Education, 51*(4), 289–301.

Bowles, C. (2003, Spring-Summer). The self-expressed professional development needs of music educators. *UPDATE: Applications of Research in Music Education, 21*(2). Retrieved July 7, 2006, from http://www.menc.org/mbronly/publication/UPDATEspring03.html#7

Bush, J. E. (2007). Importance of various professional development opportunities and workshop topics as determined by in-service music teachers. *Journal of Music Teacher Education, 16*(2), 10–16.

Conway, C. M. (2008). Experienced music teacher perceptions of professional development throughout their careers. *Bulletin of the Council for Research in Music Education, 176,* 7–18.

Friedrichs, C. (2001). The effect of professional growth opportunities as determined by California public high school instrumental music teachers (Doctoral dissertation, University of San Diego, 2001). *Dissertation Abstracts International, 62* (03), 955.
Hammel, A. M. (2007, Fall). Professional development research in general education. *Journal of Music Teacher Education, 17*(1), 22–32. Retrieved January 4, 2008, from http://www.menc.org/mbronly/publication/JMTEFall2007.pdf
Hookey, M.R. (2002). Professional development. In R. Colwell & C. Richardson (Eds.), *The new handbook of research on music teaching and learning* (pp. 887–902). New York: Oxford University Press.
Killian, J. N., Baker, V. D., & Johnson, M. D. (2006). *The perceived value of professional memberships among pre-service and early-career music educators.* Poster session presented at the 60th National Biennial In-Service Conference of MENC: The National Association for Music Education, Salt Lake City, UT.
Levin, Driscoll, & Fleeter. (2005). *Condition of teacher supply and demand in Ohio—2005.* Retrieved August 15, 2007, from http://www.ode.state.oh.us/GD/DocumentManagement/DocumentDownload.aspx?DocumentID=12577
Price, H. E., & Orman, E. K. (1999). MENC national conferences, 1984–1998: A content analysis. *UPDATE: Applications of Research in Music Education, 18*(1), 26–32.
Price, H. E., & Orman, E. K. (2001). MENC 2000 national biennial in-service conference: A content analysis. *Journal of Research in Music Education, 49*(3), 227–233.
Resnick, L. B. (Ed.). (2005). Teaching teachers: Professional development to improve student achievement. *Research Points: Essential Information for Education Policy, 3,* 1–4.
Rosenthal, R. K. (2005). *The status of music teaching in Illinois.* Retrieved August 29, 2007, from http://www.ilmea.org/documents/Status_of_Music_Teaching_in_Illinois_v.1.pdf
Tarnowski, S. M., & Murphy, V. B. (2003, Fall–Winter). Recruitment, retention, retraining, and revitalization among elementary music teachers in Wisconsin and Minnesota. *UPDATE: Applications of Research in Music Education, 22*(1). Retrieved July 7, 2006, from http://www.menc.org/mbronly/publication/UPDATEFall2003.pdf

CHAPTER 7

DEVELOPING PROFESSIONAL KNOWLEDGE ABOUT MUSIC TEACHING AND LEARNING THROUGH COLLABORATIVE CONVERSATIONS

Lisa M. Gruenhagen
Hartwick College

ABSTRACT

The intent of this case study was to generate understanding about collaborative conversations among early childhood music teachers and to explore the extent to which such conversations can function as professional development for those teachers. Through ongoing participation in 11 monthly conversations consisting of 5 to 12 music teachers, a core group of teachers emerged. These teachers' perceptions of their own individual growth and how their participation in the conversations impacted that growth illustrate the importance of engaging with colleagues in collaborative work. Through sustained inquiry that fostered individual and collective growth, the group evolved from a community of learners to a community of practice. Questions raised include (a) how to best implement collaborative professional development for groups of music teachers with diverse experience and training, (b) how to encourage participation in teacher inquiry groups, and (c) what questions need to be asked about teacher beliefs and biases and how these may manifest in teaching practices.

INTRODUCTION

The term "professional development" conjures up many images in the minds of teachers and researchers alike. In the past, professional development experiences for teachers have often been organized as in-service days, workshops or classes, and other such one-time events planned and organized by someone other than practitioners. Ball and Cohen (1999) contend these events are "often intellectually superficial, disconnected from deep issues of curriculum and learning, fragmented, and noncumulative" (p. 3). Often designed by outside experts not familiar with local contexts, "teachers are thought to need updating rather than opportunities for serious and sustained learning of curriculum, students, and learning" (p. 4). More recently, researchers have been advocating professional development that in contrast is teacher centered; is situated in practice; is an ongoing process; fosters collegiality, collaborative inquiry, and critical discourse; and is linked to improving student learning (Ball & Cohen, 1999; Cochran-Smith & Lytle, 1993; Díaz-Maggioli, 2004; Nieto, 2003; Wilson & Berne, 1999).

As director of an early childhood and elementary music program at a large community music school, I provided training, mentoring, and professional development for early childhood music teachers. My goal as director was to better understand music teacher learning while at the same time provide support for this learning. The challenge I faced in this study was creating a professional development framework for a group of teachers whose background, training, skills, and experience differed greatly. To enhance teacher knowledge and improve practice, Ball and Cohen (1999) advocate changes made in useful and manageable small steps for teachers in the context of their daily work. I began by building in a time for learning new materials and for group discussion during our faculty meetings. Initially, I asked the teachers what topics they would like to see addressed in future professional development experiences at our school. Although there were a variety of responses related to pedagogical issues and children's musical development, having time to meet together to share and develop materials and to discuss issues related to their individual teaching contexts were the most requested activities.

Of particular relevance for teachers in this early childhood music program was McCotter's (2001) study that examined teacher participation and conversation in collaborative groups. Her research focused on the group, Literacy Education for a Democratic Society (LEADS), formed in response to Carole Edelsky's (1994) challenge to educators to find "communities of colleagues who want to study and support each other and change together" (p. 257). McCotter was interested in how the LEADS group might serve as professional development for the teachers who participated. Membership in this group provided the opportunity for a different kind of personal and professional growth not found in traditional staff development programs. Of added value was McCotter's discussion of her struggles and solutions in relation to her dual role as participant and researcher. McCotter's study is one of several studies from the general education literature that share a common thread of group conversations within a teacher professional community. Many of these studies also share collaborative conversations as a framework for adult learning and are grounded in theory suggesting that meaningful knowledge is socially constructed (Brookfield, 1986; Hollingsworth, 1992; Knowles, 1984; Lave & Wenger, 1991; Perkins, 2003; Vygotsky, 1978).

Grossman, Wineburg, and Woolworth (2000) participated in, and conducted research as, members of a monthly book club they formed for a group of teachers. Rust (1999) invited 15 first-year teachers and preservice teachers to join a conversation group as part of the Sustainable Teacher Learning and Research Network Project. Over the course of the year, membership grew to include 2nd-year in-service teachers. The group met regularly in the evenings for a total of 11 times to identify questions and issues related to teaching, and to provide support to one another.

Hollingsworth (1992) organized ongoing conversations for cohort teacher groups to discuss learning to teach literacy. The teachers in the cohort taught in diverse contexts, including both urban and suburban settings. Two of the teachers were doctoral students and research assistants (who shared with the researcher the responsibility of documenting the groups' process), and the others were beginning public school classroom teachers who were former students of the researcher. Hollingsworth met with these teachers once per month for dinner and conversation. Her goal was to examine teacher learning about teaching literacy and to provide a supportive structure for the development of this learning. Hollingsworth described the teachers' ongoing dialogue and discussion as "collaborative talk," which developed into "the exchange of ideas or informal and intimate conversation" (p. 375). She labeled this kind of talk "collaborative conversation" (p. 375).

"What keeps teachers going—in spite of everything?" was Nieto's (2003, p. 389) question when she organized a group of eight high school veteran teachers from the Boston Public Schools. She met with the teachers once per month throughout the year at a local school to talk about issues, to write and reflect, and to discuss books they had read. Because Nieto did not want to dictate the agenda for every meeting, and many of the teachers had questions of their own, the group agreed that each would have the opportunity to present questions or issues.

Relevant Research in Music Education

Although music education research offers no similar examples of collaborative conversations, the literature that discusses the importance of music learning for young children and the preparation of music teachers for these children helped to frame this study. In 1967 participants at the Tanglewood Symposium examined the role of music in society and education and declared the importance of music education for all ages, from preschool through adult education, and recommended that teacher education programs be expanded and improved (Mark & Gary, 1992).

In the decades following the Tanglewood Symposium, music education researchers have examined (a) how children learn and understand music, (b) why music is important in early childhood, (c) kinds of experiences that should be available for young children, and (d) curricular practices in early childhood and elementary music classrooms (Bennett, 1991, 2005; Fox, 1993, 2000, 2003; Gruenhagen, 2002, 2004, 2005; Hornbach & Taggart, 2005; Jordan-DeCarbo & Nelson, 2002; Kim, 2000; McCusker, 2001; MENC, 2000; Miranda, 2002; Neelly, 2000; Sims, 1995). Curricular recommendations and models in early childhood music parallel those found in early childhood education and indeed Fox (2003) states that "our task to 'set the sturdy stage' for a lifetime of musical learning can be informed by current research and thinking on child development" (p. 16). Music educators have also begun to address the needs of early childhood teachers by identifying the knowledge and skills these teachers require in order to be effective facilitators of children's music learning (Fox, 1993; Neelly, 1998, 2001).

MENC: The National Association for Music Education (1994) states that music is essential in early childhood and must be provided by teachers who have received training in early childhood music. Because there are no formal certification requirements for early childhood music teaching, individuals can enter the profession with little or no training or experience in child development or children's musical development. Furthermore, no degree or coursework in music education is required to teach early childhood music. Traditionally, early childhood music teacher training has not been available through formal degree programs, but many universities now offer some courses in early childhood music (Scott-Kassner, 1999). The MENC has published standards for early childhood music learning, however, a corresponding set of expectations for the people who will teach these standards has not been established.

Although music education researchers have examined preservice music teachers' learning, studies that explore issues related to the development of in-service music teachers' professional knowledge and practice are limited. Studies that have examined the personal and professional lives of in-service music teachers have looked at (a) teaching experience, knowledge, and expertise; (b) qualities of exemplary teachers; (c) mentoring and induction processes; and (d) influence of context (Conkling & Henry, 2002; Conway, 2003, 2006; Conway, Krueger, Robinson, Haack, & Smith, 2002; Hookey, 2002; Miranda, 2002; Neelly, 2000). This body of research addresses music education practice primarily from the elementary level through high school, with limited focus on early childhood music teaching. Among Neelly's (2000) recommendations for research in the area of early childhood music teacher professional development are (a) collaborative reflection among adult learners in a community, (b) focus on teachers' issues and concerns found in the context of their daily practice, and (c) viewing teachers as change agents.

PURPOSE AND QUESTIONS

The intent of this study was to generate understanding about collaborative conversations among early childhood music teachers and to explore the extent to which such conversations can function as professional development for those teachers. The primary question that guided the study was, What happens when a group of early childhood music teachers engage in collaborative professional development? The following subquestions served to narrow the focus:

1. What do the teachers want to know? Are these desires linked to particular contexts, skills, or materials?
2. How does the group choose to go about learning, particularly in terms of collaboration?
3. Do teachers believe that collaborative conversations change their music teaching practices, and if so, in what ways?
4. Do teachers believe that collaborative conversations change student learning, and if so, in what ways?

While the term "collaborative professional development" varies in definition, Darling-Hammond and McLaughlin (1995) indicate that it involves a focus on communities of practice rather than on individual teachers, and engages educators in the sharing of knowledge.

DEFINING THE CASE

For the study, a case study approach was taken. Stake (1995) identifies two types of case studies: *instrumental* and *intrinsic*. An intrinsic case study is undertaken when the researcher is interested in understanding a specific case; the case itself is the main interest. When a researcher examines a case to provide insight into an identified issue, it is an instrumental case study. Although the case is examined in depth, it serves a supportive role that facilitates understanding about an external issue. While an intrinsic case study focuses on the important characteristics of the case "within its own world," an instrumental case study shows how concerns of researchers and theorists are discernible within the case. This study followed Stake's (1995, 2000) use and definition of an instrumental case.

Setting and Participants

This community music school had one main campus and three satellite campuses located in both urban and suburban settings. The school served approximately 4,000 students, and is accredited by the National Association of Schools of Music (NASM). The early childhood music program consisted of a core program at each of the four campuses and provided music instruction for children 6 months through 7 years of age. Total enrollment at these locations was 433 children. In addition, the early childhood music program provided music classes for children at several outreach sites in disadvantaged urban neighborhoods. These programs were held in daycare, Head Start, and early learning centers. Additionally, one program was located in a Montessori preschool program housed within an urban public school. This school did not have a regular music program. A total of 386 children, 1 year through 7 years of age, were provided music instruction at these outreach locations. Funding for these programs was provided through individual or corporate grants. In addition to music classes for children, the early childhood music teachers provided professional development opportunities in music for classroom teachers at these sites.

No formal professional development program existed for the teachers in the early childhood music program, nor was a set curriculum in place. All teachers in this program were invited to participate in the study, and details of the research protocol were discussed with them prior to the start date. They were informed that participation was completely voluntary and that they were free to withdraw at any time for whatever reason, without risk of judgment or penalty. Additionally, the teachers were assured that all names would be changed to protect identities.

The teachers met monthly for 2–3 hours for a total of 11 sessions during the 2004–2005 academic year. The meetings took place after school at my home over a light meal. In total, 12 teachers participated, including myself. Three participants attended each one of the monthly sessions, two attended 10 sessions, and three participants attended once. All participants were white; eleven were female, one male; and their ages ranged from 23 to 54. The length of time these teachers had been employed ranged from 1 month to 28 years. The teachers' expertise and experience was diverse and teaching loads varied. Eleven of the teachers taught multiple classes of varying ages in multiple contexts and locations, while one teacher taught only baby classes in one location. Table 7.1 illustrates the organization of early childhood music classes at this school.

Conflicting Roles

Although the agenda for each meeting was determined by the group, I acted as facilitator when necessary and also participated in the group conversations. My dual role as program director and participant-researcher found me at times providing materials and resources prompted by what the teachers were questioning, discussing, or requesting. At other times, I responded as a teacher-colleague who was also learning from practice. Throughout the study, I carefully considered whether these roles were in conflict. It was for me, at times, uncomfortable trying to decide how much to say, and at other times, it felt completely natural for me to interact as a full participant. I revisited McCotter's (2001) discussion of her struggles with similar dual roles. In her report, she discusses the necessity of separating her "sense of belonging from the need to observe analytically, if not objectively" (p. 687), in addition to describing her concern about validity and integrity. McCotter discusses how she dealt with these concerns by recording her thoughts in a reflective journal throughout the research process and by referring to the literature for support. Her study was a reminder to question continually my interpretations of the conversations and to look critically at each situation.

TABLE 7.1 Organization of Early Childhood Music Classes

Babies	6–12 months
Toddlers	1–2 years
Toddlers	2–3 years
Preschool	3–4 years
Kindergarten	5 years
Elementary	Grades 1–2
Children's Chorus	Grades 1–3

In addition to reviewing the literature, I recorded my thoughts and memos in a journal, and revisited it throughout the study.

As the year progressed, I reflected on ways to work with and represent the group members with integrity. In previous years, several of the teachers and I had taught together in this program. Two years prior to the study, one of the teachers had been a student of mine. Hollingsworth (1992) discusses the "shift in power" she experienced when she moved from her role as instructor to developing "a process of working with them as a co-learner and creator of evolving expertise through nonevaluative conversation" (p. 375). In addition to sitting back and listening, she describes how she struggled publicly with what she was learning. Hollingsworth indicates how this shift in role transformed her own learning, as both a researcher and a teacher educator. Moreover, she notes how this role change became an important factor "in determining the success of *teachers'* knowledge transformations" (p. 375). Throughout the year, I too struggled publicly with new insights and ideas about music teaching and learning, and about conducting research. I thought carefully about how my actions might impact the teachers and subsequently, the results of the study. In addition to implementing the above measures, I came to realize that in order to find the best possible answers to my research questions, it was necessary for me to let the conversations unfold as naturally as possible, to provide and support the opportunity for meeting together, and to supply resources and participate in the conversations as appropriate.

Sources of Data

The conversations that occurred during the 11 sessions served as primary data for the study. I audiotaped and completely transcribed all sessions and took field notes during and immediately after each meeting. Conducting individual interviews at mid-year and at the end of the project provided opportunity to gather teachers' personal histories, insights, and reflections upon individual growth and changes in their teaching practice. These interviews served as additional primary data.

Artifacts can "serve as sources of rich descriptions" of how the individual who created them "thinks about their world" (Bogdan & Biklen, 1998, p. 133) and can provide insight into the person's perceptions and assumptions around situations and the meanings they place on events and processes. The teachers participating in this study did not uniformly submit these artifacts, but there were instances where teacher-created charts, handouts, and other items were presented during discussions and interviews. During my analysis, these artifacts served as secondary data.

DATA ANALYSIS

The process of analysis began early during initial data gathering and continued as data were examined and reexamined. Guided by my research questions, data analysis consisted of a systematic search for and categorization of emerging patterns and themes. In order to generate initial categories and to propose relationships among these categories, I began with microanalysis, a detailed line-by-line analysis that combines both open and axial coding. Selective coding was then employed and involved the process of integrating and refining categories. The primary goal in this process was to illustrate relationships around a central concept. I followed Strauss and Corbin's (1998) suggestions for the integration process, including writing the storyline, creating diagrams, and writing and sorting memos.

During the analysis I periodically reviewed the research about teacher learning and learning collaboratively in communities of practice (Cochran-Smith & Lytle, 1999; Hollingsworth, 1992; Nieto, 2003; Shulman, 1997; Wenger, McDermott, & Snyder, 2002). Cochran-Smith and Lytle (1999) indicate that learning through active engagement in intentional inquiry about practice involves collaboratively reassessing context, structures, and frameworks, and includes reflecting on what knowledge is necessary and what knowledge is considered expert. Goals of teachers' work together in learning communities include "understanding, articulating, and ultimately altering practice and social relationships" (p. 281) to bring about fundamental change. Moreover, Cochran-Smith and Lytle contend "when teachers who see teaching as learning and learning as teaching work together in learning communities, they link what they learn about their own learning to new visions of what can happen in classrooms" (p. 281). These findings from teacher learning research that were focused on collaborative groupings were used for theme generation in relation to the patterns emerging in my own data analysis.

Ensuring Trustworthiness

In qualitative case study research, credibility and methodological strength is ascertained through structural corroboration. In this study, I used different data collecting techniques, such as observation, audiotaping, interviewing, field notes, and teacher artifacts resulting in multiple sources of evidence from multiple participants. Additionally, member checking confirmed the accuracy of transcriptions, working theories, and tentative findings; and the researcher's critical reflections on biases or preconceptions ensure objectivity.

EMERGING THEMES

Several broad themes emerged during analysis of the data: (a) starting, and starting over; (b) searching for structure and settling on a framework; (c) understanding understanding; and (d) evolution of practice. The first theme, *starting, and starting over*, depicts how the conversations started and the ways in which they unfolded. This theme captures the somewhat recursive process used by the teachers as they visited and revisited issues and topics, and used a variety of means to examine issues through multiple activities, resources, and materials. While examining emerging perspectives about music teaching and learning in early childhood, the teachers "zoomed in" as they focused on the details and "zoomed out" to gain a broader perspective. During the fifth and sixth sessions, a core group of teachers began to emerge, remaining together for the duration of the study. The second theme, *searching for structure and settling on a framework*, illustrates the ongoing journey of the core group as they continued to search for structure in their conversations and collaborative endeavors, finally settling on a framework for a goals and objectives project. The third theme, *understanding understanding*, portrays the depth of reflection and discussion in which these teachers engaged as they moved to define understanding in the context of early childhood music teaching and learning. The fourth theme, *evolution of practice*, synthesizes the journey of the teachers and illustrates the ways in which the teachers' practice evolved. Below is a discussion of each theme in greater detail.

THEME 1: STARTING, AND STARTING OVER

Cochran-Smith and Lytle (1999) provide a framework for examining differing assumptions about teacher learning by outlining three major conceptions of teacher learning: knowledge-*for*-practice, knowledge-*in*-practice, and knowledge-*of*-practice. Knowledge-*for*-practice assumes that there is a knowledge base that teachers need to possess in order to create an effective practice. Knowledge-*in*-practice refers to practical knowledge: the knowledge that is rooted in practice and in the reflections of teachers on their practice. The assumption here is that teachers learn from inquiry that uncovers and makes explicit embedded knowledge in the practice of master teachers. In writing about knowledge-*of*-practice, Cochran-Smith and Lytle do not distinguish between formal and practical knowledge, nor do they distinguish between expert and novice teachers. They refer instead to knowledge gained through inquiry as teachers from all career stages together "generate local knowledge of practice" through their work in inquiry communities (1999a, p. 250). This perspective assumes that knowledge is socially constructed and that it draws upon the previous experience and prior knowledge of each participant. As Rogoff, Turkanis, and Bartlett (2001) state, each member in a learning community has "valuable interests, ideas, and opinions" (p. 232) and these differences can serve as resources that enhance learning opportunities.

What These Teachers Wanted To Know

The teachers in this study began their year of conversations by exploring the nature of musical children. They wanted to know how children came to be musical; what factors influenced children's musical development; and the ways in which culture, home life, and context might impact the development of musical children. The teachers also wanted to know what musical concepts and skills should be taught to young children and at what age and developmental stage such concepts and skills could be introduced. Once topics, concepts, and skills had been identified, the teachers wanted to know how to provide sequential, developmentally appropriate music instruction.

How This Group Chose To Go About Learning

Some of the teachers at the first session were meeting for the first time, so ample opportunity was provided to socialize and to get to know one another. The teachers began to share stories, and the conversation focused on the purpose of this study and ways groups of teachers engage in collaborative inquiry. In subsequent meetings the group collaboratively developed agendas. In addition to exploring teaching and learning through the teachers' stories shared at the beginning of each meeting, conversation prompts were used to guide the groups' thinking and discussion. Some of these prompts were supplied by me; others were supplied by the teachers. As a result, discussions centered on group members' videos of their music classes, the "Nine Focusing Questions for Critical Development Teams" (Díaz-Maggioli, 2004, p. 122), children's musical development charts (Campbell & Scott-Kassner, 2006), the Pre-Kindergarten Music Standards (MENC, 1994), and various curriculum-planning frameworks (Blythe & Associates, 1998; Wiggins & McTighe, 1998).

Although many of the teachers routinely told stories *from* practice, near the beginning of the year, they didn't necessarily talk *about* their music teaching practice. They told stories about places, contexts, children, classroom teachers, aides, and parents. However, after viewing videos volunteered by two of the teachers, Josh[1] and Bette, I perceived a shift in the nature of the conversations. Some individuals became more reflective and active in the conversation while others grew quieter. Targeted questions arose, topics were explored in greater depth, and conversations became more personal. Both videos showed children participating in music classes. The first video (Josh's) took place at one of the outreach sites in an inner city neighborhood, and the second video (Bette's) took place at one of the main suburban campuses. My original expectation was that the teachers would focus their attention on the children—what they were doing musically and what the teachers were doing to foster musicianship. This is not what happened. Upon viewing Josh's video (video 1 from the outreach site), the teachers focused on the impact of culture and ethnicity on children's musical development. They wanted to know about each other; they revealed details about themselves, their backgrounds, about how they learned music, and about what music means to them. The teachers talked about their families, about their own children, and how music fits into their lives. They questioned the ways in which young children learn about music; they wondered about the influence of culture, ethnicity, and family. Initially, after viewing Bette's video (video 2 from the main suburban campus), there was silence. I invited the teachers to share any thoughts they might have or to ask questions—they erupted with a multitude of questions for Bette. Rather than discussing how children come to be musical through cultural influences, as had happened after watching the first video, the teachers asked very detailed questions related to planning, sequencing, and pedagogy. Bette's video prompted the group to think carefully about developmentally appropriate practice and to reflect deeply on teaching practice and how it impacts children's learning.

After viewing the second video, Díaz-Maggioli's (2004) nine focusing questions were introduced into the conversation. Two of the questions became focal points in the discussion: "How do you teach? Why do you teach this way?" and "Is your teaching based on specific theories about learning and teaching?" (p. 122). These questions prompted several teachers to share details of their teaching practices, reflecting on joys and successes, discussing their teaching philosophies, revealing problems, and asking for advice and ideas from the members of the group. A few of the teachers became silent or attempted to refocus the conversation. Although these teachers were originally enthusiastic about the opportunity to meet together, I sensed that perhaps they were not yet completely comfortable or ready to discuss publicly certain issues or details about their teaching practices. I hoped at this point in the year they had grown to trust me, and trust the process. I also hoped that the reason they appeared uncomfortable or hesitant to share was not because I was the program director. The teachers had indicated some general dismay in the attempt to refocus the conversation. Three revealed they were upset by recent administrative changes to the school calendar. There was a concern that these changes were negatively impacting the children and their teaching. While members of the group offered support and suggested alternatives for dealing with this situation, unfortunately it was out of our hands. Although attendance had varied throughout the year due to teaching and performance schedules, family obligations, and personal choice, within the next month these teachers stopped coming to the monthly sessions. Even though I was concerned about them and their decisions to leave the group, I was obligated to honor their prerogatives to drop out of the study.

A Core Group of Teachers Emerges

About midway through the year, during the fifth and sixth sessions, a core group of teachers began to emerge. These teachers regularly attended the monthly sessions and actively participated. While every conversation was important and informative, it was during the conversations of these latter sessions that this group of teachers began to reveal themselves on a more intimate level, discovering shared insights, questions, and passions about teaching music to young children. Over time, conversations became more focused and deeply reflective. The teachers began to take more risks by telling personal stories from practice about both triumphs and disappointments. An atmosphere of camaraderie developed, and the ongoing exchange of ideas, insights, questions, and stories resulted in the development of shared agendas that drove the groups' continuing work together.

This group of teachers ranged in age from 23 to 52 years. These teachers, whose experience ranged from novice to veteran, taught in both the on-campus programs and in one or more of the outreach programs. While all possessed at least one degree in music, they did not all possess music education degrees. This group's prior experiences in professional development varied widely and did not necessarily relate to early childhood music teaching and learning. Figure 7.1 provides a brief portrait of each of the core group teachers.

THEME 2: SEARCHING FOR STRUCTURE AND SETTLING ON A FRAMEWORK

After months of participation in collaborative conversations, the focus narrowed for the core group of teachers as they began to think about what the program needed most and what would be most helpful to new early childhood music teachers. A decision was made to outline musical goals and objectives for each age level. The group wanted to create a model with accompanying

Bette
- Bachelor's degree—Music Education
- Taught 3- to 5-year olds in this study; 1 year in current position
- Former Montessori classroom teacher—grades 2–6
- Taught 1- to 5-year olds for four years in Kindermusik studio
- Taught private piano lessons

Josh
- Bachelor's degree—Performance and Music Education
- Taught 2- to 6-year olds in this study; 1½ years in current position
- Taught 2½ years in university early childhood program
- Taught private lessons for senior adult learners

Katie
- Bachelor's degree—Intercultural Studies; Completing Master's degree in Ethnomusicology
- Taught baby classes through 7-year olds in this study; 1 year in current position
- Classroom teacher since 2002 (part-time); Taught non-music classes
- Previously part-time substitute music teacher

June
- Bachelor's degree—Music Education
- Taught 2- to 4-year olds in this study; 2 years in current position
- Concurrently in 2nd year as K–6 general music teacher and music teacher for 3- to 5-year olds in Head Start program at this elementary school

Lisa
- Bachelor's degree—Performance; Master's degree—Music Education/Flute; Completing Ph.D. in Music Education at time of this study
- Early childhood program director in this study
- Taught early childhood music classes since 1992
- Served as early childhood program director for two community music schools
- Taught elementary general music for 6 years
- Additional experiences include university teaching, work with Project Zero and WIDE World (Wide-scale Interactive Development for Educators)

Figure 7.1 Core teacher group portraits.

resources and materials that would support teachers in their planning while also educating themselves about developmentally appropriate early childhood music practice. The early stages in trying to create such a model found the core group brainstorming and webbing—recording, comparing, and connecting ideas on chart paper, around the question, "What do early childhood music teachers need to know and be able to do?" Two charts resulted from this activity and served as a reference when outlining musical goals and objectives. Having decided to begin working on one age level and the corresponding goals, objectives, and lessons for a series of fall session classes, the group examined and discussed several frameworks and templates familiar to them. These included the

Pre-K Music Standards (MENC, 1994), the developmental charts developed by Campbell & Scott-Kassner (2006), the Backward Design Method (Wiggins & McTighe, 1998), and the Teaching for Understanding Framework (Blythe & Associates, 1998). For future collaborative lesson planning, the group chose the Teaching for Understanding Framework (TfU), and utilized the TfU brainstorming chart (Blythe & Associates, 1998) as a guide in the remaining discussions. In addition to being attracted to the flexibility of the TfU framework, the group was drawn to the online curriculum planning tools and support materials that could be utilized collaboratively.

THEME 3: UNDERSTANDING UNDERSTANDING

Throughout the final conversations, primarily the 7th through 10th sessions, the core group engaged in deep collaborative reflection and thinking about the stages of children's musical development, what it means for a young child to show understanding, and what that understanding looks like. Through the telling of stories about practice and musical children, the teachers zoomed in to examine the details of children's musical understanding and zoomed out to obtain a broader perspective. The group was able to outline broad program goals modeled on the Pre-Kindergarten music standards in an effort to define understanding in the context of early childhood music teaching and learning. These storytelling experiences allowed the group to build shared meaning that enhanced understanding about sequencing, practice, context, and children's musical development. Although the model was not finished by year's end, simply because time ran out, the ongoing experience of meeting together and engaging in sustained reflection and dialogue over time moved these teachers from talk to action. The group evolved from a community of learners to a community of practice.

THEME 4: EVOLUTION OF PRACTICE

Evolution of practice as it relates to the core group of teacher-learners can be analyzed on two levels: (a) evolution of individual teacher practice, and (b) evolution of the collective group from a community of learners to a community of practice. In both cases, changes resulted from teacher learning through sustained participation in the collaborative conversations.

Evolution of Individual Teacher Practice

Research in adult education and in professional development strongly supports participation in collaborative context based learning and inquiry opportunities. This research shares a common guiding premise that teachers are capable of creating their own powerful learning opportunities when working together to problem solve around education related issues (Ball & Cohen, 1999; Cochran-Smith & Lytle, 1993; Rust, 1999; Shulman, 1997). Indeed, the teachers in this study created powerful learning experiences as they gathered together and began to tell their stories of practice. Clandinin and Connelly (1995) explain that although classrooms offer teachers privacy and a safe place to "live the stories of practice," these stories essentially remain secret stories, with the classroom becoming "a place of endless, repetitive, living out of stories without possibility for awakenings and transformations" (p. 13).

It is through the stories of practice that we begin to understand the uncertainty, unpredictability, and complexity of life in a classroom. We also begin to understand the cognitive demands placed upon teachers who must respond to and act within this dynamic system. Borko, Liston, and Whitcomb (2007) describe teaching as "a series of many choices—some predictable, some pivotal" (p. 266). They contend that teachers must be prepared "to perceive and interpret the wide variation that typifies teaching and learning situations and to manage the dilemmas that arise" (p. 266). In examining the complexities of teaching and learning, Shulman (1997) asks, "What makes teaching so difficult? How do teachers learn to manage, cope with, and eventually master those difficulties? What forms of school reform can contribute to creating the conditions for teacher learning?" (p. 505).

To understand more clearly each individual teacher's evolution of practice and to portray collectively their perceptions of their own growth and how their participation in the conversations had an impact on that growth, I have relied on Shulman's (1997) "five principles of effective and enduring learning" (p. 513) for discussion. The five principles are (a) activity, (b) reflection, (c) collaboration, (d) passion, and (e) community or culture.

Principle 1: Activity.

Authentic and enduring learning occurs when the teacher is an active agent in the process—not passive, not an audience, not a client or a collector. Teacher learning becomes more active through experimentation and inquiry, as well as through writing, dialogue, and questioning. (Shulman, 1997, p. 514)

Shulman suggests that schools must provide teachers with the kinds of opportunities and support necessary for becoming actively involved in inquiry and investigation into their own teaching and learning. Ball and Cohen (1999) indicate that "a practice-based curriculum" for teachers' professional learning

could be compelling for teachers and would help them to improve students' learning. If such teaching, and learning how to do it, became the object of continuing, thoughtful inquiry, much of teachers' everyday work could become a source for constructive professional development. (p. 6)

Through ongoing active participation in the conversations, Josh was prompted to make changes in his practice:

> I changed my practice after hearing comments of other teachers. That was something that could have never been planned unless I went to a specific workshop on setting up tonality. And here are some colleagues that I *work* with... no one told me I had to do this or that, it was after hearing the comment—it was able to provide a different perspective on things. (Interview, 7/26/04)

Katie, a 1st-year music teacher, valued the feedback she received from the group and implemented many of their ideas and materials in her own teaching practice. Although she recognized the value of sharing and discussing broad ideas during the earlier discussions, she believed the final conversations in which the core group worked specifically on outlining musical goals and objectives were most meaningful. Katie indicated that everything in her teaching practice routinely changed over the course of the year, making it difficult for her to separate her learning experiences. For her, the conversations wove together as she continually constructed new knowledge about early childhood music teaching and learning.

Participating in the collaborative conversations caused June to think more deeply about her lesson plans and to consider more carefully her goals. She explained that in addition to obtaining many new materials and resources, she also realized the impact teacher demeanor has on young children's learning. After viewing Josh and Bette's videos, June thought about the ways in which she carried herself in her own classroom and began to incorporate new modeling strategies gleaned from those video segments.

Principle 2: Reflection. Activity alone, however, will not result in learning. Learning and understanding require reflection upon what one is doing and why. Teachers need opportunities that support ongoing individual and collaborative reflection on their work. As June recalled after the first session:

> I remember feeling really bad after the first one, well, not in a bad way, in a good way. I felt bad because I think I felt intimidated a little bit. And I also felt, *challenged*, as a teacher, because people would give these great ideas, and I'd be like "Oh, *man*, I'm not doing *that* in my classroom," or "Oh, I *wish* I was doing *that*" and I felt bad in *that* kind of a way, but it was in a *good* way because it made me *think*. (Conversation, 7/11/05)

Participating in the conversations was for her a reminder "about *why* she teaches." Each conversation was "like reflection renewal, constant renewal" that encouraged her to voice her views, to define her views, and to evaluate continually what she was doing, and why (Interview, 4/20/04). Recognizing and responding to the difficult questions about practice requires reflection, honesty, flexibility, and courage to make one's practice public. But these questions are necessary if early childhood music teachers are going to develop and improve their practice and better support and develop children's musical understanding. Nieto (2003) states:

> If teachers are to develop as intellectuals, having to engage in what may be disquieting dialogue is a part of the price to be paid. In the end, this kind of dialogue (what Cochran-Smith describes as "hard talk") is a prerequisite both for developing the intellectual community that is desperately needed in schools and for imagining different possibilities for teachers and their students. (p. 79)

Katie recognized the importance of being able to talk with other teachers about her teaching practice. She valued the opportunity to ask questions and the "kind of play off each other" that happened when her colleagues discussed everyday issues and shared concerns (Interview, 7/30/05). Bette also highlighted this interplay between group members as an important aspect of her own learning:

> I know at one point I had to take time out from listening to exactly what the rest were saying to *think in my own head* how I was perceiving that word and how I wanted to describe it to them... it's been a long time since I was a *thinker* like that. (Interview, 9/9/05)

She valued the ways in which the conversations challenged her thinking and caused her to reflect more deeply on her practice. Answering the group's questions about her teaching video required Bette to describe her procedure in detail and to provide a rationale for her choices. Engaging in this kind of individual and collaborative reflection on her work caused her to focus closely on her yearlong goals and on planning developmentally appropriate procedures within her lessons.

Josh appreciated the thinking time that the conversations provided and described this experience as a true "meeting of minds":

> There's a certain part of me that needs that intellectual thinking about teaching, to be satisfied... it's important to *have that*... and it's important to really *think* about what's going on. It makes me feel *good* about teaching and trying to figure stuff out. (Interview, 7/26/05)

June echoed Josh's views, revealing her perceptions on the value of collaborative reflection:

Anytime you're forced to *voice* your views, well not forced, but you have an *opportunity* to voice your views in front of others, it causes you to actually define what they *are*... and when you work with others, *your* experience is *so enriched* because of everybody's different backgrounds and different experiences and different situations... they *bring* that to the table, and what the *group produces* is deeper than what you could have produced on your own.... (Interview, 2/23/06)

Principle 3: Collaboration. Shulman (1997) states, "There are difficult intellectual and professional challenges that are nearly impossible to accomplish alone but are readily addressed in the company of others" (p. 515). Collaboration supports active and reflective learning. When teachers have opportunities to work together, they provide scaffolding and support for each other's learning that enhances individual and collective professional knowledge. During one conversation, June said to Bette:

I took *your* staff thing... from the owls last time... I used that a lot, how you explained the staff... and I never just said, "*Look at this*" and talked about the lines and the spaces. Now I use that in my elementary school too... and I just talk to them... take it that step back, to say okay, "What are *they* seeing...." (Conversation, 7/11/05)

Katie described the value of multiple perspectives when problem solving around issues related to teaching and learning:

When you talk to other people you might get five or six [perspectives] and it might be *exactly* the point that you *need* to be going from... it *changes* you whenever you hear somebody else looking at something a different way... and it just *changes* the way that you *teach* and it also just expands the things that you have access to as far as making learning a good experience for those children. (Interview, 4/25/05)

Josh also believed the diverse perspectives that emerged during the conversations were valuable for him in his planning. I asked him if he had changed anything in his practice based on an event that might have happened or ideas that had been discussed during the conversations. He replied:

Yeah, I did think about setting up the key with my kids. Watching that videotape was like, "Yeah, I need to get these kids to sing and sing better with the pitch." It makes you think about, tune into something, that I didn't necessarily think about... when *I* was looking at that activity. I was thinking more about the improvisational nature of things, where someone else would think about the singing aspect of it... and it was like, *yeah,* I can incorporate, I can work on another mode of music-making with improvisation *and* the singing part, and let's see if we can't get that. (Interview, 3/30/05)

He indicated that he became more directed in his planning, attempting to meet more closely the children where they are at musically and developmentally. Josh began to focus more on concepts he would teach rather than just on obtaining materials and resources. He believed that his classes flowed better because of the conversations about sequencing, pacing, and strategies for working with diverse groups of children in multiple contexts. Josh indicated that through the conversations and the telling of stories from practice, he had learned how to "think differently about things" (Interview, 7/26/05). He now felt better equipped to plan his lessons because he could draw from the multiple perspectives offered by his colleagues.

Principle 4: Passion. Shulman (1997) acknowledges the "significant emotional and affective component" (p. 515) found in collaborative work. He indicates that authentic and enduring learning occurs when there is a shared passion for the material; when those involved commit to the ideas, processes, and actions of the group; and when they view the work in connection with current and future goals. June recognized and appreciated shared feelings among the group members:

> I just learned that some of things that *I* struggle with or that *I* desire, things about like, wanting a curriculum and wanting things to be sequential across the year, that those are important to *other* people too. (Interview, 2/23/06)

Bette remarked on the commitment of other group members: "I remember June saying, the one time she decided she *wasn't* able to come, she regretted it *so* much" (Interview, 9/9/05). And Josh described what this collaborative professional development experience meant to him:

> Sharing of ideas, sharing of experiences... you can talk about it, and you start thinking about things while you're verbalizing it, and then you can get feedback... the sharing of teaching... I think that a lot comes out when you share in the planning of something... and doing it in this way that is positively supporting, that is the *best* way. (Interview, 3/30/05)

Principle 5: Community or Culture. In a community, learning processes such as "activity, reflection, emotion, and collaboration" (Schulman, 1997, p. 515) are supported, legitimated, nurtured, and valued. Shulman indicates communities that embrace these principles create structures "that reduce the labor intensity of the activities needed to engage in the most daunting practices that lead to teaching and learning" (p. 515). Through her ongoing participation, June came to understand better the schools' contexts, feeling more informed and connected:

Being somebody who is only at [this school] one day a week, one of the *best* things I've learned is learning more about the climate of the school from the teachers. Because I think if you understand the school's climate and understand the student population, then it's easier to be able to meet their needs. And talking with those other teachers and things that they experience and things that they struggle with and like, feeling that it's okay if I feel those things too... that helped me learn a lot. (Interview, 2/23/06)

Katie believed the conversations provided a valuable opportunity to meet outside the work environment in a setting that supported "a different way of relating to people" (Interview, 7/30/05). Bette learned that her colleagues were open to new ideas and that early childhood music teachers often face similar challenges. She admired the dedication and perseverance of the other teachers, valuing their perspectives and feeling re-energized through her ongoing work with them.

To a Community of Practice

Wenger, McDermott, and Snyder (2002) define communities of practice as "groups of people who share a concern, a set of problems, or a passion about a topic, and who deepen their knowledge and expertise in this area by interacting on an ongoing basis" (p. 4). They indicate that people in communities of practice do not necessarily work with each other everyday, but find value in meeting together. Over time they begin to "share information, insight, and advice" and reflect on "common issues, explore ideas, and act as sounding boards" (p. 5). Together they may create tangibles such as "tools, standards, manuals, or other documents" (p. 5), but the group may also be content with conversations that merely lead to shared understandings. Wenger, McDermott, and Snyder also indicate that members of communities of practice "become informally bound by the value that they find in learning together," which supports their work and provides "personal satisfaction of knowing colleagues who understand each other's perspectives" (p. 5). June's perception about her membership in this community reflects these findings:

I'm really excited about it because, I mean, working in a public school—and I do get collaboration with other *elementary* school teachers, but trying to relate some of those ideas to *early childhood* is *so* hard because they don't *know* the things that I see and how different developmentally they are... so I'm really excited to be able to bounce ideas back with people who understand where I'm coming from. (Conversation, 11/15/04)

Additionally, Wenger, McDermott, and Snyder suggest that over time, the group develops "a unique perspective on their topic as well as a body of common knowledge, practices, and approaches" (p. 5). After observing Bette's teaching video, June described how she took one of the activities and adapted it for her own context:

> Another thing was Bette had a 2-line staff... I used the 2-line *staff* and concept of high vs. low—I could see that... it was so much *easier* for them to sing high and sing low and to recognize the difference. If I would try and have them, comparing high and low notes, playing like a kind of high and low game, they were quicker at it after *seeing* it. That was one way I saw my students improve. (Interview, 2/23/06)

Finally, Wenger, McDermott, and Snyder describe the knowledge of experts as an "accumulation of experience—a kind of 'residue' of their actions, thinking, and conversations—that remains a dynamic part of their ongoing experience" (p. 9). They refer to this type of knowledge as a "living process," as opposed to "a static body of information" (p. 9). They suggest that in order "to develop such expertise, practitioners need opportunities to engage with others who face similar situations" (p. 9). During the final session, Josh began an exchange that illustrates the importance of engaging with colleagues through collaborative work, and in particular, through *talk*:

> **Josh:** ...in learning how to think about your teaching... you can learn through your psychology classes all these philosophies, and then you get in a group like this... you sit around the table and you hear like four, five different ideas about how someone *else* is actually thinking about it—you kind of learn that it's not just a theory... like when we were chatting the *last* time, it took us awhile to *arrive* at an understanding, but eventually we did... and that just happened by *talking*...
>
> **June:** Yes, that was of my favorite moments from all of these discussions because it made me think so much, and it changed the way I think about kids, and how they learn.
>
> **Lisa:** ...we were talking, Bette, about something similar to that earlier, about *thinking* differently when we're here, or having the opportunity to just think *with* other people.
>
> **Josh:** ...definitely more of a *focused* time.
>
> **Bette:** ...mmhmm... this is *much* more reflective, where we have the time to actually let it play around in our brains a little bit...
>
> **June:** It's not a time where we're thinking, "Oh, *what* am I gonna teach next week," but "How can I best learn from other people" and "How can I *grow* from these other experiences." (Conversation, 7/11/05)

CONCLUSIONS

In this study my intent was to provide opportunity and support for teachers in the early childhood music program to meet together and to explore the extent to which collaborative conversations might serve as professional development. I believe the core group teachers experienced meaningful growth and found value in participating in ongoing conversations that were situated in local practice. At the conclusion of this study, questions remain about issues related to participation, organization, and implementation. I still wonder about how best to implement collaborative professional development with groups of early childhood music teachers whose backgrounds, experience, training, and teaching assignments vary so greatly. I wonder how those teachers who have not experienced publicly shared feedback might be encouraged to participate in inquiry groups with colleagues. What constitutes a safe environment for those teachers and what would encourage them to stay? Upon reflection of my dual role as participant and researcher, I wonder who should serve as facilitator and what kind of experience and training this persons needs. Would it be advantageous for members of the group to share facilitator responsibilities? Guskey (1995) reminds me that one size does not fit all and "there will be a collection of answers, each specific to a context" (p. 117). Educational contexts are dynamic, therefore "the optimal mix for a particular context evolves over time, changing as various aspects of the context change" (p. 117).

Teachers in this study posed important questions about children's musical development, pedagogical issues, and developmentally appropriate practice. The early childhood music profession perhaps could benefit from collaborative reflection on the existing Pre-Kindergarten music standards to determine a corresponding set of expectations for teachers who might use these standards. Because of extensive discussion among the group of teachers, I wonder to what extent the Pre-Kindergarten music standards are sufficient in providing a clear framework for early childhood music teachers? After viewing Josh and Bette's teaching videos, questions about culture, ethnicity, ability, musical behaviors, and pedagogy arose. What can we measure and know about musical children and how they come to be musical? How do we accommodate children from homes and backgrounds that may have different musical models? What questions do we need to ask ourselves about our own beliefs and biases, and how these may manifest in our teaching practices? What do we need to change in our teaching practices in order to teach these diverse groups of children?

Although this study dealt with a small sample of teachers from one community music school, I believe the findings and the questions these findings engender could be relevant for those in any type of early childhood music setting or teacher education program. Indeed, several of the teachers in this study taught at other community music schools and in public-school settings. They indicated that what they learned through participating in these collaborative conversations could be applied or adapted to other contexts. Continuing to document teachers' stories about practice, their perceptions about their own learning, about their thinking processes, and about their students' learning would result in rich portraits of contextualized learning. Portraits such as these could provide needed windows into the dynamic and complex world of music teaching and learning.

REFERENCES

Ball, D. L., & Cohen, D. K. (1999). Developing practice, developing practitioners: Toward a practice-based theory of professional education. In L. Darling-Hammond & G. Sykes (Eds.), *Teaching as the learning profession: Handbook of policy and practice* (pp. 3–32). San Francisco: Jossey-Bass.

Bennett, P. D. (2005). So, why sol-mi? *Music Educators Journal, 91*(3), 43–49.

Blythe, T., & Associates (1998). *The teaching for understanding guide.* San Francisco: Jossey-Bass.

Bogdan, R. C., & Biklen, S. K. (1998). *Qualitative research for education: An introduction to theory and methods.* Needham Heights, MA: Allyn & Bacon.

Borko, H., Liston, D., & Whitcomb, J. (2007). Conversations that renew. *Journal of Teacher Education, 58*(4), 263–268.

Brookfield, S. D. (1986). *Understanding and facilitating adult learning.* San Francisco: Jossey-Bass.

Campbell, P. S., & Scott-Kassner, C. (2006). *Music in childhood: From preschool through the elementary grades.* Boston: Cengage Learning.

Clandinin, D. J., & Connelly, F. M. (1995). *Teachers' professional knowledge landscapes.* New York: Teachers College Press.

Cochran-Smith, M., & Lytle, S. L. (1993). *Inside/outside: Teacher research and knowledge.* New York: Teachers College Press.

Cochran-Smith, M., & Lytle, S. L. (1999). Relationships of knowledge and practice: Teacher learning in communities. In A. Iran-Nejad & P. D. Pearson (Eds.), *Review of research in education 24* (pp. 249–305). Washington, DC: American Educational Research Association.

Conkling, S. W., & Henry, W. (2002). The impact of professional development partnerships: Our part of the story. *Journal of Music Teacher Education, 11*(2), 7–13.

Conway, C. M. (2003). *Great beginnings for music teachers: A guide to mentoring and induction.* Reston, VA: Music Educators National Conference.

Conway, C. M. (2006). Navigating through induction: How a mentor can help. *Music Educators Journal, 92*(5), 56–60.

Conway, C., Krueger, P., Robinson, M., Haack, P., & Smith, M. V. (2002). Beginning music teacher induction and mentor policies: A cross-state perspective. *Arts Education Policy Review, 104*(2), 9–17.

Creswell, J. W. (1994). *Research design: Qualitative and quantitative approaches.* Thousand Oaks, CA: Sage.
Darling-Hammond, L., & McLaughlin, M. W. (1995). Policies that support professional development in an era of reform. *Phi Delta Kappan, 76*(8), 597–603.
Díaz-Maggioli, G. (2004). *Teacher-centered professional development.* Alexandria, VA: Association for Supervision and Curriculum Development.
Fox, D. B. (1993). The music education of early childhood majors: All God's critters got a place in the choir. *The Quarterly Journal of Music Teaching and Learning, 4*(1), 27–35.
Fox, D. B. (2000). Music and the baby's brain: Early experiences. *Music Educators Journal, 87*(2), 23–28.
Fox, D. B. (2003). Music in early childhood: Setting a sturdy stage. *Orff Echo, 35*(2), 16–19.
Grossman, P., Wineburg, S., & Woolworth, S. (2000). What makes teacher community different from a gathering of teachers? Retrieved April 29, 2005, from http://ctpweb.org
Gruenhagen, L. M. (2002, April). *Creative problems in the elementary general music classroom: Engaging children in musical problem finding and problem-solving.* Unpublished manuscript.
Gruenhagen, L. M. (2004, March). *Music and the growing child: A powerful role, an essential ingredient.* Unpublished manuscript.
Gruenhagen, L. M. (2005, November). *Reflective practice in the elementary music classroom: An emerging picture of children's musical understanding.* Paper presented at the Conference on Music Learning and Teaching of the Center for Applied Research in Musical Understanding (CARMU), Rochester, MI.
Guskey, T. R. (1995). Professional development in education: In search of the optimal mix. In T. R. Guskey & M. Huberman (Eds.), *Professional development in education: New paradigms and practices* (pp. 117–131). New York: Teachers College Press.
Hollingsworth, S. (1992). Learning to teach through collaborative conversation: A feminist approach. *American Educational Research Journal, 29*(2), 373–404.
Hookey, M. R. (2002). Professional development. In R. Colwell & C. P. Richardson (Eds.), *The new handbook of research on music teaching and learning* (pp. 887–902). New York: Oxford University Press.
Hornbach, C. M., & Taggart, C. C. (2005). The relationship between developmental tonal aptitude and singing achievement among kindergarten, first-, second-, and third-grade students. *Journal of Research in Music Education, 53*(4), 322–331.
Jordan-DeCarbo, J., & Nelson, J. (2002). Music and early childhood education. In R. Colwell & C. P. Richardson (Eds.), *The new handbook of research on music teaching and learning* (pp. 210–242). New York: Oxford University Press.
Kim, J. (2000). Children's pitch matching, vocal range, and developmentally appropriate practice. *Journal of Research in Childhood Education, 14*(2), 152–160.
Knowles, M. (1984). *Andragogy in action: Applying modern principles of adult education.* San Francisco: Jossey Bass.
Lave, J., & Wenger, E. (1991). *Situated learning: Legitimate peripheral participation.* New York: Cambridge University Press.

Little, J. W. (2003). Inside teacher community: Representation of classroom practice. *Teachers College Record, 105*(6), 913–945.

Mark, M. L., & Gary, C. L. (1992). *A history of American music education.* New York: Schirmer.

May, W. T. (1993). *A summary of the findings in art and music: Research traditions and implications for teacher education* (Elementary Subjects Center Series No. 88). East Lansing, MI: Center for the Learning and Teaching of Elementary Subjects. (ERIC Document Reproduction Service No. ED360247)

McCotter, S. (2001). Collaborative groups as professional development [Electronic version]. *Teaching and Teacher Education, 17,* 685–704.

McCusker, J. (2001). Emerging musical literacy: Investigating young children's music cognition and musical problem-solving through invented notations (Doctoral dissertation, University of Rochester, Eastman School of Music, 2001). *Dissertation Abstracts International, 62*(02A), 504.

Miranda, M. (2002). The seasons of kindergarten: Developmentally appropriate practice in the kindergarten music classroom (Doctoral dissertation, Arizona State University, 2002). *Dissertation Abstracts International, 63*(11A), 3889.

MENC. (1994). *The school music program: A new vision.* Reston, VA: Music Educators National Conference.

MENC. (2000). Start the music: A report from the early childhood music summit. Retrieved May 24, 2002, from http://www.menc.org/guides/startmusic/stm-report.htm

Neelly, L. P. (2000). Collaborative early childhood music practice: A year in the life of a pre-kindergarten music teacher (Doctoral dissertation, University of Rochester, Eastman School of Music, 2000). *Dissertation Abstracts International, 61*(03A), 927.

Nieto, S. (2003). *What keeps teachers going?* New York: Teachers College Press.

Perkins, D. P. (2003). *King Arthur's round table: How collaborative conversations create smart organizations.* Hoboken, NJ: John Wiley & Sons.

Rogoff, B., Turkanis, C. G., & Bartlett, L. (Eds.). (2001). *Learning together: Children and adults in a school community.* New York: Oxford University Press.

Rust, F. (1999). Professional conversations: New teachers explore teaching through conversation, story, and narrative [Electronic version]. *Teaching and Teacher Education, 15,* 367–380.

Scott-Kassner, C. (1999). Developing teachers for early childhood programs. *Music Educators Journal 86*(1), 19–25.

Shulman, L. S. (1997). Professional development: Learning from experience. In S. M. Wilson (2004) (Ed.), *The wisdom of practice: Essays on teaching, learning, and learning to teach* (pp. 503–520). San Francisco: Jossey-Bass.

Sims, W. (Ed.). (1995). *Strategies for pre-kindergarten music teaching.* Reston, VA: Music Educators National Conference.

Stake, R. E. (1995). *The art of case study research.* Thousand Oaks, CA: Sage.

Stake, R. E. (2000). Case studies. In N. K. Denzin & Y. S. Lincoln (Eds.), *Handbook of qualitative research* (pp. 435–454). Thousand Oaks, CA: Sage.

Strauss, A., & Corbin, J. (1998). *Basics of qualitative research: Techniques and procedures for developing grounded theory.* Thousand Oaks, CA: Sage.

Vygotsky, L. S. (1978). *Mind in society: The development of higher psychological processes.* Cambridge, MA: Harvard University Press.

Wenger, E., McDermott, R., & Snyder, W. M. (2002). *Cultivating communities of practice: A guide to managing knowledge.* Boston: Harvard Business School Press.

Wiggins, G., & McTighe, J. (1998). *Understanding by design.* Alexandria, VA: Association for Supervision and Curriculum Development.

Wilson, S. M., & Berne, J. (1999). Teacher learning and the acquisition of professional knowledge: An examination of research on contemporary professional development. In A. Iran-Nejad & P. D. Pearson (Eds.), *Review of research in education 24* (pp. 249–305). Washington, DC: American Educational Research Association.

NOTE

1. All names have been changed.

CHAPTER 8

NOTES FOR A MOMENT IN MUSIC EDUCATION RESEARCH

Sandra L. Stauffer
Arizona State University

This invited chapter presents Sandra Stauffer's thoughts and perspectives on Chapters 2 through 7 of this volume, which she has situated in the broad landscape of research in music education.

> *The vigorous branching of life's tree, and not the accumulating valor of mythical marches to progress, lies behind the persistence and expansion of organic diversity in our tough and constantly stressful world.*
> —Gould, 2003, p. 331

Biology may seem an odd place to begin. What possible relevance does a quote from a paleontologist, even one as respected as Stephen Jay Gould, have for readers of music education research, for music educators in general, or for those sympathetic others who value arts experiences in the lives of young people and may be interested in what the authors in this volume have to say? Look again. Gould points his readers to one of the principles of contemporary biological studies: Diversity is crucial to the health of ecosystems, and healthy ecosystems produce diversity—vigorously, unpredictably, persistently.

Research Perspectives: Thought and Practice in Music Education, pages 153–169
Copyright © 2009 by Information Age Publishing
All rights of reproduction in any form reserved.

Diversity is one of the themes underlying the research collected in this volume, and diversity here is not simply a matter of varied research methodologies (though that is indeed a strength). Whether obliquely or directly, whether as a caution or conclusion, each author points to the notion that "no one size fits all"—in professional development of teachers, in the perceptions and beliefs of preservice educators, in the policies of professional organizations and the perspectives of those who study children and music, in models used to explore matters as diverse as the motivation of students in high school band or the spontaneous singing of preschool children. From our multiple perspectives as researchers, musicians, and educators, we might well conclude, as Gould does in another essay, that "variation stands out as the only meaningful reality" (1996, p. 45).

And yet, "diversity" is a curious word, or at least a word used in curious ways by English-speaking humans. Frankly, we seem a bit suspicious of diversity. Perhaps as a matter of longstanding mental habit that tends toward Platonic dualisms, "diversity" appears with "unity" in the writings of scholars in biology, multicultural education, religious studies, medicine, sociology, anthropology, and linguistics. For example, "unity in diversity" is the unofficial motto of the European Union (and a pervasive phrase in political science writings). "Unity of purpose, diversity of means" is a prominent theme in articles about quality health care (see, for example, Donabedian, 1988). We celebrate diversity, yet wish to mediate it with cohesion. We respect diversity, but want to temper it with solidarity. We consider diversity a strength, yet worry about fractionalization. At worst, we ignore diversity altogether and valorize unity under the banner of standardization, and standardization (where one size does fit all) as progress. But Gould warns us, from his biological perspective: Diversity is organic, vigorous, unstoppable, and at least a more natural state of affairs than "the accumulating valor of mythical marches to progress."

What to make of this diversity-unity conundrum, and how does it apply to music, education, and research? Diversity in the arts springs from human creativity, and our creativity appears boundless. Music making seems more richly varied every day. Similarly, the forms and formats of schooling grow increasingly diverse, even in an era when the politics and policies of education point toward types of standardization that worry and weary us. And while there may be trouble at the intersection of music, education, and policy ("Yes," a school arts administrator told me, "it would be great to have more kinds of music courses, but would they meet 'the standards'?"), music education is more varied now than it has ever been. In fact, the future of music education depends on diversity (Kratus, 2007). What connects musicians and educators, amidst variation and change, are commitments to the value and meaning of music making and to working for and with learners of all ages to create "genuinely educational and aesthetic[1] experiences" in the arts (Barone, 2007, p. 243).

And here, at the intersection of diverse practices and common purposes, the music education research community, with its array of epistemological perspectives, theoretical frames, and methodological means, seems poised on the brink of a particularly interesting moment.[2] It is not the moment of the "fractured future" that Lincoln and Denzin predict in the concluding chapter of their most recent research handbook; Lincoln and Denzin worry that "A world in which [different research methodology] sides might be heard, and the results carefully considered as differently produced and differently purposed views on social realities, now seems somewhat far away, mixed-methods advocates notwithstanding" (2005, p. 1123). Rather the editors of this volume accept diversity—of/in research *and* practice—as strength, and in doing so, they point to possibilities and potentials for the future.

Here, the editors place side by side two very different studies of professional development among in-service music educators. In these pages, readers of literature about music and young children will find three articles, each from a different inquiry perspective, that speak to their interests and merit their attention. Imagine the possibilities of placing two different kinds of studies of motivation of high school musicians alongside the one that appears in this book.

The moment this volume seems to presage is one of leveraging the strength found in a diverse music education research community already engaged in simultaneous and sometimes parallel inquiry by *publishing methodologically and theoretically diverse studies focused on a single facet of music and/in education side by side*, and then surrounding them with essays that connect to practice and inform policy. While it might seem that the music education research community has already traveled this path (certain symposium proceedings and research anthologies come to mind), the extant precedents are either not as theoretically and methodologically diverse, or not as focused on one facet of music and education, or not as diverse and focused *simultaneously* as what might be achieved.

What questions would arise, what assumptions might be questioned, how might music education researchers inform and challenge each other by publishing in one volume a collection of theoretically and methodologically diverse studies that interrogate, for example, improvisation practices among teenagers in various musical settings, or adult motivations for participating in community ensembles, or beginning string students' playing abilities, or thornier matters such as race and secondary school ensembles? Imagine, too, the ways in which a few surrounding essays or commentaries, perhaps written for a broader audience than the music education research community, might connect to and inform practitioners, policymakers, and the public. Such a project seems aligned with what Lincoln and Denzin (2005) describe as an ethic among researchers that is "communitarian, egalitarian, democratic, critical, caring, engaged, performative, social justice oriented"—an ethic in which researchers are increasingly conscious of their "responsibility and obligation to participants, to respondents, to consumers of research, and to themselves" (pp. 1117–1118).

Leveraging the strength and maturity of a music education research community composed of vibrant and independent scholars by drawing together different kinds of inquiry focused on singular or similar questions, problems, or phenomena in music and education may be a worthy project for this moment (if it is a "moment") in our history. It is not an unproblematic project, however, and one of the more vexing problems may be: Where to begin? Our possibility may be to consider where the diverse epistemologies, theoretical frames, and methodological means of the research community intersect (or do not) with some of the commonplaces[3] of music education: music practices, pedagogies, people, and place.

MUSICAL PRACTICES

Our surrounding musical universe seems to us multifaceted and immensely complex.
—Reck, Slobin, & Titon, 2001, p. 277

There seems little doubt that the "multifaceted and immensely complex" array of human musical practices, taken together, constitutes what might be described as a universal phenomenon of human musical experience. Children's singing is one practice—a pervasive practice—among many in the universe of music experience, and children's singing practices have attracted attention from diverse quarters of the research community. In this book, Whiteman's ethnographic study of children's singing and his analysis of the types, functions, and features of children's spontaneous songs provides one example of inquiry focused on this particular music making practice. There are many more. For although the study of children's musical practices is a relatively recent phenomenon (Barrett, 2003; Campbell, 2007), the diversity of research perspectives put to use in the study of children's singing is notable.

For example, scholars have investigated children's singing games on playgrounds and in other contexts (e.g., Marsh, 1995; Riddell, 1990), the ways in which children transmit their singing cultures to each other (e.g., Corso, 2003; Harwood, 1998), children's perspectives of their own musical practices, including singing (Campbell, 1998), and children's experiences of singing in their families (Custodero, 2006). Focusing on the ability through which children engage in this particular musical practice, other scholars have examined the development of children's singing voices and skills (e.g., Welch, 1985; Welch, Sergeant, & Whiter, 1995/1996), children's acquisition of singing voice over time (e.g., Miller & Rutkowski, 2003), or the relationship of singing and music aptitude (e.g., Hornback & Taggert, 2005).

Considered together, the abundance of studies about children and singing constitute what might be the equivalent of a child study movement centered on this particular musical practice.[4] And although gaps and questions remain (Why are children's singing games gendered in some places? Where are the boys? What are the perceptual and cognitive connections between the tonal gestures of language and the acquisition and/or development of singing?), the varied research perspectives brought to questions about children and singing is certainly notable. The possibility of continuing to examine children's singing practices from methodologically and theoretically diverse perspectives and, potentially, publishing different kinds of studies side by side (if such a project has any merits) seems doable.

Not all musical practices seem to merit the same multifaceted methodological attention. Ethnography and case study appear to be the preferred means of studying garage bands and rock groups. Young band and orchestra musicians seem more likely to have their perceptions measured or skills tested than to participate in sociological studies of musical meaning. Or, to take a slightly different perspective (and at the admitted risk of rather substantial oversimplification), anthropological, sociological, and ethnomusicological inquiries seem more typical of studies of community music practices, and testing and measurement seem more typical of studies of school music practices. While it may be that scholars studying musical practice are simply following the commendable practice of matching methods to research questions/problems, perhaps a bit more prodding (and even consideration of research biases) is necessary. Are questions such as "What does music making look like and sound like? How does the practice evolve? How is music transmitted? Who is involved (and who is not)? How are novices or newcomers socialized into group music making?" more appropriate for a folk fiddling group than a middle school orchestra? Are studies of finger dexterity more appropriate for school violinists than folk fiddlers? Where and why methodological diversity exists (and does not) in the study of musical practices remains a conundrum to puzzle at this moment in music education scholarship.

Two more considerations with respect to inquiry aimed at musical practices merit mention here. First, studies of musical practices grounded in the "third-wave" of feminist thinking (Lamb, Dolloff, & Howe, 2002) and critical theory perspectives have a rather short history in music education. Studies such as O'Toole's (1994) "I sing in a choir but I have 'no voice!'" signal the potential of these theoretical perspectives to turn the lens of inquiry toward matters of power relations, the politics of resource control, and discourses of uniformity and conformity in all musical practices.

Second, what shifts in inquiry might occur if we were to conceive of music listening as a musical practice rather than a behavior? Virtual spaces such as YouTube and virtual listening groups (e.g., bloggers commenting on music live, in the hall, during a wind ensemble concert[5]) create communities of listening practice, and these communities of listening practice seem as vibrant, and as worthy of study, as music making communities.

PEDAGOGIES

> *Anyone who casually wandered into one of Dewey's classes at either the University of Chicago or Columbia University expecting to witness learning by doing in the hands of a master was in for a big surprise.... In fact, all whose expectations were formed by having read one or more of Dewey's educational treatises faced a disappointment. The Great Educator, in the opinion of many, was not the greatest of teachers.*
>
> —Jackson, 1998, p. 182

First impressions can be deceiving. The apparent qualities of Dewey's delivery—a halting speech style, eye contact that often missed the students, and what seemed to be a meandering set of remarks—had a different lasting impression. Irving Edman, one of Dewey's students, states:

> ...I soon found out that it was my mind that had wandered, not John Dewey's. I began very soon to do what I had seldom done in college courses—to take notes.... Those pauses were delays in creative thinking, when the next step was really being considered.... Not every day or in every teacher does one overhear the palpable processes of thought. (Jackson, 2003, p. 184)

And Harold Larrabee, another student, noted that whatever their initial perceptions of Dewey's pedagogical shortcomings, "His students came to recognize that an hour listening to Dewey was an exercise in 'man thinking.'... One rarely left the classroom without the conviction that something intellectually *and* practically important had been said..." (Jackson, 2003, p. 184–185). While it might be tempting to conclude that the product of Dewey's teaching resides in the power of his ideas rather than his pedagogical process, Jackson comments, "Dewey himself would be among the first to point out that substance and process are inseparable" (1998, p. 185).

Pedagogy is, indeed, a complex matter—a synergy that includes not only acts of delivery, but also the instructor's philosophical beliefs and knowledge of both content and students, the nature and qualities of interactions between and among teacher and students, curricular discourses, theory-practice tensions, and the supporting/confounding influences of local and global contexts. Pedagogy is also rather ephemeral. "Teaching is a bit like dry ice," Shulman writes; in the absence of artifacts that capture its richness and complexity, "it disappears at room temperature" (2004, p. 457). Pedagogy, of which the act of teaching is a part, is (at times) similarly elusive or, at the very least, multifaceted, dynamic, and changeable in the hands and minds of educators who enact it.

Pedagogical inquiry, from case studies of classrooms to action research projects to curriculum investigations to studies examining the effects of different teaching strategies, provides opportunities to better understand the teaching-learning dynamic and to reflect on the fundamental aim underpinning these diverse kinds of research—the improvement of education. The music education research literature includes a substantial collection of studies that might be grouped under the category of pedagogy (broadly conceived), including studies of teaching and learning in school and community music making contexts, in informal and formal learning settings, among young people and adult musicians, and among preservice and novice teachers. In this book, the studies by Gruenhagen and by Bauer, Forsythe, and Kinney—two very different investigations of professional development—provide an opportunity for reflections on pedagogy.

Curiously, the music education community has examined teaching and learning in adult community ensembles and music learning among adult beginners through the lenses of adult learning models and theories, but these same adult learning models and theories have not been applied as frequently or employed as systematically in studies of in-service music teacher education or in the planning and implementation of professional development programs, where the learners are also adults. Taken together, the Bauer et al. and Gruenhagen studies point to the power of building professional development (or pedagogy for pedagogues), whether through graduate study or other means, on principles of learning. For example, in both studies, teachers point to the value of repeated experiences, whether returning to a learning group or returning to a state convention, to discuss a concern or obtain information on a specific topic. In both studies, in-service music educators identify opportunities to reflect on their teaching practices, whether in informal conversations with colleagues between convention sessions or during more conversations in a group of peers in more structured settings, as a substantial means of impacting their thinking.

In fact, the power of peer learning, or learning within a community of peers, emerges as a particularly strong finding in both studies. Practicing music teachers point to the value of learning from and learning alongside colleagues who are familiar with the local conditions or particular challenges of teaching specialties. Bauer et al. and Gruenhagen's findings, and the comments and responses of teachers in their studies, align well with the literature in general teacher education. In a summary of professional development studies, for example, Richardson and Placier (2001) note that in-service teacher education "is enhanced through dialogue, particularly dialogue with those who understand practice and the particular contexts in which one is working," and that a "discourse community" with a strong level of trust among critical friends can be a productive means of fostering growth and change among in-service teachers (p. 921).

Richardson and Placier also comment that "different teachers will respond quite differently to particular approaches" to professional development (p. 921), and certainly the findings of Bauer et al. and Gruenhagen suggest the same conclusion. Adapting instruction to meet the individual needs of learners is as crucial a principle of pedagogy for adult learners as it is for young people.

Finally, teachers in both studies valued agency. Put plainly, teachers know what teachers need, and when their voices are absent, agency is undermined. Like any other learners, they are drawn to educational experiences that are goal directed, purpose driven, and relevant to their perceived needs, and that respect them as intelligent, thinking individuals. "Figure out a way to teach people how to *think*," a teacher in the Gruenhagen study recommends, "instead of teaching them *what to do*." Perhaps no better pedagogical principle can be drawn from a research study.

PEOPLE

It takes people—living according to their particular perspectives, abilities, interests, and needs, and interacting with others in the instructional setting—to bring education alive.
—Jorgensen, 2003, p. 126

Most music education research focuses on the people who are at the core of teaching and learning—students and teachers. But many other people are involved, either directly or indirectly, in the educational enterprise—parents, families, administrators, support staff, publishers, test designers, the press, policymakers, the public; and we know relatively little about most of these people in the context of education. Music education studies that include families, for example, generally focus on parent interactions with preschool children (e.g., Berger & Cooper, 2003; Cardany, 2006; Levinowitz & Estrin, 1996), decisions about music instruction made by families who home school (e.g., Nichols, 2006), or parental support for instrumental learning (e.g., Davidson, Howe, Moore, & Sloboda, 1996). Even among the two core groups in music education (teachers and students), some striking imbalances are evident. We have more studies of (and more *kinds* of research about) preservice teachers and early career music educators than veteran teachers, and more studies of elementary-school children than middle-school learners.[6]

Methodologically diverse studies of people are particularly crucial for providing a nuanced perspective of those involved in music and education, for critiquing music education practices, and for advancing professional dialogue. For example, the observation of Bauer et al., drawn from demographic data, that the ethnicities of the music educators (in one state) bear little resemblance to the ethnicities of the students should trouble us. Placing this type of demographic data about teacher and student ethnicities next to studies that interrogate the experience of "being the other" in a culturally diverse classroom (e.g., Benhan, 2003) next to inquiry that challenges conceptions of race and "race talk" in music education from critical theory and social justice perspectives (e.g., Bradley, 2007) allows for a more informed, complex, and sophisticated conversation about race and music education than might otherwise occur.

Similarly, Miksza's psychometric study of motivation using an achievement goal framework, which appears in this volume, provides one perspective on motivation among high school band members. Examining the motivation of band students of similar ages and in similar contexts from an attribution theory perspective (e.g., Austin & Vispoel, 1998) or through case study (e.g., Renwick & McPherson, 2000), and publishing the studies side by side, could both broaden and deepen the conversation about motivations of music makers. Such a collection of studies could also have potential applications and connections to other music contexts. For example, Miksza's finding that band students are "primarily motivated to achieve for the sake of satisfying personal expectations and maximizing their experience in band" seems similar to the findings of Bauer et al. that teachers who pursue master's degrees primarily for personal satisfaction and are motivated to participate in nondegree professional development primarily to become better teachers and better musicians.

But there are more profound reasons for including epistemological perspectives, theoretical frames, and methodological means in music education research, particularly as it pertains to people. As Kincheloe and Berry note in their text on rigor and complexity in educational research, "Every aspect of human knowing—a.k.a. interpretation—is linguistically filtered, contextually grounded, power-saturated, implicated in a particular social process, shaped by narrative forms, and inscribed by tacit theories about the nature of reality" (2004, p. 87). Epistemologies matter, and "there is a subtle but crucial distinction between admitting to the possibility of diverse perspectives and acknowledging that multiple ways of understanding and constructing knowledge exist and are useful in the research process" (Barrett & Stauffer, in press). For example, Nieto's question "What keeps teachers going—in spite of everything?" (2003, p. 389), as cited by Gruenhagen in this book, begs for inquiry that engages the search for meaning (Bruner, 1990), that acknowledges the socially constructed nature of reality, that engages narrative modes of knowing (Bruner, 1986), that is grounded in theoretical frameworks that critique power relationships in education and the feminization of the teaching profession, and more.

Absent the plurality of epistemological and methodological perspectives in research about school people, we miss the local, lived, and particular (Geertz, 1983). We risk accepting as status quo data and designs that objectify and essentialize the people of music and education. Our language gives us away. "Primary teaching area" is a convenient way to organize graduate music education degrees or sessions at state conventions, but according to Bauer et al., just over one-half of the practitioners (in one state) have only one primary teaching area. What does our language speak to the rest, whose teaching lives are more diverse? What does our language say about what we believe about people? The idea that preservice teachers do not have musical knowledge (implied in the Lee and Kim study) suggests a deficit model of thinking about a particular group of people and says more about the biases of the researchers than it does about the musical abilities of the participants. And if students are not persisting in an ensemble, does that mean that students are not persisting in music (a finding/implication cited in the Miksza study)? No.

As Jorgensen notes, "A living thing cannot be standardized" (2003, p. 123), whether that "living thing" is a person, a group of people, or a practice. Certainly, each research methodology requires design structures and implementation protocols that meet the requirements of scholarly inquiry, as well as language conventions for communicating findings, results, assertions, or meanings. Each theoretical framework implies certain ground rules, inquiry techniques, and literature references. We all have our "standards." Our collective engagement in inquiry from diverse epistemological and methodological grounds, and, crucially, our care in the language we use in our scholarly work must demonstrate an ethic of respect for and responsibility toward the people at the core of music and education.

PLACE

> *The term "place" conjures up visions of locality, spatial representations of those places with which we are familiar, and those places the unfamiliarity of which intrigues us. We reside in places, go to work and recreate in places, travel daily through places that are sometimes meaningful to us and other times ignored or taken for granted. We identify with those places that played some formative (if still elusive) role in our childhood years, those places that are associated with good times or bad.*

The term "place" is imbued with emotion, defined by the boundaries it imposes on space, and informed by the utility to which space is put in our lives.
—Hutchinson, 2004, p. 11

We usually use the word "place" to refer to a physical space or a location. But places are something more. Place—our sense of place—is a socially constructed human phenomenon, and places carry meanings. A phrase in philosophy of place[7] puts it simply: space is to house as place is to home. In other words, place is a dynamic construct comprised of time plus space plus experience. Locations become places and take on meaning and sociocultural significance through our experiences, actions, and interactions over time and in the spaces we inhabit. The concept of place is also multiple in that places, for each individual, are overlapping, connected, and nested with those of other individuals, groups, societies, and cultures. We are, therefore, always multiply situated.

Although place is not the equivalent of culture, conceptions of place and culture are related, and both place and culture shape ideas about education, music, and education and music practices. The study by Kim and Lee in this volume demonstrates the power of place in shaping the ideas of preservice teachers. While preservice teachers in both Korea and the United States agreed that music learning experiences are important for young children, they disagreed (although not always at a statistically significant level) about their own perceived musical abilities, musical knowledge, attitudes, and even their thinking about who should provide music instruction for children. The authors note that some of the findings "seem to originate from cultural and educational differences" in the two countries.

Cross-cultural studies can help us understand the impact of social dynamics and place (broadly conceived). Ideas about who should teach, what should be learned when and by whom, the nature of relationship between teacher and student, and even basic definitions and fundamental concepts of "education" and "music" vary from place to place and culture to culture. On the other hand, cultural differences pose challenges to cross-cultural studies. For example, the ethic of responding to self-report about one's skills or abilities may vary according to social or cultural conventions.

There may be value in cross-place studies that examine the particularities and local differences of similar practices that occur in similar broad social and cultural contexts. What does the musical practice of high school marching band look like and sound like in Miami and Missoula? How are students' experiences similar, different, and why? How place-based are our musical practices, what elements of place create differences in similar musical practices, and what implications do differences have? In addition to studies in which "school" is an independent variable, cross-place studies conducted from an ethnographic perspective have the potential to contribute to our understanding of the impact of local cultures.

The concept of place includes more than geography or experience in specific locales, however; to reiterate, place is a dynamic construct composed of *time* plus space plus experience. Our core values about education, our beliefs about practices, our notions of the roles of teacher, student, and musician, our ideas about music and learning are complicated constructions that include historical discourses. In this volume, Miranda describes the history of early childhood education and the evolution of Developmentally Appropriate Practice (DAP)—a set of guidelines well-known in the early childhood community. Her essay demonstrates the ways in which current conceptions of children, ideas about teaching and learning, and guidelines for curriculum and practice derive from the thinking of key individuals, the debates and publications of professional organizations, and the public policies and educational initiative of various eras. Knowing the historical trajectory of ideas allows us to reconsider the perceived wisdom, challenge the power and politics of inherited canons, and move from a received past to an evolving present and an imagined future.

Philosophy of place can be particularly useful in two respects. First, it allows us to view curriculum documents and guidelines (such as DAP) as "maps"—historic documents that are "of a place." The more remote the map (e.g., a national curriculum), the more likely it is to be global and general rather than local and lived, and the more likely it is to represent a hegemonized agenda. While curriculum documents may be valuable or interesting for multiple reasons, philosophy of place allows us to see them for what they are—"fixed"—while simultaneously viewing the practices of teaching, learning, and music making—the lived curriculum—as fluid, changing, and responsive. A curriculum document might inform practice, but cannot *be* a practice. Curriculum, though impacted by a multitude of "places," ultimately rests in the hands of those who enact it.

Second, for many people, "music education" is a place-bound phrase. We say "music education," we think "public school." The connection is so powerful that the words "public school" are often silent when we speak or write about music education. Privileging "public school" has certain consequences, the most important of which is the elevation of certain forms and forums of music making and certain music learners over others. Those four words together—public school music education—whether implied or articulated, pose substantial challenges to any transformation of music teaching and learning practices, and music education research agendas, in which in which we might engage. If we want to transform, we may need to trade places.

IN CELEBRATION OF DIVERSITY...
AND COMPLEMENTARITY

"I treasure nature's bounteous diversity of species," Gould writes, continuing with a half-humorous, half-serious parenthetical, "(the thought of half a million described species of beetles—and so many more, yet undescribed—fills me with an awe I can only call reverent)" (2003, p. 344). Any enthusiasm we have for the "diversity of species" in music education inquiry should be tempered, of course, by a bit of realism. The dialectics of objectivity and subjectivity, uniqueness and universal, local and global, constant and change (the list could go on), that swirl in the back halls of research meetings and the front pages of research handbooks are not going anywhere any time soon; nor are conversations about paradigms, power, and politics. "Any methodology has inherent deficiencies and fails to capture the chaos, complexity, and contextuality of applied fields such as education, particularly in light of issues of culture, politics, values, and ideology," Smith writes, "None of [the questions that vex us] can be satisfactorily asked and answered with single research approaches" (2006, p. 458). If this book is any indication, the community of music education researchers concurs.

But I am optimistic. The "moment" this volume marks in the history of music education research seems, to me, to be a shift from contestation to complementarity—perhaps a kind of inquiry symbiosis. And although "What constitutes *complementarity* among methods or what relationships need to exist for methods to be defined as complementary, rather than merely mixed... needs careful discussion and debate" (Green, Camilli, & Elmor, 2006, p. xvii), we appear ready to have that conversation and to leverage the strength found in methodologically and theoretically diverse studies. After all, any research approach "that is intensely empirical but politically disinterested is insufficient" (Barone, 2000, p. 192) for this moment in music, education, research, and the lives of people our inquiries serve.

NOTES

1. I am mindful, here, of the debate about the word "aesthetic" in music education, particularly in the United States. Barone describes an aesthetic experience in the Deweyan (1934/1958) sense "as an event that emerges out of, but distinguishes itself from, the inchoate and formless general stream of experience"—an experience that is "life-affirming" (Barone, 2007, p. 240).
2. Denzin and Lincoln use "moment" to refer to historical moments that "are somewhat artificial... socially constructed, quasi-historical, and overlapping conventions" (2005, p. 2). Although their discussion refers specifically to qualitative research, the applications and implications are more broadly use-

ful. See their chapters at the beginning and end of *The Sage Handbook of Qualitative Research*, 3rd edition.
3. The idea of commonplaces derives from rich experiences in the Mountain Lake Colloquium, the "playshop" preceding the publication of the first *Mountain Lake Reader* (1999), and Mary Hookey's article, "Charting the Conceptual Terrain in Music Teacher Education," in that first volume, including her reference to Schwab's curricular commonplaces and her application/interpretation of Schwab's model.
4. Researchers from different epistemological perspectives and methodological traditions will likely define "practice" or "singing practice" differently. I use "practice" here in the broadest sense, acknowledging that my usage will not suit some readers, while recognizing simultaneously that, absent singing ability, there is no singing practice.
5. In the fall of 2008, various Arizona State University wind groups gave a performance in which audience members were invited to participate in various ways. One could simply attend and listen, listen while simultaneously wearing headphones through which a live running commentary on the concert was broadcast, or listen and join a live blog discussion. I joined the latter group and sat with my laptop in a section of the hall reserved for us. The experience seemed, to me, to foster a community of music listening practice.
6. Ebie (2002) found that the most frequently studied group in articles published in the first 50 years of the *Journal of Research in Music Education* was college students.
7. For more detailed explanation of philosophy of place and its potential applications to music education, see Stauffer, 2007 and Stauffer, in press.

REFERENCES

Austin, J. R., & Vispoel, W. P. (1998). How American adolescents interpret success and failure in classroom music: Relationships among attributional beliefs, self-concept and achievement. *Psychology of Music, 26*(1), 26–45.

Barone, T. (2000). *Aesthetics, politics, and educational inquiry: Essays and examples*. New York: Peter Lang.

Barone, T. (2007). Imagining Ms. Eddy alive, or, The return of the arts teacher and her personalized curriculum. In L. Bresler (Ed.), *International handbook of research in arts education, part 1* (pp. 239–244). Dordrecht, The Netherlands: Springer.

Barrett, M.S. (2003). Meme engineers: Children as producers of musical culture. *International Journal of Early Years Education, 11*(3), 195–212.

Barrett, M., & Stauffer, S. L. (in press). *Narrative inquiry in music education: Troubling certainty*. Dordrecht, The Netherlands: Springer.

Benham, S. (2003). Being the other: Adapting to life in a culturally diverse classroom. *Journal of Music Teacher Education, 13*(1), 21–32.

Berger, A. A., & Cooper, S. (2003). Musical play: A case study of preschool children and parents. *Journal of Research in Music Education, 51*(2), 151–165.

Bradley, D. (2007). The sounds of silence: Talking race in music education. *Action, Criticism, and Theory for Music Education, 6*(4), 132–162. Retrieved September 15, 2008, from http://act.maydaygroup.org/articles/Bradley6_4.pdf

Bruner, J. (1986). *Actual minds, possible worlds.* Cambridge, MA: Harvard University Press.

Bruner, J. (1990). *Acts of meaning.* Cambridge, MA: Harvard University Press.

Campbell, P. (1998). *Songs in their heads: Music and its meaning in children's lives.* Oxford, UK: Oxford University Press.

Campbell, P. (2007). Musical meanings in children's cultures. In L. Bresler (Ed.), *International handbook of research in arts education, part 1* (pp. 881–894). Dordrecht, The Netherlands: Springer.

Cardany, A. B. (2006). The ripple effect: A family's influence on music education philosophy and practice. *The Mountain Lake Reader, 4,* 75–81.

Corso, D. T. (2003). *"Smooth as butter": Practices of music learning amongst African-American children.* Unpublished doctoral dissertation, University of Illinois, Urbana-Champaign.

Custodero, L. A. (2006). Singing practices in 10 families with young children. *Journal of Research in Music Education, 54*(1), 37–56.

Davidson, J. W., Howe, M. J. A., Moore, D. G., & Sloboda, J. A. (1996). The role of parental influences in the development of musical ability. *British Journal of Developmental Psychology, 21,* 103–113.

Denzin, N. K., & Y. S. Lincoln, Y. S. (Eds.). (2005). *The Sage handbook of qualitative research* (3rd ed.). Thousand Oaks, CA: Sage Publications.

Dewey, J. (1934/1958). *Art as experience.* New York: Capricorn.

Donabedian, A. (1988). Quality assessment and assurance: Unity of purpose, diversity of means. *Inquiry-Blue Cross Blue Shield Association, 25,* 175–184.

Ebie, B. D. (2002). Characteristics of 50 years of research samples found in the Journal of Research in Music Education, 1953–2002. *Journal of Research in Music Education, 50*(4), 280–291.

Gould, S. J. (1996). *Full house: The spread of excellence from Plato to Darwin.* New York: Harmony Books.

Gould, S. J. (2003). *I have landed: The end of a beginning in natural history.* New York: Three Rivers Press.

Green, J. L., Camilli, G., & Elmore, P. B. (2006). Introduction to the handbook: What's complementary about complementary methods? In J. L. Green, G. Camilli, & Patricia B. Elmore (Eds.), *Handbook of complementary methods in education research* (pp. xv–xx). Mahwah, NJ: Lawrence Erlbaum Associates.

Harwood, E. (1998). "Go on girl!" Improvisation in African-American girls' singing games. In B. Nettl & M. Russell (Eds.), *In the course of performance* (pp. 113–125). Chicago: University of Chicago Press.

Hookey, M. (1999). Charting the conceptual terrain in music teacher education: Roles for maps and models, metaphors and mirrors. *The Mountain Lake Reader, 1,* 40–48.

Hornbach, C. M., & Taggart, C. C. (2005). The relationship between developmental tonal aptitude and singing achievement among kindergarten, first-, second-, and third-grade students. *Journal of Research in Music Education, 53*(4), 322–331.

Hutchinson, D. (2004). *A natural history of place in education*. New York: Teachers College Press.
Jackson, Philip W. (1998). *John Dewey and the lessons of art*. New Haven, CT: Yale University Press.
Jorgensen, E. R. (2003). *Transforming music education*. Bloomington, IN: Indiana University Press.
Kincheloe, J. L., & Berry, K. S. (2004). *Rigour and complexity in educational research: Conceptualizing the bricolage*. Berkshire, UK: Open University Press.
Kratus, J. (2007). Music education at the tipping point. *Music Educators Journal, 94*(2), 42–48.
Levinowitz, L. M., & Estrin, A. A. (1996). Parent-child interactions during a preschool music class: An exploratory study. *Southeastern Journal of Music Education, 8,* 156–165.
Lincoln, Y. S., & Denzin, N. K. (2005). Epilogue: The eighth and ninth moments—qualitative research in/and the fractured future. In N. K. Denzin & Y. S. Lincoln (Eds.), *The Sage handbook of qualitative research,* (3rd ed., pp. 1115–1126). Thousand Oaks, CA: Sage Publications.
Marsh, K. (1995). Children's singing games: Composition in the playground? *Research Studies in Music Education, 4,* 2–11.
Miller, M. S., & Rutkowski, J. (2003). A longitudinal study of elementary children's acquisition of their singing voices. *Update: Applications of Research in Music Education, 22,* 5–14.
Nichols, J. B. (2006). *Music education in homeschooling: A phenomenological inquiry*. Unpublished doctoral dissertation, Arizona State University, Tempe.
Nieto, S. (2003). *What keeps teachers going?* New York: Teachers College Press.
O'Toole, P. (1994/2005). I sing in a choir but I have no voice. *Visions of Research in Music Education, 6*(1). Retrieved September 15, 2008, from http://www-usr.rider.edu/~vrme/v6n1/vision/otoole_2005.htm.
Reck, D. B., Slobin, M., & Titon, J. T. (2001). Discovering and documenting a world of music. In J. T. Titon (Ed.), *Worlds of music: An introduction to the music of the world's peoples* (pp. 277–302). Belmont, CA: Schirmer.
Renwick, J., & McPherson, G. E. (2000). "I've got do my scale first!": A case study of a novice's clarinet practice. In C. Woods, G. B. Luck, R. Brochard, F. Seddon, & J. A. Sloboda (Eds.), *Proceedings of the sixth international conference on music perception and cognition*. Keele, UK: Keep University, Department of Psychology. CD-ROM.
Richardson, V., & Placier, P. (2001). Teacher change. In V. Richardson (Ed.), *Handbook of research on teaching* (pp. 905–947). Washington, DC: American Educational Research Association.
Riddell, C. (1990). *Traditional singing games of elementary school children in Los Angeles*. Unpublished doctoral dissertation, University of California-Los Angeles.
Shulman, L. (2004). *The wisdom of practice: Essays on teaching, learning, and learning to teach*. San Francisco: Jossey-Bass.
Smith, M. L. (2006). Multiple methodology in education research. In J. L. Green, G. Camilli, & Patricia B. Elmore (Eds.), *Handbook of complementary methods in education research* (pp. 457–475). Mahwah, NJ: Lawrence Erlbaum Associates.

Stauffer, S. L. (2007). Place, people, purpose: Persistent and productive tensions in music and teacher education. In Rideout, R. (Ed.), *Policies and practices: Rethinking music teacher preparation in the 21st century* (pp. 77–94). Amherst, MA: University of Massachusetts.

Stauffer, S. L. (In press). Placing curriculum in music education. In T. Gates & T. Regelski (Eds.), *Action for Change in Music Education*. Dordrecht, The Netherlands: Springer.

Welch, G. (1985). A developmental view of children's singing. *British Journal of Music Education, 3,* 295–303.

Welch, G. F., Sergeant, D. C., & Whiter, P. J. (1995/1996). The singing competencies of five-year-old developing singers. *Bulletin of the Council for Research in Music Education Bulletin, 127,* 155–162.

ABOUT THE CONTRIBUTORS

William I. Bauer is the Director of Music Education and Associate Professor at Case Western Reserve University, where he teaches undergraduate and graduate level classes in music education research, music cognition and learning, instrumental music education, and music instructional technology. He has published articles in leading journals in music education and is currently the editor of *Contributions to Music Education*. His research and writing focus on music teacher education, music cognition, and the applications of technology to music teaching and learning.

Mark Robin Campbell is Associate Professor of Music Education at the Crane School of Music, SUNY at Potsdam, where he teaches undergraduate and graduate courses in music teaching, learning, philosophy, and curriculum. His research focuses on the thinking and socialization processes of preservice music teachers. He is editor of several collections of works and is author of numerous published articles and studies.

Elliot W. Eisner is the Lee Jacks Professor Emeritus of Education and Emeritus Professor of Art at Stanford University. Professor Eisner was trained as a painter at the School of the Art Institute of Chicago and studied design and art education at the Institute of Design, Illinois Institute of Technology. He received his PhD from the University of Chicago.

Professor Eisner's contributions to education are many. He works in three fields: arts education, curriculum studies, and qualitative research methods. He has been especially interested in advancing the role of the arts in American education and in using the arts as models for improving educational practice in other fields. He is the author or editor of 16 books addressing these topics, among them *Educating Artistic Vision, The Educational Imagination, The Enlightened Eye, Cognition and Curriculum, The Kind of Schools We Need,* and most recently, *The Arts and the Creation of Mind,* published by Yale University Press. He has lectured on education throughout the world.

Professor Eisner has served as President of the National Art Education Association, the International Society for Education Through Art, the American Educational Research Association, and the John Dewey Society.

Jere L. Forsythe is Associate Professor of Music Education in the School of Music at Ohio State University, where he teaches introduction to music education and supervises student teachers at the undergraduate level, a course in classroom management for masters' students, and doctoral seminars in psychological foundations and music teacher education. His scholarly research topics include teacher education, philosophy of music education and experimental research studies.

Lisa M. Gruenhagen is Assistant Professor and Coordinator of Music Education at Hartwick College, where she teaches courses in music teaching and learning, curriculum, and world music. Her research focuses on children's musical understanding and on processes of collaborative inquiry in music teacher education and professional development programs. She has presented her research at the American Educational Research Association Annual Meeting, the Symposium on Music Teacher Education, the Music and Lifelong Learning Symposium, and the Conference on Music Learning and Teaching sponsored by the Center for Applied Research in Musical Understanding.

Mary Ross Hookey retired as Associate Professor of Music Education at Nipissing University, North Bay, ON, Canada, after teaching in the undergraduate, preservice, and Master of Education programs. Her ongoing research relates to the roles and professional development of music educators, music teacher educators, and generalist teachers as music educators. She has published on music education and professional development in journals and books.

Jinyoung Kim is Assistant Professor of Early Childhood Education at the Department of Education, College of Staten Island, City University of New York, where she teaches undergraduate and graduate courses in music for early childhood/elementary education, psychological foundations of early childhood, and curriculum. Her research focuses on preserivce and inservice classroom teachers' music integration. She is the author of many books and research articles on music education. She is also a songwriter who has published music albums of children's songs.

Daryl W. Kinney is Assistant Professor of Music Education at Ohio State University, where he teaches undergraduate and graduate courses in instrumental music education. His research interests, which include music teacher education, musical and nonmusical outcomes of school music participation, and music perception and cognition, may be found in the *Journal of Research in Music Education*, the *Bulletin of the Council for Research in Music Education*, the *International Journal of Music Education*, the *Journal of Music Teacher Education*, and the *Empirical Musicology Review*.

Seung Yeon Lee is Assistant Professor of Early Childhood Education at Ewha Womans University, Seoul, Korea, where she teaches undergraduate and graduate courses in infant and toddler education, early childhood teaching strategies, child rights and welfare, and multicultural education. Her research focuses on infant-caregiver relationships and infant-teacher education. She and Jinyoung Kim co-authored the book *Music Education for Early Childhood Teachers* in Korean.

Martina Miranda is an Assistant Professor of Music Education in the College of Music at the University of Colorado at Boulder, where she teaches elementary music methods courses, graduate music education courses, and supervises practicum placements and student teachers. Her areas of specialization include early childhood music, elementary general music, general music methodology, and children's folk song literature.

Peter Miksza is Assistant Professor of Music Education at the University of Colorado at Boulder. He teaches undergraduate methods courses as well as graduate psychology and research courses. His research interests lie in the investigation of effective music practice and issues related to music teacher training. His publications can be found in several prominent music education research journals.

Sandra L. Stauffer is Professor of Music in Music Education at Arizona State University, where she teaches undergraduate and graduate courses. She has written for general music textbooks, curriculum projects, and symphony orchestra programs, and she has worked with composer Morton Subotnick on the development of music software for children. Her recent research and publications focus on creativity in music and on children and adolescents as composers, and narrative inquiry in music education.

Matthew D. Thibeault is Assistant Professor of Music Education at the University of Illinois where he teaches undergraduate and graduate courses. He writes frequently on issues of general music, technology, and qualitative approaches to understanding music education. His recent research focuses on technology-based general music projects for ensembles and teaching creative rights in the classroom.

Linda K. Thompson is Associate Professor of Music Education at Lee University, Cleveland, Tennessee, where she teaches undergraduate and graduate courses, including music methods, curriculum, and research. Additionally, she is the coordinator for the graduate music education program at Lee. Her research interests include teacher education and preservice teacher thinking and beliefs. She has published in both music education and music therapy journals.

Peter Whiteman teaches undergraduate and graduate music education and creative arts courses at the Institute of Early Childhood, Macquarie University, Australia, where he also convenes the Honors program. His research interests encompass early childhood music education and musical development, emergent symbol systems, and reconstructed childhoods. He is the author of journal articles and book chapters, and his research has been presented in a range of international symposia.

Advances in Music Education Research, the official book series of the AERA Music Education Special Interest Group (SIG), is an edited and peer-reviewed publication whose purpose is to strengthen the research and educational base of music education. Titles in the series reflect the interests of AERA Music Education SIG members and include a broad range of disciplinary and interdisciplinary subjects and diverse methodologies.

Research reports accepted for publication in *AMER* represent the work of members of the Music Education SIG. For AERA and the Music Education SIG membership information, visit www.aera.net or contact the current chair of the Music Education SIG.

Information for the submission process for *AMER* is available on the Music Education SIG Web site http://www.aera.net/Default.aspx?menu_id=192&id=1079 or by contacting the editor(s).

Readers are encouraged to respond to an article in a current or past volume of *AMER* and/or to present a position on topics and issues related to research in music education. Responses will appear in the *Dialogue Column* of the volume. For submission criteria and guidelines for the *Dialogue Column,* contact the editor(s).

Editorial Correspondence
Correspondence should be sent to the editor(s):

Linda Thompson	**Mark Robin Campbell**
School of Music	Crane School of Music
Lee University	State University of New York at Potsdam
Cleveland, TN 37312	Potsdam, NY 13676
E-mail:	E-mail:
lthompson@leeuniversity.edu	campbemr@potsdam.edu
Telephone: (423) 614-8067	Telephone: (315) 267-3229

Printed in the United States
217353BV00002BA/6/P